PROFILES IN AMERICAN HISTORY

Significant Events and the People Who Shaped Them

Volume 3: *Indian Removal to the Abolition Movement*

Indian Removal
Black Hawk, John Ross, Winfield Scott

Industrialization
Samuel Slater, Eli Whitney, Harriet Hanson Robinson

Women and Reform
Sarah Grimké and Angelina Grimké Weld, Susan B. Anthony, Amelia Jenks Bloomer

Plantation System
James Henry Hammond, Harriet A. Jacobs, Mary Boykin Chesnut

Slave Resistance
Denmark Vesey, Nat Turner, John Quincy Adams

Antislavery Movement
David Walker, William Lloyd Garrison, Frederick Douglass, Sojourner Truth, Harriet Beecher Stowe

Volume 4: *Westward Movement to the Civil War*

Westward Movement
Christopher "Kit" Carson, Marcus Whitman and Narcissa Prentiss Whitman, John Sutter

Mexican War
José Antonio Navarro, Sam Houston, Zachary Taylor, John Charles Frémont, Jr., and Jessie Ann Benton Frémont

Transcendental and Romantic Movements
Henry David Thoreau, Margaret Fuller, Nathaniel Hawthorne

Pre-Civil War Controversies
Stephen Douglas, Dred Scott, John Brown

Civil War
Abraham Lincoln, Robert E. Lee, William Tecumseh Sherman, Martin Delany, Anna Carroll, Mathew Brady, Walt Whitman

(Continued on inside back cover)

PROFILES IN AMERICAN HISTORY

Indian Removal to the Antislavery Movement

1784

Iroquois forced to give up lands west of Niagara River in Treaty of Fort Stanwix, first American-Indian Treaty.

1786

Reservation system begins for Iroquois.

1793

Eli Whitney invents the cotton gin. New England shippers increase amount of slaves imported.

1798

Whitney contracts with the U.S. government to produce 10,000 muskets, which he builds using interchangeable parts.

1808

Congress outlaws importing slaves; slave trade within the United States increases.

1820

Textile mills begin appearing along rivers in New England and the Middle Atlantic states.

1825

President James Monroe proposes removal of all Indians east of Mississippi River.

1838

Cherokee relocated to Oklahoma along the Trail of Tears.

1848

Elizabeth Cady Stanton and Lucretia Mott organize the Seneca Falls Convention for women's rights.

1863

All slaves are freed after January 1 by Emancipation Proclamation.

PROFILES IN AMERICAN HISTORY

Significant Events and the People Who Shaped Them

3

Indian Removal to the Antislavery Movement

JOYCE MOSS
and
GEORGE WILSON

U·X·L
AN IMPRINT OF GALE RESEARCH INC.

PROFILES IN AMERICAN HISTORY:
Significant Events and the People Who Shaped Them

VOLUME 3: INDIAN REMOVAL TO THE ANTISLAVERY MOVEMENT

Joyce Moss and George Wilson

Staff
Carol DeKane Nagel, *U•X•L Developmental Editor*
Thomas L. Romig, *U•X•L Publisher*

Christine Nasso, *Acquisitions Editor*

Shanna P. Heilveil, *Production Assistant*
Evi Seoud, *Assistant Production Manager*
Mary Beth Trimper, *Production Director*

Mary Krzewinski, *Cover and Page Designer*
Cynthia Baldwin, *Art Director*
Arthur Chartow, *Technical Design Services Manager*
Barbara J. Yarrow, *Graphic Services Supervisor*

The Graphix Group, *Typesetting*

This book is printed on acid-free paper that meets the minimum requirements of American National Standard for Information Sciences—Permanence Paper for Printed Library Materials, ANSI Z39.48-1984.

ISBN 0-8103-9207-0 (Set)
ISBN 0-8103-9210-0 (Volume 3)

Printed in the United States of America

Published simultaneously in the United Kingdom
by Gale Research International Limited
(An affiliated company of Gale Research Inc.)

ITP™
The trademark ITP is used under license.

Contents

Reader's Guide

The many noteworthy individuals who shaped U.S. history from the exploration of the continent to the present day cannot all be profiled in one eight-volume work. But those whose stories are told in *Profiles in American History* meet one or more of the following criteria. The individuals:

- Directly affected the outcome of a major event in U.S. history
- Represent viewpoints or groups involved in that event
- Exemplify a role played by common citizens in that event
- Highlight an aspect of that event not covered in other entries

Format

Volumes of *Profiles in American History* are arranged by chapter. Each chapter focuses on one particular event and opens with an overview and detailed time line of the event that places it in historical context. Following are biographical profiles of two to seven diverse individuals who played active roles in the event.

Each biographical profile is divided into four sections:

- **Personal Background** provides details that predate and anticipate the individual's involvement in the event
- **Participation** describes the role played by the individual in the event and its impact on his or her life
- **Aftermath** discusses effects of the individual's actions and subsequent relevant events in his or her life
- **For More Information** provides sources for further reading on the individual

Additionally, sidebars containing interesting details about the events and individuals profiled, ranging from numbers of war casualties to famous quotes to family trees, are sprinkled throughout the text.

Additional Features

Maps are provided to assist readers in traveling back through time to an America arranged differently from today. Portraits and illustrations of individuals and events as well as excerpts from primary source materials are also included to help bring history to life. Sources of all quoted material are cited parenthetically within the text, and complete bibliographic information is listed at the end of the entry. A full bibliography of scholarly sources consulted in preparing the volume appears in the book's back matter.

Cross references are made in the entries, directing readers to other entries in the volume that elaborate on individuals connected in some way to the person under scrutiny. In addition, a comprehensive subject index provides easy access to people and events mentioned throughout the volume.

Comments and Suggestions

We welcome your comments on this work as well as your suggestions for individuals to be featured in future editions of *Profiles in American History.* Please write: Editors, *Profiles in American History,* U·X·L, 835 Penobscot Bldg., Detroit, Michigan 48226-4094; call toll-free: 1-800-877-4253; or fax: 313-961-6348.

Preface

"There is properly no History; only Biography," wrote great American poet and scholar Ralph Waldo Emerson. *Profiles in American History* explores U.S. history through biography. Beginning with the first contact between Native Americans and the Vikings and continuing to the present day, this series offers a unique alternative to traditional texts by emphasizing the roles played by significant individuals, including many women and minorities, in historical events.

Profiles in American History presents the human story of American events, not the exclusively European or African or Indian or Asian story. But the guiding principle in compiling this series has been to achieve balance not only in gender and ethnic background but in viewpoint. Thus the circumstances surrounding an historical event are told from individuals holding opposing views, and even opposing positions. Slaves and slaveowners, business tycoons and workers, advocates of peace and proponents of war all are heard. American authors whose works reflect the times—from James Fenimore Cooper to John Steinbeck—are also featured.

The biographical profiles are arranged in groups, clustered around one major event in American history, though each individual profile is complete in itself. But it is the interplay of these profiles—the juxtaposition of alternative views and experiences within a grouping—that broadens the readers' perspective on the event as a whole and on the participants' roles in particular. It is what makes it possible for P*rofiles in American History* to impart a larger, human understanding of events in American history.

Acknowledgments

For their guidance on the choice of events and personalities, the editors are grateful to:

Jonathan Betz-Zall, Children's Librarian, Sno-Isle Regional Library System, Washington

Janet Sarratt, Library Media Specialist, John E. Ewing Junior High School, Gaffney, South Carolina

Michael Salman, Assistant Professor of American History, University of California at Los Angeles

Appreciation is extended to Professor Salman for his careful review of chapter overviews and his guidance on key sources of information about the personalities and events.

For insights into specific personalities, the editors are grateful to Robert Sumpter, History Department Chairman at Mira Costa High School, Manhatten Beach, California.

Deep appreciation is extended to the writers who compiled data and contributed the biographies for this volume of *Profiles in American History:*

Diane Ahrens
Dana Huebler
Lawrence K. Orr
Robert Sumpter
Colin Wells

The editors also thank artist Robert Bates for his research and rendering of maps and illustrations and Paulette Petrimoulx for her careful copy editing.

Introduction

The American nation teamed with activity in the early 1800s. New inventions and social relationships emerged. Factory towns appeared in the North while plantation agriculture spread throughout the South. As common citizens set up businesses, the experiment in democracy continued. The people exercised their voice in government, electing officials and petitioning Congress. Meanwhile, a few pivotal events occurred in government and society that polarized opinions and profoundly changed the way people viewed Native Americans, women, and African Americans.

The United States government adopted a policy calling for the physical removal of tribes from choice pieces of property in the East. The Indian nations dealt with the threat of removal in different ways. The Shawnee, for example, chose to fight it, while the Cherokee met with various American leaders to prevent it. In either case, the tribes struggled to survive as distinct peoples on their own lands against odds that proved too great to overcome.

Meanwhile, new inventions in the textile industry resulted in the rise of mill towns on New England lands once occupied by Indians. Children, the first laborers in these factories, were soon followed by women. Although domestic duties continued to be viewed as their primary responsibilities, women discovered other opportunities to labor outside the home. They founded new schools and passed out Bibles, and eventually took up the controversial issues of the day, such as the abolition of slavery.

Given the new inventions in the textile industry, the demand for cotton soared—and so did the use of slaves. Their population rose from 1.5 million in 1820 to 4 million in 1860. Since the nation's birth, some Americans were disturbed by the contradiction between slavery and the notion of liberty for all. While Northerners grew more concerned about the rising number of slaves, Southern planters who were economically dependent on their labor fiercely defended the institution.

Strict rules governed the behavior of slaves in the South, as owners tried to control their "property" and curb the influence of Northerners. In response, many black Southerners—free and slave—took matters into their own hands. Though they resisted slavery in different ways, most dramatic were the attempts at outright rebellion.

In the first half of the nineteenth century, men and women, both white and black, forged a movement to end slavery in the nation. To keep the issue in the public eye, abolitionists petitioned Congress, persuaded crowds that the institution was morally wrong, and published fiction and nonfiction works exposing slavery's evils.

Picture Credits

The photographs and illustrations appearing in *Profiles in American History: Significant Events and the People Who Shaped Them,* Volume 3: *Indian Removal to the Antislavery Movement* were received from the following sources:

On the cover: **Courtesy of The Library of Congress:** Harriet Hanson Robinson, Frederick Douglass, Black Hawk.

Courtesy of The Library of Congress: pages 7, 15, 25, 35, 43, 51, 61, 73, 86, 89, 101, 111, 124, 127, 132, 147, 177, 183, 189, 206, 217, 229, 237, 241; **courtesy of the Oklahoma Historical Society:** page 19; **The Bettmann Archive:** page 66; **courtesy of The Garrison Papers, Sophia Smith Collection, Smith College Library:** page 91; **courtesy of The Smithsonian Institution:** page 117; **The Schomburg Center for Research in Black Culture, The New York Public Library, Astor, Lenox and Tilden Foundations:** page 144, 205; **Radio Times Hulton Picture Library:** page 165.

Indian Removal

1784
Iroquois forced to give up lands west of Niagara River in Treaty of Fort Stanwix, first American-Indian treaty.

1786
Reservation system begins for Iroquois.

1794
After losing Battle of Fallen Timbers, Ohio Valley Indians forced to deed territory in Treaty of Greenville.

1814
Ohio Valley Indians lose Battle of the Thames and sign second Greenville Treaty. Creek lose Battle of Horseshoe Bend and give up land in Alabama and Mississippi.

1825
President James Monroe proposes removal of all Indians east of Mississippi River.

1830
Choctow removed from Mississippi to Indian Territory.

1832
Black Hawk leads Sauk east across Mississippi River, which results in Bad Axe Massacre.

1835
Osceola fights to preserve Seminole lands in Florida and Georgia; **Winfield Scott** sent to defeat him.

1838
John Ross supervises removal of Cherokee to Oklahoma. Scott oversees removal for U.S. government.

1842
Seminole removed to Indian Territory.

1876-1877
Sioux and Cheyenne win Battle of Little Big Horn but are afterward defeated and removed to reservations.

1886
Apache and Navajo removed from lands in New Mexico and Arizona.

1890
Sioux fight U.S. troops in Battle of Wounded Knee, the last major clash between Indians and the U.S. government.

INDIAN REMOVAL

The removal of Indian peoples from their American homelands began soon after the arrival of the Europeans. In the early 1600s, tribes such as the Pequot began to die out due to warfare and diseases they caught from the European colonists. This type of removal was mostly unplanned. After the Revolutionary War, however, United States leaders adopted a policy of intentional removal. The first Indians affected were the Iroquois, who had sided with the British in the war. As early as 1786, they were forced to live on reservations, lands set aside for them by the new Americans.

In 1789, Henry Knox, the nation's first secretary of war, explained United States policy. Indian peoples were recognized as the rightful owners of North American lands, which could lawfully be taken only by the Indians' consent or by conquest in a just war. In either case, a treaty would seal the transfer of ownership. The goal of this policy, prompted by the great demand for Indian lands, became the removal of tribes to areas west of the Mississippi River.

The treaty strategy worked. Many Indian leaders agreed to exchange a portion of their tribal lands for trade goods, yearly payments, and the promise that no more demands would be made on their territory. The central and state governments gained vast areas in this way. While this was the main goal of the U.S. policy, other goals were to encourage Indians to live like whites and to pre-

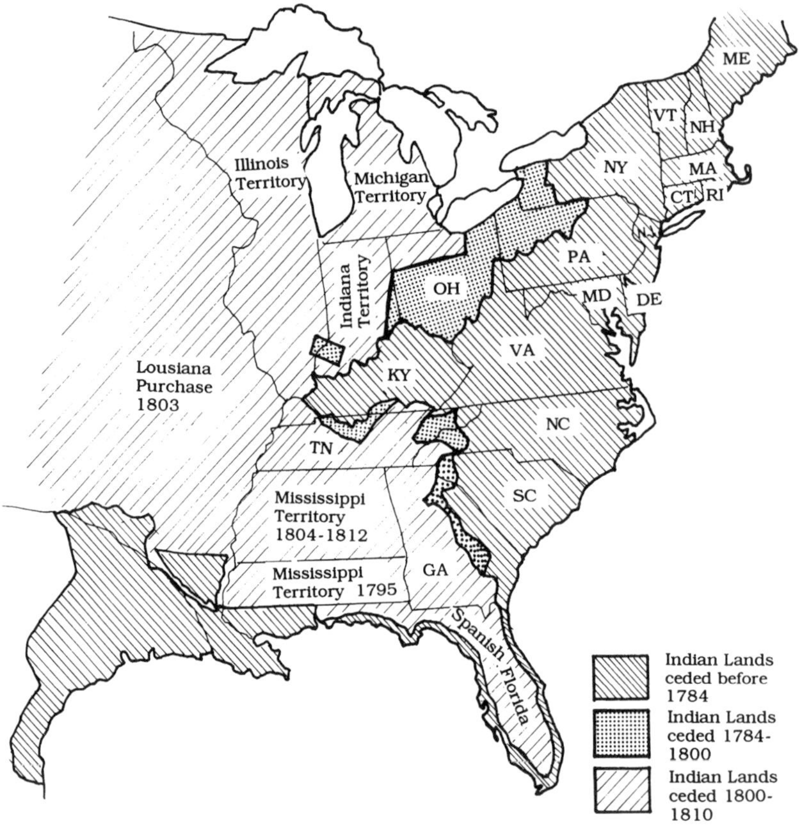

▲ **Indian lands ceded to settlers, 1784-1810**

vent dishonest land deals. Yet whites often tricked Indians into selling land at prices far below its value.

A number of other problems arose too. First, most Indian societies did not practice individual ownership of land. Instead they viewed *all* members of a tribe as the rightful occupants of the nation's lands—an individual chief had no authority to deed them away. Second, Indian nations frequently were forced to sign treaties—they did not do so of their own free will. The Iroquois, for example, after being defeated, were threatened with more war unless they signed the Treaty of Fort Stanwix, which gave to the United States their lands west of the Niagara River. Third, the policy had a loophole that worked to the advantage of the new Americans: the right to take lands in case of a just war. In the century after 1789, wars broke out periodically. With less manpower and weaponry, Indian armies fought valiantly, but they often lost. The United States considered all these wars just and itself entitled to the losers' lands.

With Iroquois power broken in the East, the government moved to acquire territory in the Old Northwest—the region stretching north and west from the Ohio to the Mississippi rivers. In the War of 1812, Tecumseh led an army of tribes to preserve Indian lands in the region but was ultimately defeated. Indian power in the Old Northwest was broken, and the war moved south, where the Creek Indians also lost land.

Indian policy focused fully on the South after the war. Government leaders sought removal of five southern nations—the Choctaw, Chickasaw, Seminole, Creek, and Cherokee. These nations, called "civilized" because they had blended some of the ways of whites into their own lifestyles, posed a special threat. But American policymakers had argued that Indians were "savage"—they could not exist peacefully alongside whites—and had to be moved off choice land areas in the East. The five tribes sought to disprove this argument.

In the 1820s, President James Monroe, pressed by new demands for land, proposed removal of the southern tribes; the next president, Andrew Jackson, pursued the policy. There was some disharmony in government when the Supreme Court ruled in *Worcester v. Georgia* that the state of Georgia had no legal right to remove the Cherokee, and the state and President Jackson ignored the ruling. In 1830, Congress also approved removal, voting for funds to place southern tribes west of the Mississippi River. Vastly outnumbered, the Indians were left with little choice other than to leave.

The 1830s became the decade of removal. In 1832, due to a grave misunderstanding, the government crushed **Black Hawk,** a chief of the Sauk Indians in Illinois and Wisconsin. Led by Osceola, Seminole Indians rose up against removal in 1835, beginning a seven-year war in Florida. The government sent **Winfield Scott** to crush the Seminole, but before that was achieved Scott was called

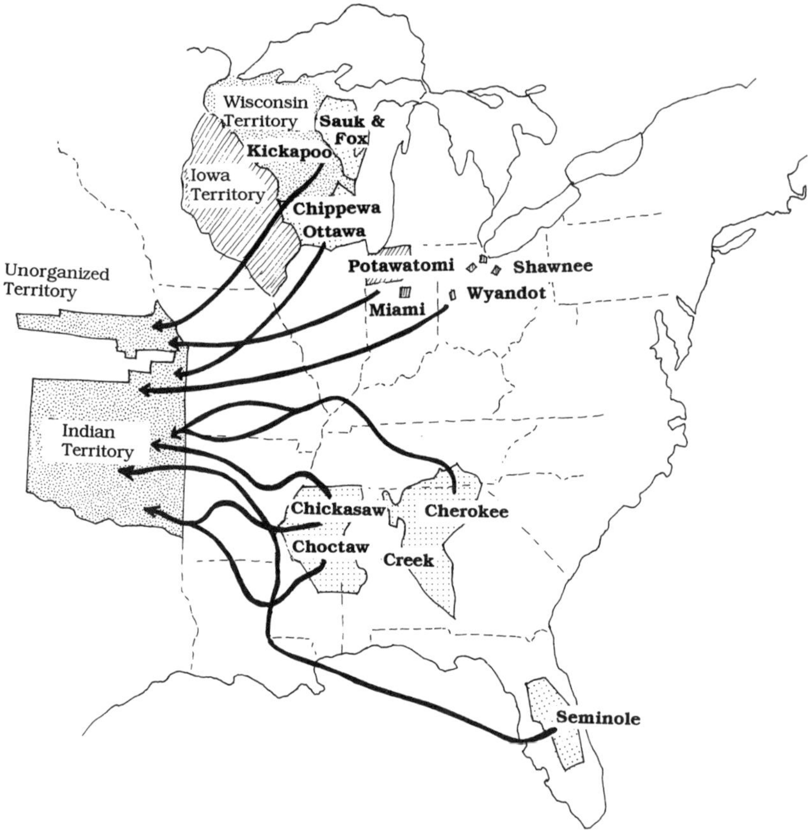

▲ **Indian removal, 1820-1840**

away to oversee the removal of over 13,000 Cherokee from Georgia. The Cherokee traveled along what they called the *Nuna-da-ut-sun'y,* or "Trail of Tears," to vacant land in present-day Oklahoma, which the government set aside as Indian Territory. Thousands perished along the way due to disease, starvation, and winter cold, and thousands more died from hunger and sickness the first year after arriving. The removal cost $6 million, which the government paid but then deducted from the $9 million it owed the Cherokee for their eastern lands. Chief **John Ross** supervised the Cherokee removal. Some tribes had fought against removal. Others, like the Cherokee, had held peaceful meetings with the government to combat it. Yet no strategy seemed to work. By 1844, except for a few small communities in New York, Michigan, and

Florida, removal of all tribes east of the Mississippi River was achieved.

Disputes over Indian lands would continue west of the Mississippi River. The state of Texas demanded that the federal government remove the Apache as early as 1845. In 1851, Congress passed the Indian Appropriations Act, which collected western tribes onto reservations to protect the stream of oncoming pioneers. The reservation system became popular around the mid-1800s. Conflicts with the Sioux in South Dakota ended in their forced removal to reservations in 1877. By 1886, the last Apache had been moved from tribal lands in Arizona to prisons in Florida and then to Oklahoma.

Meanwhile, the other Indian societies placed in Oklahoma began to adjust. But their territory here would soon be threatened too. Indian lands and tribal identities would continue to exist, however, surviving the new threat just as they had the devastating removals to Oklahoma earlier in the 1800s.

Black Hawk

1767-1838

Personal Background

Sauk and Fox. By the early nineteenth century, the Sauk (or Sac) Indians had merged with their Fox neighbors and spread along the Mississippi River from western Illinois to Prairie du Chien in present-day Wisconsin. The Fox occupied several villages on the east side of the river, while the Sauk, for the most part, spent their summers in Saukenuk (near present-day Rock Island, Illinois). There were about a hundred lodges in Saukenuk. Made of bark, blankets, or animal skins, each lodge housed one or more families. The families raised corn, beans, and squash. After the fall harvest, they would move across the river to hunt buffalo and elk in what is now Iowa. The Sauk trapped for furs to trade with the British and Americans. For over a century, they, as well as the Fox, had been dependent on white traders for guns, ammunition, cooking utensils, and blankets.

Career and family. The man known to whites as Black Hawk was born Ma-ka-tai-me-she-kia-kiak (Black Sparrow Hawk) in the year 1767. Like most of the boys in his tribe, Black Hawk learned to hunt and fish at an early age.

Black Hawk's father was a head chief in the Sauk council, and the boy wanted to follow in his footsteps. First he needed to prove himself as a "brave" by injuring or killing someone in battle. Once a

▲ Black Hawk

Event: The Black Hawk War.

Role: Black Hawk, a chief of the Sauk Indians, fought the last war between Indian tribes and whites east of the Mississippi River. He first resisted, then signed, a treaty calling for his tribe to move west of the Mississippi. Accepting an invitation by the Winnebago, he recrossed the river into Illinois to live with them. The move led to a war in which Black Hawk and his followers held off a vastly superior force for months before they were slaughtered.

brave, he could become a war chief by showing leadership qualities in battle. A warrior normally held this title only as long as he maintained his reputation for courage and skill and could persuade men to follow him into battle. By the age of fifteen, Black Hawk had become a "brave" by wounding an enemy. It was in later fighting with the Osage Indians that he earned the title of war chief. By the age of forty-five, he had killed thirty of this enemy's warriors.

Black Hawk was strong and independent-minded. As a young man, he recognized the dangers of rum and cognac and decided never to drink the "fire water." Although liquor flowed freely among his people and was often traded to the Indians by the large fur companies in exchange for pelts, Black Hawk abstained from drinking alcohol throughout his life.

Another custom of the Sauk was polygamy. Most successful warriors married more than one wife. Black Hawk married young as others did, but he took only one wife, Asshewaqua (Singing Bird). The two remained loyal to each other throughout their lives.

In religion and war, however, Black Hawk was a traditional Sauk. Nearby tribes were accepting Christianity, but the Sauk and Fox continued to practice their old religion. Since fighting was important to the Sauk, the warriors were ever-ready for battle and relied on the Great Spirit to give them direction in war. Before leading a war party, Black Hawk fasted and prayed to the Great Spirit for a sign by which to rally his men. They trusted his instincts and followed him. He took great care when forming his war parties, personally interviewing each possible warrior, and proved to be a good judge of men. As a result, Black Hawk won a reputation as a fearless and able leader in battle.

White settlers. By the end of the 1700s, the Sauk were coming into contact with more and more white traders and settlers. The Indians decided, for their own protection, to sign the Treaty of Greenville in 1795. It promised that the Sauk would be received into the friendship and protection of the United States on an equal basis with other Indian tribes. Black Hawk was twenty-eight years old and a Sauk war chief when this treaty was signed. Despite their treaty with the Americans, the Sauk remained friendly with the British, who had been their longtime friends and trading partners. In fact, the Sauk had sided with the British during the American Revolution. They continued their regular visits to British trading posts in the late 1700s and early 1800s. These trips often took them near the new American settlements in the area.

In August 1804, after a fight between whites and Sauk travelers ended in the deaths of three settlers, some Sauk leaders agreed to travel to St. Louis and arrange a permanent peace. There they were plied with liquor and food, then asked to sign a treaty. The treaty traded fifteen million acres of Sauk land in Illinois, Wisconsin, and Missouri to the American government in return for $2,274.50 and an annual payment of $1,000. Although the Sauk party did not represent the tribal council or include most of the war chiefs, the Americans considered this treaty binding on the whole Sauk nation. The drunken Sauk party had even sold the land on which their principal city, Saukenuk, stood. White squatters began immediately to settle on Sauk territory—land that the majority of Sauk protested they had never agreed to sell. Black Hawk and some other war chiefs argued that the treaty was not binding.

Tensions grew between the two sides until, in 1808, the Americans built Fort Madison in disputed territory on the west bank of the Mississippi River near the mouth of the Des Moines River. Black Hawk led a party of Sauk in a demonstration against its construction. In 1809 he tried to take the fort by surprise during a supposed trading trip. Pretending to entertain the whites with a war dance, warriors attempted to stage an attack but withdrew when confronted with a loaded cannon. Black Hawk had planned to massacre the troops.

War of 1812. Three years later, the War of 1812 erupted between Great Britain and the United States. The conflict led to a break between Black Hawk and the majority of Sauk and Fox. While most of their warriors chose to remain neutral in this war, Black Hawk led a minority group that supported the British.

A broken promise strengthened his decision. Americans had pledged to the Sauk and Fox that Fort Madison would furnish them with the supplies they needed for survival. When the Indians arrived in late summer of 1812, they found no supplies available. Shortly after that, a British trader arrived at Saukenuk, which the

Sauk had continued to occupy. He delivered two boatloads of supplies for Black Hawk's people, convincing the war chief that the British were more reliable than the white Americans.

With the British. A group of the warriors traveled from Saukenuk to Green Bay on Lake Michigan, where Robert Dickson, a trader, was recruiting Indians of all tribes to fight for the British. Black Hawk was with the group but hesitated to join the British in battle. Eager for Black Hawk's support, Dickson presented him with a medal and gave him command of all forces at Green Bay, calling him General Black Hawk. The new general reluctantly agreed to fight. He led his men in attacks on Fort Meigs and possibly in the Battle of the Thames, under the Shawnee leader Tecumseh. Fighting without much success, Black Hawk and his followers returned to Saukenuk.

Keokuk. Black Hawk returned to find that the Sauk had a new war chief. In his absence, an American expedition had threatened the town, and the elders had prepared to abandon Saukenuk. Keokuk, a Sauk who had never killed an enemy, persuaded the council to let him talk. In a fiery speech, he begged his people to stand and fight. When no Americans showed up after this speech, Keokuk was an instant hero. Black Hawk and Keokuk began a long rivalry for tribal leadership.

Fighting the Americans. The rivalry was interrupted when Black Hawk resumed fighting in the War of 1812. In July 1814, he led an attack on three American keelboats on the Mississippi, setting one on fire by shooting a flaming arrow into its sail. His warriors boarded the burning boat and killed and scalped those aboard. Angered by this attack, the Americans sent General Zachary Taylor with 430 men to burn Saukenuk. They were not, however, aware that the British had reinforced the Sauk town with troops and artillery. Under unexpected fire, Taylor's men retreated. Black Hawk was disappointed that the Americans chose not to fight. He continued to support the British until the end of the war.

Saying "I have fought the Big Knives and will continue to fight them till they are off our lands," Black Hawk went on attacking the Americans even after British support stopped (Hagan, p. 76). His raids continued for a year, then stopped because the Sauk and Fox decided to make peace with the Americans. The warriors signed a treaty that reconfirmed the sale of Indian land in 1804. Black Hawk was one of the signers. They agreed also to exclude British traders from Saukenuk, but Black Hawk continued to believe in the British and to wear the king's medal.

The lead mines. In 1822, lead mining brought floods of white settlers to northwestern Illinois. They worked the mines side by side with the Sauk and Fox. The white settlers took over old Sauk hunting grounds, forcing the Sauk to hunt on Sioux land. Fighting erupted between the two tribes. As conditions around the mines grew more tense, it was decided that a party of Sauk and Fox should travel to Washington to meet with government officials. Keokuk, a friend of the Americans, went. Black Hawk did not. Afterward, in making tribal decisions, Keokuk became a strong champion of peace with the United States.

First removal. Settlers continued to move into the Saukenuk area while the government agent urged the Sauk to relocate across the river. Black Hawk and some of the Sauk refused to leave. By 1829, white settlers had begun taking Indian cornfields and bullying the Sauk. One settler started selling liquor in his store, against the rules of the Sauk. Black Hawk led a group of Sauk into the store, rolled out the barrels of liquor, used tomahawks to break them, and poured out the contents.

Governor Reynolds and the army. These and other incidents led John Reynolds, the governor of Illinois, to organize a militia to force the remaining Sauk to move. At the same time, General Edmund D. Gaines organized six companies of United States infantry as much to protect the Sauk from Reynolds's "wildcat army" as to persuade the Sauk to leave. Black Hawk carefully considered the situation, deciding that resistance was hopeless. When, in late June, the militia stormed Saukenuk, they found that Black Hawk and his followers had already crossed the Mississippi River. Shortly afterward, he and twenty-seven other Sauk and Fox chiefs appeared at Fort Armstrong near Saukenuk to sign articles of agreement. The Americans chose to recognize Keokuk as the head chief of the Sauk and Black Hawk, now sixty-one, was forced to submit to him.

Decision to fight. Conditions for the Indians continued to worsen. Keokuk tried to arrange a meeting with President Andrew Jackson in Washington but was refused. Black Hawk had remained inactive until he learned of this snub by the president. "Then and there ... the old Sauk decided to return to Saukenuk in the spring" (Hagan, p. 139). Some discontented Winnebago, Kickapoo, and Potawatomi joined Black Hawk and his followers. Bolstered by this support, the war chief decided to fight, and the episode that came to be known as the Black Hawk War was about to begin.

Participation: The Black Hawk War

Return home. By 1832, the village of Saukenuk had been destroyed, but an old ally, White Cloud, invited Black Hawk's followers to live in his village of Winnebago Indians located just up the Buck River. Feeling that he was responding to a direct order from the Great Spirit, Man-ee-do, Black Hawk led 400 braves with their families east across the Mississippi River, bypassing the old village to head up the Rock River. White Cloud, however, began to worry about breaking the signed agreement with the Americans. He reported Black Hawk's move to the authorities.

Black Hawk intended to stop at White Cloud's village, then move on to settle peacefully among the Potawatomi twelve miles farther up the Rock River. He told this to John Dixon, whose trading post was on the way, and warned an American official that his people would fight if the soldiers tried to stop them.

White reaction. News of Black Hawk's "invasion" wrought hysteria among the white settlers. Although there were no reports of any settlers being bothered by the Indians during their move upriver, Governor John Reynolds called out the militia. Among the men who volunteered to fight the Indian party was a young lawyer named Abraham Lincoln. Altogether, 1,600 militiamen were recruited for the action. They had no military training, however, and were nearly useless as a fighting force.

Meanwhile, the collection of rebellious Indians began to meet with disappointments. The main groups of Winnebago and Potawatomie Indians in northern Illinois and southern Wisconsin refused to take them in. Black Hawk had been promised by a Canadian Indian, Neopope, that the British would provide supplies, but none came. Reluctantly, he decided to swallow his pride and return to Iowa.

Misunderstanding and ambush. Meanwhile, the militia was approaching. Black Hawk sent a group to its camp to inform the soldiers that his people wanted to peacefully retreat across the Mississippi. In his autobiography, Black Hawk described the event:

> I immediately started three young men, with a white flag [of truce], to meet them and conduct them to our camp, that we might hold council with them, and descend Rock River again.... After this party had started, I sent five young men to see what might take place. The first party ... were taken prisoners. The last party had not proceeded far, before they saw about twenty men coming towards them in a full gallop. They ... were pursued, and two of them overtaken and killed! (Black Hawk, p. 123)

It had all been the result of a misunderstanding. The untrained militia, none of whom understood the Sauk language, had suspected the Indians were trying to trick them with the white flag. They continued to fire, killing two more messengers. The militia then set out after the rest of the Indians, but were ambushed by Black Hawk and forty warriors. At Old Man's Creek, the two forces battled, losing eleven militiamen and three Indians. The militia fled in panic from what came to be known as the Battle of Stillman's Run, named after a militia captain, Isaiah Stillman.

The war had begun in earnest. Winnebago and Potawatomi tribesmen who had earlier wanted nothing to do with Black Hawk now joined him. Potawatomi war parties attacked several settlements. At Ottawa, Illinois, they shot, tomahawked and mutilated the bodies of fifteen settlers and kidnaped two teenage girls. (The girls were later released.) News of this massacre created widespread panic in Illinois. Thousands fled toward Lake Michigan and the safety of the village of Chicago.

Retreat. Still trying to move back across the Mississippi River, Black Hawk decided to travel through the Wisconsin wilderness. To cover his retreat, he sent war parties against white settlements in Illinois and Wisconsin. He hoped that these small but deadly skirmishes would distract the settlers long enough for his followers to escape through the wilderness. By late June, most of his people were in southern Wisconsin, foraging for food near Lake Koshkonong. They were having problems. Some had begun to die of starvation. Potawatomi and Winnebago warriors who had recently joined the party began to desert. At this point, Black Hawk felt his only hope was to reach Iowa, where he could rejoin Keokuk or escape into the Great Plains. The American soldiers in pursuit of him, however, had discovered his trail.

On July 21, 1832, the troops finally caught up with Black Hawk's rear guard near present-day Sauk City, Wisconsin. In what became known as the Battle of Wisconsin Heights, the Americans lost one soldier and the Sauk lost five warriors. Though the Americans had more men and superior weapons, they hesitated, perhaps remembering Stillman's Run, and the Sauk managed to slip away.

The only hope for Black Hawk and his followers was to outrun their pursuers. Old, sick, and starving Indians dropped along the trail. Many were killed and scalped by the troops. Black Hawk finally reached the Mississippi River at the mouth of the Bad Axe River (near present-day Victory, Wisconsin). With 500 followers, he hoped to cross the Mississippi, but found the path blocked by an American steamship, the *Warrior,* that carried troops and artillery.

Once more Black Hawk sent a party under a white flag to offer surrender. Once more there was misunderstanding. The captain of the ship suspected the white flag was a trick and requested that just two Indians come aboard. There was no trustworthy translator and the Indians did not understand his request. The *Warrior* opened fire on the Indians. Black Hawk and his group were trapped.

Bad Axe Massacre. The next day, August 2, 1832, the soldiers and militiamen caught up with the Sauk. In what became known as the Bad Axe Massacre, the troops killed dozens of Indians, including women, children, and the elderly. Those who made it across the Mississippi were killed by Sioux Indians who had joined the fighting on the side of the Americans. Only about 150 Sauk survived. Black Hawk escaped and fled to a Winnebago settlement.

▲ **The Bad Axe Massacre**

The Black Hawk War, now virtually over, had cost the lives of 72 soldiers and settlers and between 450 and 600 Indians.

Aftermath

Cholera. An indirect result of the war was the spread of Asiatic cholera to the Midwest. The disease had spread from Asia to Europe in 1831 and was brought to New York by immigrants. Troops recruited from the East Coast carried it to Detroit, Chicago, Galena, and Saukenuk. It spread throughout the Midwest, killing thousands on both sides of the war. The epidemic proved to be far more deadly than the Black Hawk War.

Surrender. Black Hawk and White Cloud surrendered after the Winnebago were persuaded to give them up. They were escorted to St. Louis by Lieutenant Jefferson Davis, future president of the Confederate States of America. Black Hawk described Davis as "the young war chief who treated us with much kindness" (Nichols, p. 268). For several months the two Indians were held at Jefferson Barracks, then they were taken to the East Coast. The Americans hoped to impress them with the wealth and power of the United States.

Black Hawk. Black Hawk was sent to Fort Monroe in Virginia, then to meet President Jackson. He was paraded through the streets of eastern cities like a captured animal, but the public greeted him "as a brave, romantic symbol of the wild frontier and treated him like a hero." The tour seemed to soften Black Hawk's attitude toward the Americans. In New York he said, "Brother, we like your talk, We will be friends. We like the white people, they are very kind to us. We shall not forget it" (Tebbell and Jennison, p. 205).

The Movements of the Sauk Indians

Before 1816	Settled at Green Bay, Wisconsin.
1816	Ceded land to United States, moved onto Fox land.
1824	Merged with Fox Indians.
1832	Removed from east of the Mississippi to central Iowa.
1842	Removed to Osage land in Oklahoma.
1857	325 Sauk buy land and move to Tama, Iowa.
After 1857	Other Sauk spread to Kansas and Nebraska.

In 1837, Black Hawk returned to Washington, D.C., accompanying Keokuk and other Sauk to negotiate with the government. Once again, the Indians were forced to sign away a large tract of land in exchange for a small sum of money.

In the last few months of his life, Black Hawk found himself the object of admiration among Iowa settlers. He was often invited to the territorial capital to attend sessions of the legislature. His last public appearance was at a Fourth of July celebration in the town of Fort Madison, Iowa, the namesake of the fort he had tried to capture in 1809. After receiving a toast, he spoke:

> A few summers ago, I was fighting against you. I did wrong, perhaps, but that is past. It is buried. Let it be forgotten. Rock River was a beautiful country. I loved my towns, my cornfields, and the home of my people. It is now yours. Keep it as we did. (Tebbell, p. 286)

Black Hawk died in his lodge on October 3, 1848. His wife, Singing Bird, survived him.

The Sauk and Fox. The Sauk and Fox were forced to accept a harsh peace settlement, which included giving up a 50-mile-wide strip of Iowa land in exchange for $660,000 and some supplies. In later years, the followers of Keokuk were moved to Kansas and then to Oklahoma. Some returned to Iowa, where today they have a settlement at Tama. Other Sauk and Fox live in Kansas, but the largest reservation sits in Oklahoma. In 1989, the Wisconsin legislature passed a resolution expressing regret and sorrow for the Black Hawk War and the Bad Axe Massacre.

For More Information

Black Hawk. *Black Hawk.* Edited by Donald Jackson. Chicago: University of Illinois Press, 1964.

Eby, Cecil. *"That Disgraceful Affair," the Black Hawk War.* New York: W. W. Norton and Company.

Hagan, William T. *The Sac and Fox Indians.* Norman: University of Oklahoma Press, 1958.

Nichols, Roger. "Black Hawk War Remembered." *Sac and Fox News,* June 1, 1990.

Tebbell, John, and Keith Jennison. *The American Indian Wars.* New York: Harper Brothers, 1960.

John Ross

1790-1866

Personal Background

Scotch-Cherokee family. John Ross's grandfather, John McDonald, moved from Inverness, Scotland, to London, England and then to Georgia in America. There he settled at Fort Loudoun and married Anna Storey, a young woman who was half Cherokee Indian. This marriage made McDonald a member of the Cherokee, and he lived among them with his new wife. In time the two had a daughter, Molly.

The Rosses. When Molly had grown into a beautiful young woman, there chanced to pass through the region a traveling tradesman, Daniel Ross. Caught by Cherokee warriors and threatened with death as a spy, Daniel was rescued by McDonald and, in the process, met Molly. The two were married in 1785. They too chose to live among the Cherokee, while Daniel set up trading posts in one part of the Cherokee nation and then another. The couple had nine children. John, born October 3, 1790, at Tahnoovayah (now Rossville), Georgia, was the third oldest. His brother Lewis was his nearest boyhood companion.

Molly died while the two boys were young, but not before she had taught them to love Cherokee ways. After Molly's death, the boys' grandmother took over their upbringing and taught them about their Scottish heritage.

▲ **John Ross**

Event: The removal of the Cherokee Indians from their native lands.

Role: As head chief of the Eastern Cherokee, John Ross stubbornly resisted the loss of his people's original homeland. He met with federal authorities to negotiate on the tribe's behalf. When removal became inescapable, he supervised the Cherokee journey and continued to lead the nation in its new home in Indian Territory (Oklahoma).

Childhood. There was an uneasy merging of the two cultures in the boys' upbringing. Grandfather John McDonald and father Daniel insisted on raising the children as Scots. John Ross and his brother were to be given a good education and to learn the manners and dress of the Scots. Later, John would always remember one childhood incident. When he was about seven years old, the family was planning to attend the Green Corn Festival of the Cherokee, an affair in which the Indians dressed in their finery to sing and dance in celebration of the harvesting of the first corn. John's grandmother had prepared a fine Scot suit for him to wear for the Cherokee festival. No one was more uncomfortable than John Ross when the other Indian boys teased and chided the dapper young Scot on the first day of the festival. A tearful night convinced the older generation to let him return the next day in his everyday clothes of buckskin. From then on he preferred to dress like the Cherokee boys around him and play Cherokee games.

Education. Still, John Ross's grandparents and father insisted that he grow up as a Scotch-American. To ensure that his sons would be properly educated, Daniel Ross started a school near their home and hired John Barber Davis as the teacher. The Ross boys learned to read and write English, after which they spoke English at home and broken Cherokee at play. John completed his formal education at the Kingston Academy in Tennessee, then began a career in business as a partner with his brother and John Meigs (son of U.S. Indian agent M. J. Meigs) at Ross's Landing.

Involvement with the Cherokee. John Ross grew to be a slender young man of medium height with blue eyes and brown hair. Because most Cherokee men were taller than he, Ross became known as Little John or Little John Scot. He quickly gained a reputation for hard work, absolute honesty, and thoughtfulness. He also began taking an interest in the affairs of the Cherokee nation, then led by a head chief named Pathkiller and a Cherokee council whose spokesman was a giant of a man called Ridge. Young Ross would sit in the audience at meetings of the tribal council and, although not permitted to speak, would afterward discuss the issues at hand with individual council members. They learned to respect him for his clear thinking and problem-solving ability.

Ross's first real venture into the affairs of the Cherokee came

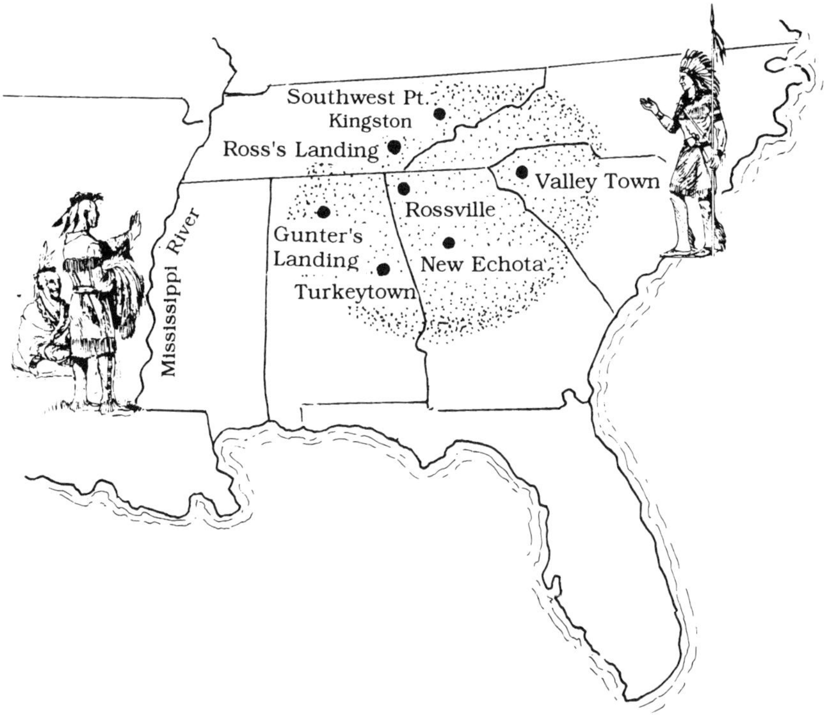

▲ **Cherokee land, circa 1800**

at the request of the U. S. Indian agent M. J. Meigs in 1809. The Cherokee people were already in disagreement about whether or not to listen to white settlers urging them to move eastward. Some Cherokee had already separated from the Eastern Cherokee and moved to Arkansas. Meigs needed to establish good relations with the Arkansas group and decided to send them gifts. Ross was just nineteen years old when he was asked to lead a party to deliver the gifts. He and three aides started on Christmas Day to travel to Arkansas. The journey began by boat upriver toward the Mississippi. After a sixty-day trip that ended with the boat capsizing and half the presents being lost, Ross and his small group decided to continue the remaining 200 miles of the journey on foot. The party made it in just eight days with no further losses. They returned to Ross's Landing in April. Ross had earned a new reputation for courage. Before he turned twenty-three, he would be nominated for a place on the Cherokee council by his friend Ridge.

Tecumseh. In 1811, many of the Indian tribes were in turmoil. A powerful Shawnee chief, Tecumseh, was riding among them, forecasting doom unless all the tribes banded together to resist the invasion of their lands by whites. Ridge attended a meeting that Tecumseh had called with the neighboring Creek. Unlike Tecumseh, the leaders of the Creek nation had been urging their people to act peacefully, like the Cherokee, to establish rights to their own lands. Many of the Creek and Cherokee thought Tecumseh's proposals outlandish and dangerous, but a few agreed with him. A small group of young Creek warriors, who became known as "Red Sticks," decided to heed Tecumseh's words. They began a rampage of murder and destruction among the white settlers in their Georgia territory. Even some of the Creek were frightened and called for help. In response, General Andrew Jackson arrived to search out and subdue the Red Sticks.

Battle of Horseshoe Bend. Part of a military leader's task was to recruit soldiers, and Jackson needed more men. He tried to recruit among the local white settlers and then asked for help from the Cherokee. Ridge gathered about 800 Cherokee recruits, for which Jackson rewarded him with the rank of first lieutenant. The chief's bravery in battle soon won him a promotion to major in 1814.

Ridge was a highly respected Cherokee leader but was handicapped in dealing with the whites because of his poor command of English. He solved this problem by recruiting young John Ross as his interpreter with the rank of lieutenant. Ridge's Cherokee troops joined some American troops under General John Coffee in pursuit of the Red Sticks.

Jackson's forces, along with those of Coffee and Ridge, caught up with about 1,000 Red Sticks in upper Alabama. Barricading themselves on the banks of the Tallapoosa River, the Red Sticks had built a large and strong breastwork where the river arched. The barricade protected them on the land side while the river, curving like a horseshoe, defended them on two sides and in the rear. Behind them, canoes lined the riverbank in case they needed to make a quick escape.

Jackson attacked the breastwork with artillery, but the Red Stick fortress held firm. Meanwhile, General Coffee's troops and

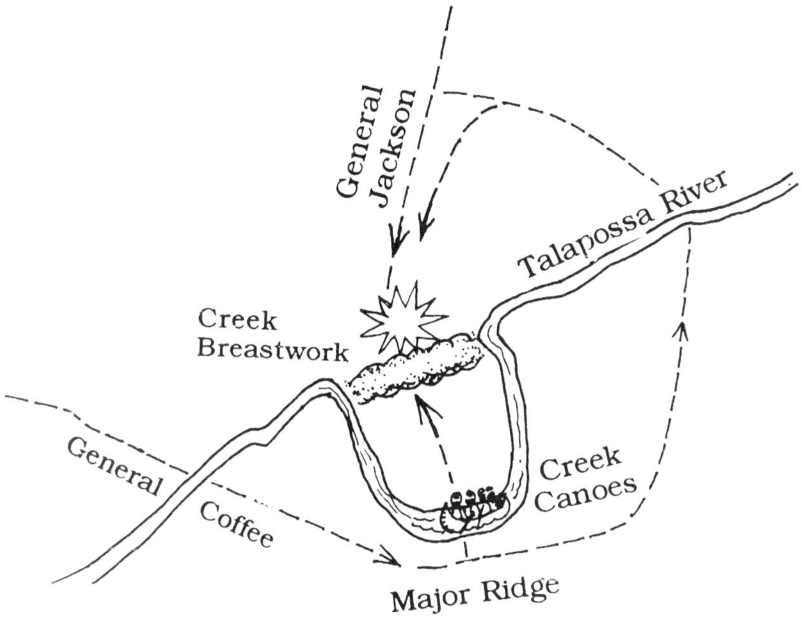

▲ **The Battle of Horseshoe Bend**

Major Ridge's Cherokee regiment attacked from the side and then crossed the river to approach from the rear. Ridge's Cherokee tried to attack from the river's edge but were helpless with the river between them and the enemy. A pause to regroup gave the major time to think out loud about the possibility of taking the Creek canoes so that his men could get on the same side of the river as the Red Sticks and behind their breastwork. Ross and two other Cherokee promptly jumped into the river. Under Red Stick fire, the three swam to the canoes. Although one of them, known as the Whale, was wounded, they hauled back the canoes. The Cherokee could now cross the river and attack the Creek from the rear.

In the end, the Red Sticks were almost destroyed. A total of 557 Red Sticks lay dead in their fortress and another 350 were killed in the water as they tried to flee. Perhaps 100 escaped, many of them wounded. The American and Cherokee counted 50 dead and 135 wounded.

Marriage. In 1813, Ross had married Elizabeth Brown Henley. Part Cherokee, Elizabeth was known by her Indian name,

Quatie. The marriage lasted until Quatie's death in 1839. In those twenty-six years the couple had six children, five of whom survived infancy. Much of this time, Ross spent long periods in Philadelphia and Washington as a negotiator for the Cherokee nation. Since Quatie could not read or write English, she did not communicate with her husband during these periods, which were difficult for the Ross family.

The Family of John and Quatie Ross

Sons (all fought for the Union in the Civil War)
- James McDonald (1814; killed in the Civil War)
- Allen (1817)
- Silas Dinsmore (1829)
- George Washington (1830)

Daughter
- Jane (1821; married Indian agent R. J. Meigs)

Cherokee council. In 1823, Ross and a farmer named Charles Hicks became members of the Cherokee tribal council. Since Head Chief Pathkiller had become old and weak and Major Ridge preferred to remain speaker for the council, Hicks was made assistant head chief. Ross, Major Ridge, his son John Ridge, and Hicks soon found themselves in negotiations with the United States government, which hoped to remove all the Cherokee to land west of the Mississippi River.

Participation: Removal of the Cherokee

The problem of removal. Every president since Thomas Jefferson had faced the problem of separating Indian and white societies. For many years, Congress and various presidents had discussed the Cherokee "problem." At the same time, many Cherokee had decided it would be wise for them was to adopt some of the ways of white settlers. Major Ridge had become a wealthy landowner with his own slave-worked plantations. Charles Hicks was a successful farmer, an occupation not usually adopted by Cherokee men. Ross himself had become a successful trader and plantation owner. Meanwhile, tensions continued to grow between the Indians and whites vying for land. By the 1820s, the major question on the white side seemed to be whether to remove the Cherokee gradually or immediately. John Quincy Adams had favored gradual removal but did little to encourage it (see **John Quincy Adams**). The burden of solving the problem often fell on state governments, which was the case in Georgia.

A traitor. In 1823, Ross, Major Ridge, and Hicks were

▲ **Major Ridge**

appointed by the Cherokee council to meet with Georgia representatives about their situation. Before the agreed-upon date, however, some Georgians had worked to influence the Cherokee. They had made one Cherokee chief a general and offered him bribes in return for his help in convincing other Cherokee to agree to give up their lands. Before the meeting began, "General" McIntosh contacted committee chairman Ross and the others, offering each $2,000 or $3,000 to agree to give up Cherokee lands in that state. General McIntosh then put his offer in writing. Ross received a note that promised $2,000 to any of Ross's friends if they would agree to sign treaties giving up Cherokee land. Outraged, Ross decided to use this note at the meeting. Without comment, he handed it to the clerk, who, with the Georgia representatives present, read it to the assembled negotiators. General McIntosh left the meeting in disgrace, followed soon by the Georgia representatives. The plans to take Cherokee land had been momentarily stopped.

Head chief. Ross was beginning to feel that the Cherokee could best protect their own interests by unifying under a constitution, a set of common rules and purposes, like that of the white people. He and Major Ridge began to create one. By the annual council meeting of 1827, they were prepared to recommend the adoption of a Cherokee constitution. Meanwhile, that year had been a somber one for the Cherokee nation. Old and beloved Head Chief Pathkiller had died and, surprisingly, so had Assistant Head Chief Hicks. On the recommendation of Major Ridge, the council chose Ross to be acting head chief. He took charge at a difficult time. Ridge and Ross wanted to keep peace with the whites but settlers were pressing for Cherokee land—and the Cherokee people were beginning to divide over the issue. In addition, missionaries had arrived to set up schools. They were popular with some Cherokee and disliked by others. Mostly, the missionaries advised the Cherokee of their right to keep the land.

Georgia land claims. In the midst of a rebellion within the tribal council, the state of Georgia decided to take action against the Cherokee. Some nervous chiefs blamed the missionaries for their difficulties and wanted to force them to leave. These chiefs also wanted to reinstate old tribal laws that did not permit individual Cherokee to sell tribal lands. Major Ridge voted to enforce this old law but cautioned the chiefs to remain calm and to work together. As a symbol of the nation's unity, he planned and paid for the building of a capital city, New Echota.

The *Cherokee Phoenix*. Ross was also searching for ways to unite the Cherokee nation. Sequoyah, a Cherokee Indian, had invented a written language by 1821, and many Cherokee could read and write in their own language. Seizing on this common language, the head chief ordered special printing type and began the first Indian newspaper in the United States, the *Cherokee Phoenix*.

The paper contained articles by Ross and reports of council actions in both English and Cherokee. But all these efforts—the Cherokee language, Major Ridge's New Echota, and the *Cherokee Phoenix*—failed to hold the nation together.

In 1828, the Georgia Legislature claimed that Cherokee lands fell under state control. In the same year, John Quincy Adams was replaced as president by Andrew Jackson, who was anxious to be rid of the Indian problems with the settlers. The situation grew more tense in the next year with a new discovery on Cherokee land—gold. White gold hunters flocked onto the lands, ignoring Cherokee rights. The Cherokee council sent Ross and others to Washington to plead with Jackson. They soon found that, against the advice of his cabinet and military officers, the general whom they had aided in the Creek War would do nothing to help them.

Government investigation. At Ross's pleading, Secretary of War John Eaton sent General John Coffee to investigate reports that Georgia was illegally occupying Cherokee land. Coffee advised the Cherokee that they had the real rights to the land but should not expect government aid. The Cherokee, he said, should drive the whites off their land themselves. Ignoring Chief Ross's request for patience, Major Ridge decided to do as Coffee suggested. He gathered some warriors and drove off about thirty white settlers, killing a few in the process. This resulted in even more tension between whites and Indians. Georgians threatened to burn the homes of Ross and Ridge, who were forced to place armed guards around their properties. Ridge's independent "attack" was the beginning of a rift between the two most powerful men among the Cherokee.

Cherokee appeals. Major Ridge could not believe that his old friend Andrew Jackson would not come to his people's aid. He took his own group of Cherokee to Washington to plead with the president. At first Jackson refused to see them, and when he finally agreed to speak with Ridge, he refused to lend his support.

Ross, meanwhile, placed his hope in the Supreme Court. Cherokee claims were considered in several cases in 1831. Chief Justice John Marshall sided with the Cherokee. In three separate decisions, the state of Georgia was ordered to withdraw its claim to

Cherokee land. Georgia ignored these decisions, and President Jackson refused to enforce the ruling of the court.

John Ridge. Major Ridge's son, John, had suffered ill health and, therefore, was not a strong candidate for Cherokee political office. However, John had gone north to school and become a capable lawyer. He had spent a great deal of time in places where he could measure white feelings and intentions. When, on a petition by John Ross, the Supreme Court ruled that the state of Georgia had no right to Cherokee land and Jackson refused to act, John Ridge felt that the Cherokee would lose everything. He began to plead for the Cherokee to sell their land and move. Major Ridge, who had been a outspoken champion of remaining on the land, now changed his position to side with his son. The minority of Cherokee who joined them became known as the Treaty Party.

Ross continued to side with the more conservative Cherokee and urged the people to hold onto their land. Under him, the tribal council had renewed the old law that forbade the selling of any Cherokee land under the penalty of death. The state position was that the Indians could sell the land to the state or lose it to the state. Since the Cherokee, by their own rule, could not sell the land, Georgia began to take choice bits of Cherokee land to sell to white settlers. Hundreds of acres of Major Ridge's plantation were sold in 1832 along with 160 acres of John Ridge's plantation. The large home of John Ridge was sold the next year. The Cherokee were told they would be paid for the land if they agreed to leave the state. The Ridges agreed to move but Ross refused to barter with the state and moved to a cabin in Tennessee.

Kitchen Chiefs. During all this turmoil, Ross had converted to Methodism. In 1833, the American Board of Missions advised him to move west of the Mississippi River. At the board's request, he again traveled to Washington to hear of the government's offer to relocate the Cherokee. He returned home unconvinced, only to find that the Ridges had persuaded twenty-five chiefs to sign a petition against him. His own brother, Andrew, leader of a powerful group of non-chiefs who called themselves Kitchen Chiefs, was now willing to give up his land under government terms.

Divided Cherokee nation. Soon there were two Cherokee

parties in Washington working for different purposes: John Ross campaigned for the government to allow Cherokees to stay on some of their land while giving up other land; John Ridge and Andrew Ross were negotiating a treaty of complete removal. Andrew was the one who made the final deal, but the terms were too harsh even for the champions of removal. Major Ridge refused to sign. John Walker, another chief, and David Vann, the wealthiest of all Cherokee, negotiated privately with Secretary of War Lewis Cass. Finally, they also refused to accept the government's terms. Ross, of course, refused to consider the government offer all along.

Impeachment. Now completely disillusioned, the Cherokee tribal council met in 1834 amid quarreling and threats. One council member, Elijah Hicks, presented a petition for the impeachment of the three council members who had most strongly sided with the government—John Ridge, Major Ridge, and David Vann. Even though two of them had finally refused the government offer, all three were impeached. John Walker, another champion for abandoning Cherokee land, was killed traveling from the meeting. Ross raised funds to defend the two men accused of the murder.

The Treaty Party. In October, 1834, the Cherokee council met again. Conditions were growing desperate, so desperate that the council voted to send a new delegation led by the Treaty Party to Washington. They were to reach a final agreement with the government. Ross and John Ridge, both members of the delegation, represented the two major factions of the Cherokee nation.

Ross now realized that the split in the Cherokee nation would weaken it and end in removal. He began pleading for the best terms possible for his people. He suggested selling some Cherokee land to the United States, but proposed allowing those Cherokee who so desired to stay on their land and become full citizens.

The terms of removal. By 1835, only the terms of the removal were in question. Ross suggested selling the land for $20 million, the amount he estimated would be needed to settle the 12,000 or 13,000 people on new land. The United States Senate declined. The government believed that $5 million was enough to pay the Cherokee. Ross withdrew his proposal to sell. In the end, John Ridge agreed to sell the Cherokee land to the United States for

$4.5 million and an annual sum for schools in the new territory. The Eastern Cherokee were to migrate west to join the 1,000 Cherokee who had moved there earlier.

Arrest. John Ridge suggested to the president that a respectful letter of friendship to the Cherokee would ease the tense situation. To make sure that this letter was received and accepted, Major Ridge and John Ridge announced that they were organizing the 1835 tribal council. Open war developed between the Ridge faction and Ross's Cherokee government. Finally, in November, the two sides agreed to send another group of twenty people to Washington to complete the terms of removal. That expedition was never organized, however, for on November 7, 1835, Georgia guards arrested Ross, claiming he was illegally living among the Cherokee. He and a house guest, who also was arrested, were imprisoned in a log cabin where two corpses of Cherokee warriors hung. Ross was soon released and his friend moved to other quarters, but the doom of the Cherokee was sealed as the Ridges now tried to speak for the whole Cherokee nation. On December 29, 1835, twenty chiefs of Ridge's Treaty Party met at New Echota to sign an agreement giving up Cherokee land. The tribe was given until May 23, 1838, to remove themselves from the land.

The Ridges quickly sold their land to the government. Major Ridge headed west with a bankroll of $27,000. Meanwhile, Ross also traveled—first to Washington to plead for more time, then around the Cherokee nation advising the people to stand firm for fair treatment from the government.

Deadline for removal. May 1838 came and passed with most of the Cherokee still holding on to their land. In desperation, the United States assigned General Winfield Scott the task of removing them. Demanding that his officers treat the Indians as kindly as possible, Scott declared that all Cherokee should be rounded up and placed in prison camps pending their removal west. By June 19, all the Cherokee remaining in the East were held in three camps. At this point, Ross focused on getting adequate treatment for those 11,000 Cherokee to be removed. He went to work for the officers supervising the removal. At the same time, he proposed to Scott that he be placed in charge of the removal effort. Finally, over the protests of President John Tyler, Scott contracted with Ross to supervise the removal. Ross organized and equipped the traveling parties; the Cherokee would walk several hundred miles to the new land. Had Ross not taken charge, the removal might have been much worse than it was.

Removal. The first Cherokee migrants had gone to Arkansas, then moved to Kansas, and finally settled in Oklahoma. The majority of the Cherokee would walk to Oklahoma. Ross agreed to move all the people if the government would pay the costs—$772,393 if the trip was successfully completed in eighty days. But the trip, which came to be called the Trail of Tears, was so difficult that hundreds of Cherokee died on the way. The Cherokee took off in groups, with the first one leaving in May 1838. A traveler described the sight:

> We met several detachments in the southern part of Kentucky.... The last detachment which we passed on the 7th [of December] embraced rising two thousand Indians.... The sick and feeble were carried in waggons ... many ride on horseback and multitudes go on foot—even aged females, apparently nearly ready to drop into the grave were traveling with heavy burdens attached to the back ... on the sometimes frozen ground, and sometimes muddy streets, with no covering for the feet except what nature had given them. (Foreman, p. 306)

It took roughly ten months for all the detachments to reach their destination, the travelers in some cases walking 800 miles. Lasting much longer than the government planned, the removal cost an additional $486,939. About 4,000 died during the capture-and-prison-camp period and the removal itself. Altogether, Ross claimed a total of 13,149 Cherokee and other Indians removed under his supervision. Ross and Quatie were among the last to depart, starting their journey by boat in very cold weather. Sadly, Quatie was one of those to die on the trip.

Aftermath

Chief in a new land. Arriving in Oklahoma in 1839, Ross again found himself in an uneasy atmosphere. A few hundred

Cherokee had moved west before Ross's group at the first sign of turmoil with the whites. They had been joined by the migrants in Major Ridge's Treaty Party. Together these Cherokee formed a new, comfortable society. They were willing to accept the Ross group, which outnumbered them by nearly ten to one, but only on their conditions and under their laws. Ross suggested that a council be held to reduce differences between old and new immigrants.

Six thousand Cherokee attended this conference in the new land. The majority was strongly in favor of a government such as the one they had formed in the East. In frustration, the chief of the Oklahoma Cherokee, the earlier migrants, walked out of the council. Ross again became head chief of the Cherokee nation.

Murder. Now Ross's followers demanded that the old laws be enforced. One of these called for the death penalty to anyone selling Cherokee land without approval of the council. The new council found that some of its old members had been guilty of dealing independently with the United States government, among them the Ridges and Elias Boudinot, the first editor of the *Cherokee Phoenix.* According to old tribal law, these men should be sentenced to death. The council knew, however, that Ross was a fair man and would not agree to a death sentence. Members decided to take matters into their own hands.

Warriors drew lots to see who would be selected for the murder parties. About twenty-five men were assigned for each murder. Without Ross's knowledge, parties went out and killed John Ridge and Major Ridge as well as most of the others who had been found guilty. Major Ridge's nephew, Chief Stand Watie, escaped. He would later take out his anger on Ross by burning his house down.

Mary Stapler. Ross continued to negotiate for fair terms for the Cherokee. He traveled to Washington to get money for schools and the sum promised for the removal, which was finally paid in 1841. On one of his many trips east to crusade for the Cherokee cause, Ross met Mary Bryan Stapler. In 1841, at the age of fifteen, Mary began to write letters to Ross. Although he was thirty-six years her senior, the two were married at Philadelphia, Pennsylvania, in 1844. Ross and his new wife built a home at Park Hill, Oklahoma, which they called Rose Cottage. Here the two lived happily until the Civil War, with Ross continuing as head chief of the Cherokee and Mary as his closest companion and adviser.

Civil War. The Civil War created new dissension among the Cherokee. At first Ross kept them neutral, but by October 1861, the Cherokee council had decided to side with the Confederacy. Ross pleaded with the council, and the following year it resumed its earlier position of neutrality. Late in 1862, however, pressure from the United States resulted in the Cherokee nation joining the Union. Ross went to Washington in 1863 to sign the agreement.

Confederates and Unionists. The damage had been done, however; Cherokee warriors had by this time enlisted on both sides of the conflict. One who joined the rebel cause was Chief Stand Watie, who became a capable Confederate general. It was General Stand Watie who oversaw the burning of the Ross home.

By that time, however, Ross and Mary had fled from the Confederate invasion of Cherokee land. They were in Philadelphia when she died on July 20, 1865. But Ross continued to fight for his Cherokee people. He was in Washington, again pleading for government support of the Cherokee, when he died on August 1, 1866.

For More Information

Eaton, Rachel Caroline. *John Ross and the Cherokee Indians.* Chicago: University of Chicago Libraries, 1921.

Ehle, John. *Trail of Tears: The Rise and Fall of the Cherokee Nation.* New York: Doubleday, 1988.

Foreman, Grant. *Indian Removal.* Norman: University of Oklahoma Press, 1972.

Moulton, Gary E. *John Ross Cherokee Chief.* Athens: University of Georgia Press, 1978.

Winfield Scott

1786-1866

Personal Background

The Scott family. One of Winfield Scott's grandfathers had come from Scotland to Bristol, England, and then to Virginia, where he hid from the law until a general amnesty for all British law violators was decreed in 1747. Scott's other grandfather had been part of a group seeking to overthrow the British king. Another relative, William Winfield, had been the wealthiest man in the colonies. Winfield Scott's parents, William Scott, once a captain in the Revolutionary Army, and Ann Mason Scott, inherited some of this wealth. The couple lived on a large farm about fourteen miles from Petersburg, Virginia. It was here that Scott was born June on 13, 1786.

Early years. Scott's father died when he was six years old, leaving his mother to raise him alone. He credited her and two teachers with his training in manners as well as his passion for books. In fact, Scott gave all credit for his success in later life to his mother, who died when he was seventeen. After a year of high school, he went on to enter college.

In his later years, Scott wrote about his life, describing school days that were not challenging and studies to which he paid little attention. He did, however, recall two of his teachers: James Hargrave, a Quaker tutor, and James Ogilvie, with whom he studied for a year in high school in Rappahannock County, Virginia, before enrolling in William and Mary College in Williamsburg, Virginia.

▲ **Winfield Scott**

Event: Removal of the Indians from east of the Mississippi River.

Role: As one of the leading generals of the United States Army, Winfield Scott was called upon by various United States presidents to remove first the Sauk and later the Seminole and Cherokee from their lands in the East to Iowa and Indian Territory (Oklahoma).

Scott long remembered one incident about this period of his life. At age seventeen, he had nearly reached his full adult height—six-feet four-inches tall—which in those days made him a giant of a man. One day as he walked through town, a loud noise attracted him; he rounded a corner to find his teacher, James Hargrave, a slight man, being attacked by one of the town's biggest bullies. One blow from Scott knocked the bully down. But Hargrave believed in Quaker principles of peacefulness and grabbed Scott to stop him from fighting. Hampered, Scott fell victim to several blows from the bully before he could free himself. He then punched the brute again and ended the battle. The episode made the boy aware of his great physical strength. Years later, Hargrave would say that he had not wanted Scott to fight, but since he did, the teacher was glad that he had not lost.

A lawyer. Scott left college after one year of study to read for the law with a prominent attorney, David Robinson. Shortly thereafter, Scott began his own practice, "riding the circuit" to provide legal aid wherever it was demanded. In 1807, an incident that would affect his life for years brought him to Richmond, Virginia. The former vice-president of the United States, Aaron Burr, was being tried for treason. Scott joined the throng of young lawyers who gathered to watch the proceedings. Convinced of Burr's guilt, Scott was sorry that he had not been punished and made an example of. Furthermore, he was certain that Burr's cohort General James Wilkinson was equally guilty and should have been punished also. Later, Scott made his views public, angering Wilkinson, who by then was major general of the army. From that time on, the two shared a common dislike for one another.

Jefferson's embargo. The events of 1807 began to shape Scott's future. On July 2, President Thomas Jefferson took action against Britain by closing American harbors to international trade. Jefferson felt that depriving the British and French of American goods would force them to make more favorable trade agreements. British ships of trade and war ignored the ban, however, and waited offshore ready to steal into any cove to conduct trade. Jefferson, who had deliberately reduced the size of the army as part of his plan to have a weak central government, now needed troops to keep the British out, so he called for a militia.

Hearing of the president's need, Scott rode twenty-five miles in one night to borrow a friend's old uniform and report for duty. After joining he was made a lance-corporal and given charge of a small group patrolling a section of coastline. One night during a patrol he and his men intercepted a British rowboat that had put ashore from one of the larger ships. The men in the rowboat had picked up supplies illegally and were headed back to sea. Scott arrested them and held them until a higher authority ordered him to release the men and the boat, but not the supplies. This experience was his introduction to the politics of army life. Corporal Scott thought it ridiculous to send the men back with only a warning—not to do it again.

Army life in the early 1800s. When Jefferson began to challenge the British with his policies, there was no official, organized United States army. Commanders received ranks according to the number of men they could recruit. The system produced officers who were often poorly prepared to lead their charges in combat. Adding to the disorganization, most officers did not want to take orders from anyone else. Officers and their units fought when and where they pleased and refused combat or other active duty when it appeared to offer no chance of personal gain.

But more serious and committed than most, Scott applied to President Jefferson for a permanent position in the army. Impressed with the eager young man, Jefferson soon called on him to serve with the rank of captain. In 1808, Scott organized his company in Norfolk, Virginia, and proceeded as ordered to New Orleans, Louisiana. James Wilkinson, the general whom Scott had openly charged with treason at the trial of Aaron Burr, was then in charge of the army in the South. The two men heartily disliked each other, but they held an uneasy truce for two years. In 1810, their conflict came to a head with the court-martial of Scott for remarks against his commanding officer. Although in the end he was only scolded, Scott left the service to resume his law practice.

War of 1812. The army was still a disorganized patchwork when another need for a fighting unit arose. In the northwest, Indians and British were at war with Americans. Scott was called to service and doubly promoted to the rank of lieutenant colonel. He was placed in charge of recruiting and then commanding the Second

Artillery, a "flying" artillery unit, which could travel fast because it carried light equipment.

Once the unit was formed, Scott requested action, seeking an assignment in Canada (in present-day Ontario). Arriving there on October 4, 1812, when the battle at Queenston was winding down, he reported to Brigadier General Alex Smyth. Scott pleaded to be allowed to join in the battle. With American forces badly battered, Scott's unit was positioned on a high post overlooking the British forces. Left alone to defend the heights, Scott soon saw how greatly the enemy outnumbered his force. A message asking for reinforcements brought only a reply from the commanding officer that none of the other unit commanders was willing to help. Overpowered, Scott began a retreat, but the British kept up a hot pursuit even as the Americans stumbled down a steep slope. Only about a third of the men reached the bottom of the hill, and Scott had no choice but to surrender. His men were taken prisoners, then paroled (left free on the promise that they would not resume the fight). Scott was finally returned to the Americans in exchange for British prisoners. In spite of the defeat, he had shown himself to be courageous in battle and soon was promoted to the rank of colonel and placed in charge of a new regiment.

This regiment joined General Henry Dearborn near Niagara, in present-day Ontario, and Scott soon became the general's chief of staff. He took on many duties throughout the war, including leading troops at Niagara, helping in the successful attack on Fort George, and joining the force that battled at Stoney Creek. This last battle went poorly for the Americans, who were forced to retreat to Fort George. Commanding the rear guard in this retreat, Scott recovered to help American naval forces in the fighting at Burlington Heights and York. He also fought at Kingston, where he was wounded in one arm and struck by a cannonball in the chest.

Scott's leadership in battle had, by March 1814, earned him the rank of brevet brigadier general. (The term "brevet" indicated that this was an honorary, wartime rank.) Scott made headquarters at Buffalo, New York, from where he joined in crossing the Niagara River and capturing Fort Erie in Canada. On March 5, 1814, he joined the Battle of Chippewa, in which his strategy and leadership earned him credit for the American victory. Moving on to the Battle at Lundy's Lane, near Niagara Falls, Scott added to his reputation as a capable leader. Congress rewarded him with a gold medal and promotion to brevet major general.

After the war. Scott grew so popular among Americans that he was asked to be secretary of war in 1815. His goal, however, was to be in command of the army, so he refused the position, withdrew from public life, and traveled to Europe. After this long rest, Scott returned to reveal a more self-centered and ambitious side of himself. He vied with General Edmund Gaines for overall control of the army. Scott and Gaines quarreled for years about who should have the senior position.

Andrew Jackson. Scott was hotheaded, but so careful in his work and speech that his associates began to call him "Old Fuss and Feathers." His habit for stating his mind and trying to justify his statement with seemingly endless explanation won him an enemy, Andrew Jackson. In charge of the army in the South, Jackson found the lack of organization in the war department unbearable. Lower-ranked officers continually made decisions for themselves. Sometimes these officers received their orders directly from the secretary of war instead of from their commanding general. One officer sent on a surveying mission by Jackson ended up in New York City at the command of the secretary, who did not bother to tell Jackson about the change. Jackson exploded. He sent out a command to all his officers that they should not respect an order from the war department. The command riled politicians throughout the states.

> **Theodore Roosevelt's Description of Winfield Scott**
>
> "Scott had many little vanities, and peculiarities of temper and disposition, at which it is easy to laugh; but these are all of small moment.... He was a fearless, honest, loyal, and simple-hearted soldier who served the nation with entire fidelity and devotion." (Horne, p. 342)

When Scott visited New York and dined with Governor De Witt Clinton, Jackson and his command were the main topics of conversation. Scott told Clinton that he thought Jackson had overstepped his authority and should be reprimanded by the president. Gossip traveled quickly, and Jackson soon read about Scott's remark in the newspapers. Angrily, he wrote to Scott challenging him to a duel. Scott declined. Jackson then challenged Clinton to a duel. He too declined.

Peacetime army. When Scott rejoined the army in 1821, he encountered several changes. A few generals had retired, and Jackson had resigned from the military to enter politics. The army named Scott as head of the army of the East and his old opponent General Gaines as head the army of the West; both were given the permanent rank of brigadier general. Secretary of War John C. Calhoun oversaw these changes. For a time Scott experienced little action and, in 1825, thought of resigning to enter politics. He wanted to support Calhoun, who was then fighting for states' rights in Congress. However, Scott's resignation was refused.

About this time, the position of general in charge of the entire army opened up, and Gaines and Scott, the two highest-ranking officers, renewed their dispute over who had seniority. Disturbed by their squabbling, their superiors decided that neither of them should be commander in chief. Instead, a major general during the War of 1812, Alexander Macomb, was appointed to head the United States Army. Scott and Gaines would continue to head the armies of East and West and alternate with each other every few years.

Court-martial. But Scott's ego again took command. He wrote a letter to the secretary of war stating that Macomb had been an officer junior to him and that he would not take orders from the new commander. For his stubborn refusal to cooperate, he was immediately court-martialed and was relieved of his command. With no one to command and no official army duties, Scott again headed for Europe. Andrew Jackson had just been elected president.

Scott returned in 1830 to command forces in Atlanta. It was a tense time in the South. As early as 1799 various states had taken issue with laws made by the federal government. Some states had even nullified, or declared illegal, some federal laws. In 1828, Scott's old friend, Calhoun, had written an article defending South Carolina's right to take such action. Now in 1830 Georgia was refusing to accept federal decisions concerning the land of the Cherokee Indians. Scott was sent to calm the "nullifiers." His demonstration of military strength combined with patient explanations of the central government's position eased tensions and made him popular with the military and the public once again.

Participation: Indian Removal

Black Hawk War. With promises and persuasion, the government had finally convinced the Sauk and Fox Indians to give up their land in Illinois and move west across the Mississippi River. But its failure to live up to its commitments made the U.S. government's actions unacceptable to the Indian war chief Black Hawk. He had decided to take his followers back east to live with the Winnebago Indians; this tribe, however, refused him. A disappointed Black Hawk tried to return west. Misunderstandings arose, that led to a long chase, a massacre of some Indians, and the capture of Black Hawk (see **Black Hawk**). For a time during the chase, President Andrew Jackson was unsure of the outcome and felt he needed stronger military leadership in this Black Hawk War. The war was being fought in General Gaines' region, and he logically should have taken charge. Gaines, however, was opposed to forced removal of Indians from their homelands.

Swallowing his personal dislikes, Jackson turned to Scott because of the general's excellent military record. Scott arrived in the area as the Black Hawk War was ending. At the same time, thousands of white settlers, who had hurried to Chicago for protection while Black Hawk was being chased, were returning home. Angry at all Indians, these whites began raiding and looting Indian communities and were joined in their rioting by the soldiers. Scott immediately stopped his troops from disfiguring Indian bodies or taking scalps. When peace had returned, Scott oversaw the treaty-making at which the Sauk signed away their long-standing rights to land along the eastern border of the Mississippi. Standing tall and in full uniform, Scott must have shocked some Indian representatives with his great size and with his claim that he was the "Great White Warrior" come to make permanent peace with them.

Seminole. Jackson earlier had made a name for himself by defeating the Creek Indians in the South and battling the Seminole in Georgia and Florida. After he became president, the military in 1832 had finally convinced the head chief of the Seminole to leave the Georgia/Florida land and move his people west. But two years had passed with only a few of the Seminole moving. The United States government finally decided to force the Seminole to leave. Fighting

▲ Scott at age 75

broke out between the military and the Indians. About the time most of the fighting was dying down, Secretary of War Lewis Cass sent Scott to Florida to handle the situation. Generals Winfield Scott, Zachary Taylor, and Sidney Jesup fought against the forces of the great Seminole chief Osceola. His people were eventually defeated, with 3,824 of them moving to Oklahoma in 1843. By then, however, Scott had left to command the removal of the much larger group of the Cherokee.

Cherokee. A similar situation was taking place among the 12,000 or 13,000 Cherokee Indians in Tennessee, Alabama, and

▲ **Scott returned from the Mexican War a hero**

Georgia. The government worked to split up this large and powerful nation with bribes and by offering to buy pieces of its land from individual Indians. Some Cherokee had become large landholders, building plantations not unlike their white neighbors. Cherokee law prescribed the death penalty to anyone selling property without Cherokee council approval, but the government's tactics were winning out. Finally, Cherokee leaders agreed to removal to Indian Territory (present-day Oklahoma).

Scott arrived in time to supervise the removal, establishing his headquarters at New Echota, the Cherokee capital:

> Under Scott's orders the troops were disposed at various points throughout the Cherokee country, where stockade forts were erected for gathering in and holding the Indians preparatory to removal. From these, squads of troops were sent to search out

> with rifle and bayonet every small cabin hidden away in the coves or by the sides of mountain streams.... Men were seized in their fields, women were taken from their wheels and children from their play. (Foreman, p. 287)

A large sum of money had been appropriated to equip the thousands of Cherokee for the long walk to the new land, but Congress was slow to provide the money. The Indians began their move without the full provisions promised them. Scott ordered his soldiers to treat the Indians with the utmost respect. To ensure fair treatment, he contracted with Chief John Ross to supervise the trip (see **John Ross**). John Tyler was then president, and was furious when he learned of this agreement. He ordered Scott to withdraw the contract, but Scott continued to respect its terms. More than 13,000 Cherokee made the move to Oklahoma. The emigrants, including Indians and their black slaves, traveled in groups of about 1,000 each. In July the death and sickness suffered by the first detachments prompted Scott to postpone the removal until September, when the weather would present less hardship. There were whites who cursed Scott for his kindness. In spite of the general's attempt to be helpful, and of his putting their own leader in charge of the removal, several thousand Cherokee died in the detainment camps and during their journey along what became known as the Trail of Tears.

Aftermath

Army chief. Scott briefly entertained ideas about political office. In 1838, he had contended with Henry Clay and William Henry Harrison to be the Whig party candidate for president. He urged selection of one of the other men and the sixty-two votes first given to him finally helped Harrison to win the nomination.

In 1841, Scott finally reached his greatest goal: he became major general and commander in chief of the army. In charge when war erupted with Mexico in 1845, he took a force of 12,000 men there.

Mexican War. As soon as his troops arrived in Mexico, Scott invaded and captured Vera Cruz. Victories at Puebla, Contreras, Curubuso, Molino del Rey, and Chapultepec were costly; Scott's force was reduced to 8,000 men. With these men, he marched on Mexico City and took over the national palace. This nearly ended the Mexican War. Scott, whose victories dazzled the military and public back home, turned over his command to W. O. Butler and returned a hero to the United States. Another gold medal was struck for him by Congress. With victory came the territories of New Mexico and California, newly won parts of the United States.

Presidential candidate. Now the Whig party sought to capitalize on Scott's popularity. In 1852 he was nominated as that party's presidential candidate. John P. Hale and Daniel Webster were also candidates, as was Franklin Pierce, representing the Democrats. Pierce earned 254 electoral votes; Scott, 42.

Three years later, the government brought back into use a special military rank, lieutenant general, so that it could honor Winfield Scott with that title.

Civil War. Scott was still in charge of the army when the Civil War erupted. He organized the Union troops for the long struggle and made early preparations to defend the capital. However, by 1861 he was seventy-five years old and ready to retire. He turned over the command to General George McClellan and once more visited Europe. Returning home, he settled at West Point, where he died on May 29, 1866. He is perhaps best remembered for his writing about regulations for the army and about infantry tactics, and for his campaign in the Mexican War, which some felt to be the greatest in recent military history.

For More Information

Elliott, Charles Winslow. *Winfield Scott, The Soldier and the Man.* New York: The Macmillan Company, 1937.

Foreman, Grant. *Indian Removal.* Norman: University of Oklahoma Press, 1972.

Horne, Charles F. *Great Men and Famous Women.* Vol. 2. New York: Selmar Hess, 1894.

Industrialization

1789

Englishman **Samuel Slater** sails to America with secrets of British textile manufacturing.

1790

Slater begins operations at the first water-powered cotton mill in the United States, in Pawtucket, Rhode Island.

1793

Eli Whitney invents the cotton gin, which cleans cotton fifty times faster than old methods.

1798

Whitney contracts with the U.S. government to produce 10,000 muskets, which he builds using interchangeable parts.

1820

Textile mills begin appearing along rivers in New England and the Middle Atlantic states.

1821

The Merrimack Manufacturing Company establishes mills at Lowell, Massachusetts. All steps of cotton production are brought together under one roof.

1830

Majority of workers at Lowell mills are women aged fifteen to twenty-nine.

1833

Harriet Hanson Robinson begins work in the Lowell mills.

1840

The first issue of *The Lowell Offering,* a journal written by mill girls, is published.

1845

Irish immigrants form 8 percent of work force in Lowell.

1860

Irish immigrants form nearly 50 percent of work force in Lowell. Immigrant males begin to displace female workers.

INDUSTRIALIZATION

The United States in 1776 was not yet an industrial nation. Manufacturing was small-scale and spread across the countryside. Small businesses—sawmills, blacksmith shops, grain mills—appeared here and there, employed two or three workers, and mostly sold their wares to the local people.

In the late 1700s, dramatic changes began to take place elsewhere in the world that would affect the way people worked and lived in America. New inventions and methods for harnessing power enabled people to use machinery to produce goods. This period of new inventions came to be called the Industrial Revolution, and it ushered in new social and business patterns that have continued to the present day.

The Industrial Revolution began in England with several key inventions. For centuries people had produced fabric by hand: spinning the raw fiber into thread, weaving the thread into cloth, and, finally, sewing the finished cloth into clothing. Most of this work was done at home on a piece-by-piece basis. Also in effect at the time was the apprentice system. The student-apprentice worked for a master craftsman at his shop in exchange for training in the craft.

England's new inventions sped up the process of cloth manufacturing. The first major invention, designed in 1733 by John Kay, was a loom with a flying shuttle. The shuttle is a tool that weaves threads crosswise in making fabric. Instead of pushing the shuttle by hand and walking from one side of the loom to the other, weavers could pull a cord that sent the shuttle "flying" across the loom. The new flying shuttle made the weaving process three times faster.

Now cotton spinners could not supply the weavers with spun fiber quickly enough. In 1767, John Hargreaves solved this problem by inventing the spinning jenny. It enabled one craftsman to spin seven to eight threads at once; later, as the design was refined, that number rose to eighty. Not everyone welcomed the spinning jenny. When it was first used, hand spinners rioted and smashed early models of the new machine, convinced that it would put them out of work.

Before long, Richard Arkwright posed a far more serious threat to hand spinners. In 1769, Arkwright patented the water frame, a large spinning machine powered by running water. Two years later, he set up a water-powered mill in Cromford, England. Arkwright could use low-paid, unskilled workers to run his operation. In fact, children, with their small, nimble fingers, were well-suited to the factory work. Arkwright took a partner, Jedediah Strutt, and became hugely successful. Soon England's cotton industry was booming.

The British government closely guarded its inventions. It forbade machine makers from leaving England, and anyone caught smuggling out manufacturing secrets faced up to twelve years in jail or fines as high as 200 pounds.

Across the Atlantic, American manufacturers struggled to copy the English machinery. In 1789, **Samuel Slater,** who had served as an apprentice under Strutt, immigrated to America. He memorized the secrets of textile manufacturing before leaving England. Within a year, Slater set up the first water-powered cotton mill in America.

Located in Rhode Island, Slater's mill had an immediate impact on the American cotton-processing market. Americans could now buy cloth made in the United States for nine cents a yard; before, they had paid as much as fifty cents a yard for English fabric. Soon mills sprung up next to rivers all over New England.

Not long after Slater's mill began operating, **Eli Whitney** made another major contribution to the American cotton industry. In 1793, Whitney developed the cotton gin, which made it possible to clean cotton fifty times faster than before. Southern planters profited greatly, and the use of slave labor in the South grew.

Northern mill owners increased their demand for cotton from the South, where plantation owners began to devote most of their slave labor to producing this single crop. Different social patterns developed in the regions. In the South, slave labor continued to grow, and work life remained closely tied to the home. In the North, wage labor became popular, work life was now separated from the home, and more factory towns appeared. Meanwhile, industry tied the regions to each other.

Whitney himself did not profit much from the cotton gin, but he soon made a second contribution to American industry. In 1798, he signed a contract with the federal government to produce 10,000 muskets in two years. To meet his quota, Whitney developed a system for producing standardized, or interchangeable, parts. He invented machinery that produced each part accurately over and over again. Any one of these standardized parts could be used with any other part to build a musket. Later, other manufacturers began using interchangeable parts to produce goods. In the process, the pace of industry quickened. Items were manufactured in quantities never before thought possible and prices for finished goods dropped.

By the 1850s, industry had become a key feature of American life, with textile manufacturing in the lead. Most of the New England mills produced cheap cloth, using machines to perform the dozen or so steps needed to produce the cloth. Workers made sure the machines operated properly and quickly.

Mill owners at first employed children, and then women, as cheap labor. One mill girl, **Harriet Hanson Robinson,** wrote about her work experience, providing readers a half-century later with an insightful glimpse into a world gone by. By the time Robinson wrote of her experience, immigrants, many of them male, had largely replaced the New England mill girls in the factories. Mill towns grew overcrowded and filthy. Meanwhile, the mill owners raced to produce goods faster, in larger quantities, and for less money than ever before. Even in Robinson's day, factory owners attempted to cut costs by lowering their workers' pay. The New England mill girls went on strike to protest these wage cuts, beginning the long fight for factory workers' rights in the new democracy.

Samuel Slater

1768-1835

Personal Background

In 1789, a ship bound from England to America harbored a twenty-one-year-old man taking one of the biggest risks of his young life. Posing as a farmer on his way to the new country, Samuel Slater was actually an industrial spy taking secrets of the powerful and profitable English manufacturing industry to the United States. He carried no papers or blueprints with him, but held all the valuable information in his head. During his years working as an apprentice to the owner in English cotton mills, Slater had memorized all of the machine parts and the complicated manner in which they worked together.

None of his fellow passengers would have doubted he was a farmer, for he had the sturdy build and ruddy, wholesome complexion of a man who had spent his entire life in the English countryside. Still, the risk was great. If caught, Slater could face a fine of 200 pounds or twelve years in jail. England had enacted strict laws to prevent its profitable industrial secrets from reaching other shores. But Slater knew that Americans would pay top dollar for his valuable knowledge, and he was ready to establish himself as a successful manufacturer in the young country. Not only did he achieve this goal, but Slater managed almost singlehandedly to set the course of American industry.

▲ Samuel Slater

Event: Industrial Revolution in America.

Role: Dubbed the "Father of American Manufactures" by President Andrew Jackson, Samuel Slater played a key role in American industry by introducing the machine spinning technology to mass produce cotton yarn in the United States.

Early years. Samuel Slater was born on June 9, 1768, in Belper, England, the fifth child and first son of William and Elizabeth Slater. His family was respected in their community and was fairly well-off. They lived in Holly House, a large, two-story, stone structure that had been passed down to William through generations of Slaters. William made his living farming and selling timber, and Elizabeth, when she could spare time from her duties as a mother, spent hours at the spinning wheel. From the wool of the sheep that her husband raised, she made yarn and wove it into clothing on the loom.

From his early years, Slater was a hard-working, serious, and thoughtful boy. His father wanted him to have a solid education, so he was sent to the local school to learn to read, write, and work with numbers. At home, Samuel helped around the farm, gathering eggs, chopping wood, and tending the livestock. His inside chores included winding the wool that his mother spun into spools of yarn. One of his earliest mechanical efforts was to make a steel spindle that helped in winding the wool.

Apprenticeship with Jedediah Strutt. Samuel Slater grew up in an environment that greatly influenced his life's work. He had been born within a year after Richard Arkwright built the world's first spinning mill in Hockley, England. He was raised in Derbyshire County, England, within walking distance of two spinning mills owned by Jedediah Strutt, one of England's leading manufacturers. Slater's father was a friend of Strutt's, so it was not unusual for the young boy to visit the busy, loud mills. There he watched with fascination as the complex machinery spun cotton into yarn.

In 1782, William Slater helped Jedediah Strutt in purchasing land and water-power rights along the River Derwent for a cotton mill that Strutt planned to build. At the time, Samuel was fourteen, about the age at which boys usually began an apprenticeship to learn a trade that would see them through life. After spending a trial period working as a clerk in the new mill, Slater had to decide whether to formally sign on as an apprentice under Strutt. His father could offer little guidance in making the decision or arranging the details. William Slater had injured himself falling from a wagon, and when his son approached him for help, he told the boy, "You must do that business yourself, Samuel; I have so much to do and so little time to do it in" (Cameron, p. 13). Soon after, William Slater died.

Samuel Slater left his boyhood behind at this point in his life. With characteristic caution, he spent time carefully considering a career decision. He had no desire to get stuck in a trade that would not prove profitable or, at least, offer him security later in life. In making up his mind, Slater met with Strutt to find out all he could about the new industry and what its future held. Strutt soon convinced the serious young man that he could expect a solid future if he stayed in the business of spinning cotton.

Beginning in 1783, Slater signed on to serve a six-and-one-half year apprenticeship under Strutt. He moved in with Strutt at his home in nearby Milford and began to learn the tools of his chosen trade. Strutt appreciated his luck in finding a bright, hard-working apprentice and became like a second father to the boy. Though Slater now lived only a long walking distance from his family home, he sometimes went as long as six months without visiting his family. He preferred instead to spend his days off studying the spinning equipment at the mill.

Mill life. At the mill Slater took his place among many other laborers. Most were even younger than he. Children's tiny, quick hands made them most suited to work at many of the duties performed in the mills.

The process for turning raw cotton into finished cloth was quite involved. First the cotton was cleaned. Before the cotton gin was invented in 1793 (see **Eli Whitney**), workers had to remove the tiny seeds from the small puffs of cotton by hand. Next, the cotton fiber was carded, which means that it was brushed between two metal combs so that all the fibers ran in one direction. Then, a drawing machine stretched the carded cotton into a loose yarn. Finally, the loose yarn was stretched and twirled by moving spindles into a final tight yarn.

Work in the mill was fast and tedious, and the noise from the whirring, rattling, and clashing of the crude machinery could at times be deafening. Slater, who as an apprentice was required to learn every phase of the spinning process and the function of each machine, soon proved his worth to Strutt. He invented a device that helped distribute yarn more evenly on a spindle. Strutt rewarded the young man with a shiny guinea, a hefty sum in those days.

By the time Slater reached the end of his apprenticeship, he had learned everything there was to know about the business and mechanics of spinning cotton. Now, he was ready to strike out on his own. Hearing of the high prices paid in America to people who could design and build cotton-spinning machinery, Slater left his native country to make his home in America. There he would establish himself as a leader in American industry.

Inventions Important to the Textile Industry

Flying Shuttle: John Kay, 1733. Mounted on small rollers so it could roll back and forth across a wooden rail, the flying shuttle enabled weavers to simply pull a cord to make the shuttle "fly" across the loom. Before this, they had to push the shuttle by hand across the long stretch of woven fabric, going from one side of the loom to the other.

Spinning Jenny: James Hargreaves, 1760s. Early spinning wheels could produce only one thread at a time. The spinning jenny used multiple spindles, making it possible for a person to spin up to eight threads at once.

Water Frame: Richard Arkwright, 1768. The water frame, a large spinning machine powered by a rushing river, produced stronger thread than any spinner could on a traditional spinning wheel. Arkwright set up the first spinning mills in England, along the country's fastest rivers. With his system, cotton could be spun onto thousands of spools in one factory.

Participation: Building American Industry

American industry in the late 1700s. Several important eighteenth-century English inventions made that country a powerful leader in the Industrial Revolution. England closely guarded the secrets of these inventions by forbidding machinery to be exported and mechanics or manufacturers to leave the country. While England profited magnificently from its production of manufactured goods, the United States, whose main business was agriculture, could only watch with envy and continue to depend on the far-off country for many of its goods.

When Slater arrived in America in 1789, some citizens, including Secretary of Treasury Alexander Hamilton, believed the country should begin to compete in the world market and develop its own trade and industry. Producing its own goods would give the newborn country even more independence from England. Hamilton felt the federal government should encourage the growth of industry. President Thomas Jefferson, however, disagreed: he wanted America to remain a land of independent and self-sufficient farmers and craftspeople. In the end, in part to Slater's fateful immigration to the new country, Hamilton's preference would win the day.

Partnership with Moses Brown. A few weeks after arriving in New York, Slater learned of a businessman in Rhode Island who was setting up a new cotton mill. Slater immediately wrote him a letter:

> Sir—A few days ago I was informed that you wanted a manager of cotton-spinning, etc., in which business I flatter myself that I can give the greatest satisfaction, in making machinery, making good yarn, either for stockings or twist, as any as that is made in England; I have had opportunity, and oversight, of Sir Richard Arkwright's works, and in Mr. Strutt's mill upward of eight years. (Cameron, p. 37)

Moses Brown must have thrown up his hands in delight when he received Slater's letter. The businessman had invested in cotton machinery that he later discovered to be faulty. Now he was trying somehow to make a financial return on his investment. In Slater, Brown had found a man who could turn his mill into an operating concern. He invited Slater to come to Rhode Island and offered him a share in the profits of the business.

Pawtucket, Rhode Island. Slater was twenty-one years old when he first met Brown at the Providence shipyards in January of 1790. If Brown felt any initial dismay at Slater's youth, he was soon reassured by the sense of confidence and security that Slater inspired in people. He had the finest qualifications, having worked under the most important textile manufacturer in the world, Richard Arkwright. What's more, Slater had an air of calm assurance and serious intelligence that went well beyond his years.

The two new partners wasted no time in getting down to business. They traveled by horse and buggy to Pawtucket, a small village a few miles north of Providence. The building that housed Brown's machinery stood at the edge of the Blackstone River. Slater looked at the rushing waters of the powerful river with approval; he knew this was an excellent site for a mill. His spirits fell, however, when he saw the outdated, poorly constructed machinery that Brown had purchased. He realized there was no way these machines could ever produce fine cotton yarn.

Slater told Brown the machines were useless, and the two discussed their next move. They decided Slater would have to build the machinery for the mill himself. Confident that his mechanical skill and keen memory would enable him to build the machines he had seen in operation since boyhood, Slater promised to Brown in a signed agreement: "If I do not make as good yarn as they do in England, I will have nothing for my services, but will throw the whole of what I have attempted over the bridge." (Cameron, p. 47).

Construction. Slater set to work building three carding machines, two water-frame spinning machines, and one drawing frame. He set up a machine shop at the workplace of Sylvanus Brown, a local woodcraftsman. David Wilkinson, son of a local ironworker with whom Slater was staying, forged iron parts for the machinery. Local carpenters also contributed their skills. Slater and his crew worked day and night building the machines, and it was here that Slater's true mechanical genius came to light. The designs he had copied were complex and involved detailed patterns of moving, interworking parts. That he built such machines from memory was an amazing feat. Even more incredible was that he was able to build them using only the crude tools and parts he had on hand.

The men who helped him, most of whom were much older than he, easily took orders and direction from the younger man. Moses Brown, who, along with William Almy, put up the money for the operation, maintained a strong trust in the man he had met only months earlier. Slater's extreme confidence in himself and in his skills made others feel comfortable with his judgment and ability.

Gearing into operation. Slater and his crew worked for eight months perfecting the new machines. But as they neared completion, Slater almost gave up on the project. The carding machines he had built refused to function properly. Fearing that the failure would cause the others to lose faith in him, Slater entertained thoughts of running away and abandoning the project entirely. But Sylvanus Brown would not let the inventor give up until he found a solution. Finally, on December 20, 1790, operations at the mill were ready to begin.

In the early hours of dawn on that icy winter day, Slater

worked at the water wheel to break off the large chunks of ice that had formed on the wheel. (He was to perform this same chore many winter mornings for years to come to keep his mills running.) With his hands rubbed raw, he watched as the wheel slowly began to turn, gathering speed as he removed more ice. Upstairs in the mill, the machinery began to grind into motion. Soon after, the new mill, which came to be called the Old Mill, spun the first cotton produced in America by water-powered machinery.

The Old Mill. The spinning machines spun cotton onto seventy-two spindles at the mill. About ten employees worked there, all of them children between the ages of seven and twelve. They worked six full days a week, with Sundays free. Each morning the children awoke before dawn to the sound of the mill's bell calling them to work. Slater proved to be not only an excellent mechanic but a fine manager. He watched closely over all the operations of the mill, making sure each part ran smoothly. He controlled the flow of cotton and made sure that all machines operated at a steady pace.

Soon the mill was producing more yarn than the company had orders for. His partners, Almy and Brown, worried that a large supply of cotton would pile up in their warehouse with no one to sell it to. Therefore, Almy, Brown, and Slater decided to take orders for finished cloth from the local New Englanders. They hired weavers to weave the cotton yarn into yards of cloth. However, these weavers could not weave fast enough to keep up with the output of the busy mill. To solve this problem, Slater convinced his partners to look at another option besides selling finished cloth. In order to increase profits, he reasoned, they should sell yarn not only in New England but all over the country.

Because of Slater's business sense, the new mill in the tiny Rhode Island village was having far-reaching effects on the American cotton market. The price of cotton cloth went down because of the abundant supply of cotton yarn coming from Slater's mill. Americans could now buy cloth made in their own country for nine cents a yard; imported English fabric had cost forty to fifty cents for a yard. Proud of his company's success, Moses Brown sent a letter to Alexander Hamilton. He wrote that his mill had proved that "mills and machines may be erected in different places, in one year, to make all the cotton yarn that could be wanted in the United States" (Cameron, p. 60).

Expansion. As the company grew, the next logical step was to expand. In 1793, the partnership of Almy, Brown, and Slater built a second mill, later known as the Old Slater Mill, along the Blackstone River. This time Slater, remembering the winter mornings he spent hacking away chunks of ice from the frozen water wheel, instructed builders to enclose the water wheel on one end with wood so that it would not freeze. Once workers had finished construction, this new and larger mill soon prospered; by the turn of the century, the Old Slater Mill employed 100 workers.

In 1801, Slater branched out on his own to build the White Mill, across the river in Massachusetts. He went on to build, either alone or with partners, mills located at several New England sites, including a mill at Slatersville, near the Massachusetts border; the Green Mill, in Oxford, Massachusetts; and the Bell Mill and Island Mill, both in New Hampshire.

Mills spread through New England. Before long other New England towns, using Slater's model, began building mills along the rushing waters of the region's powerful rivers. By 1815, 165 cotton mills were in full operation in New England. By the mid-1800s, Slater's creative techniques had left a lasting mark on American industry. His successful spinning mill machines had brought about a huge increase in the amount of cotton grown in the United States—from 2 million pounds in 1790 to 80 million pounds in 1835. By then, America grew almost half of the cotton in the world. For the first time in history, Americans began leaving their farms to work in the new mill towns. With Slater's industry, America had established itself as a fighting force to compete in the world manufacturing market.

Aftermath

Marriage and family. While living at the Wilkinsons in his early years in Pawtucket, Slater met and fell in love with their seventeen-year-old daughter, Hannah. Less than two years after he arrived in Rhode Island, they were married. Hannah was a woman after Samuel's own heart, for she made her own mark on the American textile industry. In 1793, she devised a way of making strong cotton thread to use for sewing. At the time seamstresses used strong linen thread for sewing, but its rough texture made sewing difficult. Hannah realized that if she could twist two strands of fine cotton yarn together, a strong, smooth thread would be the result. This thread is still in use today, labeled two-ply No. 20.

Samuel and Hannah's marriage was a happy one. Between 1798 and 1802, Hannah gave birth to four children, three of whom died in infancy; the last, Samuel, born in 1802, grew to be a somewhat sickly child. In the next ten years, Hannah had five more sons before she died in 1812. Left with the responsibility of raising six young sons, Slater began looking for another wife. In 1817, he proposed to widow Esther Parkinson, who had been married to one of Slater's friends. He wrote Esther a frank and businesslike letter, which said in part:

> I have been inclined for some time past to change my situation in life, and have at times named you to my brother and sister for a partner.... Now if you are under no obligation to anyone, and on weighing the subject fully, you should think that you can spend the remainder of your days with me, [write] me soon to that effect. (Cameron, p. 123-24)

The proposal was hardly romantic. Yet the marriage seems to have been a happy one. Slater's six sons adored Esther and blossomed under her motherly care.

Final years. Samuel Slater passed away in 1835, at the age of sixty-six, from complications of several diseases. He died a rich man, leaving an estate worth over a million dollars. Throughout the land he was recognized as an important American industrialist. Two presidents, James Monroe and Andrew Jackson, had visited the powerful manufacturer to see his mills in operation. The mills and machines that Slater introduced to America had changed the young country from a farming to a largely industrial society. After his death, Slater's youngest son, Nelson, carried on the management of the mills until his own death in 1888.

For More Information

Cameron, E. H. *Father of American Manufactures.* Freeport, Maine: The Bond Wheelwright Company, 1960.

Simonds, Christopher. *Samuel Slater's Mill and the Industrial Revolution.* Englewood Cliffs, New Jersey: Silver Burdett Press, 1990.

Eli Whitney

1765-1825

Personal Background

Family. Eli Whitney was born on December 8, 1765, in Westborough, Massachusetts, a town about forty miles east of Boston. His parents, Eli and Elizabeth, had married in January of that year and lived on a farm that Elizabeth had inherited from her parents. Much of young Eli's childhood was difficult and unhappy. His mother became a near invalid after the birth of her last child, leaving five-year-old Eli to share some of the burden of caring for his two younger brothers and older sister. The housekeeper that his father hired to help out probably did more harm than good; in front of the children, she called their helpless and dying mother ugly names.

In 1779, two years after Elizabeth died, Eli Whitney's father married a widow named Judith Hazeldon. Judith was an older woman with ten children, two of whom she brought to live at her new home. The Whitney children could not have been too happy with their new stepmother, although out of respect and love for their father they kept these feelings to themselves. Judith was cold, ungiving, and uncaring toward her stepchildren and favored her own children over them. Eli's sister, Elizabeth, later gave an account of the harsh and neglectful treatment her brother had received from their stepmother and stepsisters. When Eli was sick in bed recovering from an almost fatal infection, he was "grossly

▲ Eli Whitney

Event: Industrial Revolution in America.

Role: Eli Whitney's invention of the cotton gin gave America the ability to profitably produce a valuable national product and helped turn the country into an economic power. Later, Whitney's use of standardized parts to build muskets helped revolutionize manufacturing in the United States.

neglected." He knocked on the floor with his cane for help, but for hours his stepmother and stepsisters ignored him:

> Directions were left for him to take medicine once an hour ... he knocked and knocked again, became weary.... After being alone five hours and a half, he heard Father come home. He knocked. Father went to his chamber. He told Father how he had been neglected and said he could not endure it. (Mirsky and Nevins, p. 44)

His stepmother did, however, appreciate Eli's toolmaking skills. When he crafted a knife to replace a broken one, her feelings toward him seemed to have softened somewhat.

The one guiding and caring force in Eli Whitney's childhood was his father. Eli Whitney, Sr., was a hard-working farmer who served as justice of the peace, participated in town politics, and was well-respected within the community. Weighing 300 pounds, he was an affectionate father who cared deeply for his children's welfare. Even when his second wife tried to stop him, he remained devoted to his children and continued to look out for their best interests. Whitney's love and respect for his father is apparent in the fact that he continued to write frequent letters to him throughout his lifetime.

Toolmaking and mechanical skills. The Whitney farm housed a well-stocked workshop for making and repairing tools, furniture, and farm equipment. From an early age, Whitney showed an amazing skill for working with tools and making knives, nails, and hatpins. Once, when his family had gone to church, he took apart his father's watch to study how it worked and then put it back together again perfectly before they returned. Later, when he was twelve, he made a violin that produced as beautiful music as a violin crafted by a skilled artisan. His sister wrote that "as soon as he could handle tools he was always making something in the shop and seemed not to relish working on the farm" (Mirsky and Nevins, p. 25).

Preparing for an education. For reasons unknown, Whitney decided at the late age of nineteen that he wanted to pursue a college education. He chose to attend Yale College in New Haven, Connecticut, but first had to spend four years preparing for the difficult entrance exam. Studying at Leicester Academy in the summers, he earned his living by teaching school in the winters. Often he was just a few weeks ahead of his students in the material they studied. Seeing Whitney's hard work and determination, Whitney, Sr., finally agreed to fund his son's college education against the strong protests of his wife.

Yale. Whitney entered Yale in 1789, halfway into the school year; at twenty-three, he was years older than most of his classmates. For the next four years, he lost himself in his studies, learning subjects ranging from English grammar, Latin, and Greek, to science, philosophy, and law. Most days began at 5:00 a.m. and usually ended well after suppertime. Students were required to attend daily prayer services, take classes, study, and recite lessons.

Whitney excelled in his studies and made full use of the college's well-stocked library. He joined a book-buying club and was elected to the Phi Beta Kappa fraternity. Always, however, the problem of money loomed over him. Although his father continued to send him the money he could, Whitney constantly had to scrimp and borrow. By the time he graduated in 1792, he was heavily in debt.

Southward bound. Although he intended to work as a lawyer after graduating, Whitney accepted a teaching post in New York because he needed to start earning money as quickly as possible. When that position fell through, however, he was forced to accept an offer to work as a tutor in South Carolina. He was not happy about the prospect of living so far from home in a region whose climate, customs, and landscape varied so greatly from the world in which he had grown up. Before leaving, he wrote a letter to his father that indicates his lack of enthusiasm and misgivings about this major move:

> After mature consideration I have concluded to go.... The climate of the Southern States is something unhealthy but I hope by temperance and Prudence to withstand it. If I should find my health declining, I shall return, if possible before it is too late.... If I should have good success I shall make something handsome, but I may have bad luck and lose all. The world is a Lottery in which many draw Blanks, of which may fall to my share. (Mirsky and Nevins, p. 59)

Little did he know it, but Whitney had not drawn a blank. The move South shaped his destiny and set him on course for achieving his life's work.

Participation: Growth of American Industry

Economics in the late 1700s. When Whitney headed south to begin his life after college, America was a young country struggling to establish itself as an economic power. Although the rich land held abundant natural resources—including vast stretches of forests, large mineral deposits, and fertile soil—America did not have the manpower or the industry to turn these resources into manufactured products. As a result, Americans relied on Europe for most of their manufactured goods and were forced to pay high import prices for them.

It was clear that the country needed a way to become more economically independent. Many thought the solution was to produce a valuable item that could be traded with Europe. Others, like Alexander Hamilton, believed the answer lay in promoting the growth of American manufacturing and industry. Inventors and craftsmen searched for new and better ways to build and produce goods.

Whitney would help solve America's economic problems in two ways: his invention of the cotton gin would enable Americans to produce in large quantities a profitable product; later, his use of interchangeable standardized parts would boost American industry by enabling manufacturers to make goods more quickly and in larger numbers than ever before.

Mulberry Grove. After arriving in the South, a second twist of fate brought Whitney closer to his destiny. When the job he had accepted in South Carolina fell through, he ended up living at the plantation of Catherine Greene. This young widow, whose warm, lively, and entertaining manner made her popular throughout the South, owned a large plantation outside of Savannah, Georgia. After her husband's death, Greene had asked Phineas Miller, her children's tutor, to manage the plantation. Miller struggled to make the plantation profitable, working to raise crops such as corn and rice in the fields.

Whitney had accepted Greene's invitation to stay at Mulberry Grove on his way to South Carolina. He could not have been there very long before hearing some of the complaints of the local farmers. Southern farms grew mostly rice, corn, indigo (for making dye), and tobacco, none of which yielded a very large profit. Cotton, farmers knew, could bring a large profit because of the booming British textile industry; mills that produced cotton yarn and cloth could use as much cotton as could be grown. Also, thanks to Samuel Slater's new cotton mills in Rhode Island, the American cotton industry was growing rapidly (see **Samuel Slater**). The problem was that the cotton that grew best in the South had small green seeds with a velvety covering (as opposed to long black seeds with a smooth coat), which made it extremely difficult to clean; a slave could clean just a pound of cotton a day. The resulting poor-quality cotton could be used only for making coarse fabric. Southern farmers wanted to find a way to clean their cotton quickly and adequately so that they could have a profitable crop.

With his natural mechanical genius, Whitney could not help but ponder the problem and think about the kind of machine that would be necessary to clean green-seeded cotton. Just a few days after arriving at Mulberry Grove, an idea suddenly came to him. Whitney discussed his idea with Miller, and the two formed a partnership in which Miller would fund the operation and both would share in the profits. Ten days later, Whitney had constructed a small working model of the cotton gin.

The cotton gin. Whitney's invention involved a roller covered with short wire hooks, which revolved against a grooved plate. While the plate held the seed, the wire hooks caught the cotton fibers and pushed it along. Then another roller, which was smaller than the first and covered with bristles, brushed the cleaned cotton from the wire hooks. The invention made it possible to clean ten times as much cotton as any previous method. Besides this, Whitney's cotton gin cleaned the cotton much better than earlier methods, resulting in an end product that was much smoother and cleaner and therefore more valuable.

By the spring of 1793, Whitney had applied for a patent for his invention and had moved back to New Haven to set up a workshop

▲ **Replica of a 1793 cotton gin.**

to build more gins. Although he was challenged by several problems that came up during construction, he eventually produced six working cotton gins. Around the same time, the patent for his invention was approved. Southern farmers clamored to find out about the new device and were eager to use it to clean their harvested cotton.

Far-reaching effect. The cotton gin brought prosperity to the South as well as lasting and far-reaching changes to the entire country. While reducing labor in cotton production, the gin created employment for thousands of people since more acreage could now profitably be devoted to cotton. Farmers could pay off their debts and, at the same time, their land increased in value with the new crop. The cotton gin also made southern farmers depend even more on slavery; they relied on hardy slaves to pick the cotton under the burning sun and they used the weaker and older slaves to run the gins. Any hopes of freeing slaves were dashed for several generations. Cotton production was also important on a national level. American cotton mills could use cotton from their own country and not have to pay high prices for imported cotton. Also, cotton gave the United States a valuable commodity to trade with Europe.

Business problems. Understandably, Whitney expected to become wealthy with his important invention; unfortunately, this did not happen. As he and Miller worked at building their business, they faced many setbacks and difficulties. In 1795, a fire burned Whitney's New Haven workshop, destroying tools and many of the parts intended for use on twenty gins under construction. After the fire, Whitney wrote:

> For more than two years I have spared no pains nor exersion to systimatize and arrange my business in a proper manner—This object I had just accomplished.... But my prospects are all blasted, and my labour lost. I do not, however dispair and hope I shall not sink under my misfortunes—I shall reestablish the business as soon as possible, but it will be a long time before I can repair my loss. (Green, p. 69)

Meanwhile, farmers resented paying to have their cotton ginned. Ignoring Whitney's patent, they hired artisans to build illegal copies of the relatively simple machine.

Miller and Whitney struggled to deal with these problems. They sued patent offenders (people who copied their idea), and began to lease gins and to sell the right to manufacture their machine. When financial pressures increased, Catherine Greene, who had married Miller in 1796, donated money from her estate to help save the partnership from ruin. After a time, Whitney began to withdraw from operations, leaving most of the responsibility of the failing business to Miller.

Finding a new line of work. At a time when he expected to be living well off the profits of his invention, Whitney was, in fact, heavily in debt once again. Adding to his misery was the jealousy that the marriage of Greene and Miller seems to have aroused in him. Although he had never expressed it, Whitney seems to have been in love with the warm-hearted and engaging Catherine. When the business all but failed, he wrote despondently to Miller of the contrast in their positions at this very low point in his life. They had both failed at a business, but Miller, Whitney noted, had financial means separate from the business as well as a loving and charming wife. Whitney, on the other hand, though he had "ever looked forward with pleasure to a connection with an amiable and virtuous companion of the other sex" could not, at that point, "*even think* of Matrimony" (Green, p. 98). In fact, Whitney would not marry until well into middle age and after Catherine Greene had died.

Whitney's depression was understandable. He had worked hard and tirelessly for three long and stressful years and was hardly better off than when he began. He could not think of marriage because he had nothing to offer a potential wife. Now, from his workshop in New Haven, he began to explore other avenues to make a profit from his mechanical genius.

A government contract. Before long, Whitney decided that working with the United States government would be a safe and profitable way of doing business. In 1798, he wrote to Secretary of the Treasury Oliver Wolcott proposing to contract with the government to make 10,000 to 15,000 muskets. At the time, war with France seemed likely and the American army and navy needed firearms.

The country lacked the labor force necessary to build a large number of muskets quickly. Arms makers built muskets by hand one at a time, fitting parts together as they made them for an individual musket. Using this technique, the U.S. armory produced only 1,000 muskets in three years. At this rate, the country would not have enough firepower to successfully fight a war with a major power like France.

Whitney knew that if he could devise interchangeable parts for muskets he could build them at a much faster pace. Furthermore, he could employ less skilled laborers because all they had to do was fit together the parts he produced. They did not need to file or hand tailor the finished parts. He and Wolcott agreed to a contract whereby Whitney would produce 10,000 muskets in twenty-eight months. With a $5,000 advance and another $5,000 soon to come, Whitney set about fulfilling the terms of his contract.

Musket making. To produce this many muskets so fast, Whitney had to depart from the traditional method of crafting products one at a time. To do this, he looked at muskets in terms of the various individual parts that went into making them. Next, he had to invent and build machinery that could produce each individual part consistently and accurately. Every part that each of the different machines turned out had to be exactly the same. Any one of these standardized parts could be used with any other part in building a musket. As Whitney described it, "The tools which I contemplate are similar to an engraving on copper plate from which may be taken a great number of impressions exactly alike" (Green, p. 121).

Whitney did not invent this idea of interchangeable or standardized parts. Other people in America and the world were hard at work inventing labor-saving technology. However, Whitney was one of the first to carry out and perfect what came to be called "the interchangeable system." This important contribution places him at the forefront of the growth of American industry.

A working mill. To accomplish his objective, Whitney first needed to find a site that offered water power to operate the machinery he would be using. After deciding to build a mill in Mill Rock, outside of New Haven, he once again faced many setbacks and problems, which caused him delay after delay. He had to wait months before he was granted title to the mill site. That winter, poor weather delayed construction and the mill was not completed until January 1799. Meanwhile, yellow fever in Philadelphia, Pennsylvania, then the nation's capital, set back the delivery of materials. The quarantine also prevented Whitney from buying the high-quality iron and steel that could be found in that city. The weary inventor began to wonder if he could meet the terms of the contract: "I have now taken a serious task upon myself & I fear a greater one than is in the power of any man to perform in a given time—but it is too late to go back" (Green, p. 113).

Although Whitney did not meet the terms of his contract, he was successful in carrying out his plan of using an interchangeable system to build muskets. In 1801, government officials, who had waited nervously for some results, were more than satisfied when Whitney traveled to Washington, now the capital, to demonstrate his clever technology. Spreading a large supply of various lock parts across a table, he showed his audience how he could pick up any part and fit it into any other and still produce a working device. Later, President Thomas Jefferson wrote of Whitney:

> He has invented moulds and machines for making all the pieces of his locks so exactly equal, that take 100 locks to pieces and mingle their parts and the hundred locks may be put together as well by taking the first pieces which come to hand. This is of importance in repairing, because out of ten locks, e.g. disabled for the want of different pieces, 9 good locks may be put together without employing a smith. (Green, p. 133)

With their faith in Whitney confirmed and the threat of war diminished, the government officials were content to let Whitney work at a slower pace. He finally fulfilled the contract in 1809, eleven years after starting work. Although he had made little profit from the project, Whitney had established himself as a talented engineer and a creative manufacturer. The interchangeable system he had developed and perfected would carry over into all other types of American manufacturing. Soon the country would be using this new manufacturing approach to produce goods at a rate faster than anyone ever thought possible.

Aftermath

Domestic comfort. For a quarter of a century, Whitney had devoted himself to his business. Although he had friends and family, he spent the majority of his time working and had little time for a personal life. Finally, in 1817, at the age of fifty-two, he married thirty-one-year-old Henrietta Edwards, the daughter of a friend and a woman he had known for years. Over the next eight years, the couple had four children, the youngest of whom died while still a baby.

After his initial struggles, Whitney's business had grown and prospered; also, he had invested wisely. He was now a fairly wealthy man, and his family lived comfortably. Generous with his money, Whitney had helped many a friend out of debt. At the time of his death, he had loaned more than $70,000 to friends in need.

Final invention. In his last years, Whitney suffered from a painful illness. An enlarged prostate gland made it difficult for him to urinate, which caused him unbearable pain. He used his mechanical skill to invent a device that would help him urinate. Of this invention, Whitney's friend Benjamin Silliman noted: "Nothing he ever invented, not even the cotton gin, discovered a more perfect comprehension of the difficulties to be surmounted, or evinced more efficient ingenuity" (Green, p. 185).

His invention probably helped Whitney live longer than doctors had expected. When he died in January 1825, Eli Whitney left behind a lasting legacy. Two of his nephews, Philos and Eli Blake, carried on their uncle's business and kept it strong and profitable until Eli Whitney III was old enough to assume responsibility.

For More Information

Alter, Judith. *Eli Whitney.* New York: Franklin Watt, 1990.

Green, Constance McLaughlin. *Eli Whitney and the Birth of American Technology.* Toronto: Little, Brown & Company, 1956.

Mirsky, Jeannette, and Allan Nevins. *The World of Eli Whitney.* New York: Collier Books, 1952.

Harriet Hanson Robinson

1825-1911

Personal Background

Family and early years. Harriet Hanson Robinson was born on August 2, 1825, in Boston, Massachusetts, the second of four children born to William and Harriet Hanson. When she was six years old, Harriet's father died, leaving her mother with the difficult task of feeding and caring for four young children. At the time, it was not unusual for a family to break up because of financial need, but Harriet's mother was determined to keep her family together. When a concerned neighbor offered to ease her burden by adopting young Harriet, Mrs. Hanson said, "No; while I have one meal of victuals a day, I will not part with my children" (Robinson, p. 17). These words stayed with young Harriet, who wondered for many years what the word "victuals" meant.

With help from her husband's friends, Mrs. Hanson set up a small shop in Boston, selling food, candy, and firewood. The family lived in a room behind the shop, sleeping in one bed, "two at the foot and three at the head" (Robinson, p. 17). In spite of their poverty, the children went to school every day and Harriet also attended a sewing school on Saturdays.

Mrs. Hanson's struggle to support her family became increasingly difficult. When her sister suggested she join her in Lowell, a booming mill town about twenty miles northwest of Boston, to man-

▲ **Harriet Hanson Robinson**

Event: The participation of women in American industry.

Role: From childhood to early womanhood, Harriet Hanson Robinson worked as a "mill girl" in the cotton mills of Lowell, Massachusetts. Years later, she wrote an account of her experiences, that gave a view of mill life and the first female workers in the early days of American industry.

age a boardinghouse for mill workers, Mrs. Hanson did not hesitate. In 1832, she piled her four children into a canal boat and traveled the short journey up the Middlesex Canal to Lowell.

New England mill towns. Samuel Slater's introduction of spinning technology (see **Samuel Slater**), combined with advances in weaving technology, such as power looms, pushed the cotton spinning and cloth weaving industries to the forefront of American industry. As businessmen rushed to profit from the booming textile industry, new mills were quickly constructed. Large mill towns began to spring up all over the New England countryside, along the region's powerful rivers, especially the mighty Merrimack.

One of the most successful mill owners was Francis Cabot Lowell, a Harvard graduate from a wealthy Boston family. Taking advantage of the demand for cloth brought on by the War of 1812 and with financial help from his family, Lowell established the Boston Manufacturing Company. It was a mill complex that, under Lowell's guidance, used the power loom to its greatest advantage. Located at Waltham, the Boston Manufacturing Company was the first factory in which all processes from raw material to finished product were performed in one building. From the spinning of the cotton to the weaving of the finished cloth, all work was done in this one mill.

Instead of turning to very young children for labor, as Slater had done, Lowell believed that young women would suit his purposes perfectly. His employees did not need to be strong, only intelligent and hard working. Lowell knew, however, that in order to attract young women to the mills, he would have to offer safe, respectable working and living conditions. Single women living on their own feared for their safety and avoided circumstances that would stain their reputations. Lowell solved this problem by setting up boardinghouses run by responsible, trustworthy matrons, like Robinson's mother, and instilling a strict moral code in both the mills and the surrounding town.

Later, larger mills were built at Lowell, Massachusetts, along the Merrimack River. These mills used power looms, which required workers with nimble hands for smooth operation. The Merrimack Manufacturing Company employed both women and young girls, and the Hanson family moved to this new and larger city.

Life at the mills. In Lowell, Mrs. Hanson worked as hard as ever. She managed a house of forty boarders, taking care of all the cooking, cleaning, and shopping. Now her income was steady and secure. The children continued with their school, but also helped with the housework. Harriet washed many sinkfuls of dishes, standing on a crate to reach the sink.

At age ten, Harriet went to work in the mills. Her mother needed the extra income and Harriet wanted to help out. She was sent to work as a doffer—a worker who took full bobbins off the spinning frame and replaced them with empty ones. The work was fairly easy; doffers were needed only fifteen minutes out of every hour. "The rest of the time," she later wrote, "was their own, and when the overseer was kind, they were allowed to read, knit, or even to go outside the mill-yard and play" (Robinson, p. 19).

When she was older, Harriet became a drawing-in girl, one of the more desirable positions in the mill. Drawing-in girls drew in the threads of the warp through the harness and the reed, making the beams ready for the weaver's loom. (The warp is the thread that runs lengthwise in a fabric. The harness raises and lowers warp threads on the loom. The reed is a movable frame that separates the warp threads.) Though it required skill and a nimble and steady hand, this job was not very demanding. Since the drawing-in girls were paid by the piece, not by the hour, they could work at their own pace. If they chose to read, they could, and Harriet often took the opportunity to open a book while she worked. Throughout her childhood, books were extremely important to Harriet. She spent much of the precious free time she had each day reading.

When she was fifteen, Harriet took two years off from working in the mills to attend Lowell High School. Here, in a wooden schoolroom located above a butcher shop, Harriet learned French, Latin, and English grammar and composition. Her composition titles—including "Poverty Not Disgraceful" and "Indolence and Industry"—give a glimpse into her attitudes about life. She felt that hard-working poor people were just as worthy as wealthy people and she hated laziness. A photograph of her during this time shows a strikingly beautiful young women with piercing black eyes, ringlets in her long hair, and a brave, confident face.

After high school, Harriet joined in many of the literary groups that had sprung up around Lowell. She even began writing and publishing her own poetry. In fact she met her husband, William Robinson, when she took some of her poetry to the Lowell *Journal,* where he worked as an editor.

Chronicle of early mill life. Harriet left the mills at age twenty-three. She later wrote of her experiences in a book called *Loom and Spindle, or Life Among the Early Mill Girls,* published in 1898. Although many historians believe that Robinson paints an overly bright and rosy picture of life in the mills during this time, Robinson claimed that hers was an accurate account of her experiences and that working conditions did not worsen until after she left in 1848. It is important to keep in mind, however, that Robinson's circumstances may have been more favorable than most. She lived with her family (many girls had left homes far away to work in the mills); she held a skilled but relatively easy job that allowed time for reading; and she worked in the very early days of the industry, when workers were still allowed to perform at their own pace. Nonetheless, her account captures a time in history when women began to see their position in society change as they had the opportunity to become wage earners and to educate themselves.

Participation: Early American Industry

Who were the mill girls? Assured of a safe environment and attracted by the cash wages and the chance to earn a living for themselves, women from all over New England flocked to the mill towns to work. They called themselves mill girls.

According to Robinson, mill girls included farmer's daughters aching for city life, women from fine families who did not really need the money but wanted to be in a cultured and stimulating environment, "women with past histories" (Robinson, p. 39), married women running away from husbands who had mistreated them, and unmarried women who had been dependent on relatives for their support. Robinson's moving account of this last group gives a clear idea of how strongly women were affected by the opportunity to earn their own income:

> How well I remember some of these solitary ones!... I can see them now, even after sixty years, just as they looked,—depressed, modest, mincing, hardly daring to look one in the face, so shy and sylvan had been their lives. But after the first pay-day came, and they felt the jingle of silver in their pockets ... their bowed heads were lifted, their necks seemed braced with steel, they looked you in the face, sang blithely among their looms or frames, and walked with elastic step to and from their work. (Robinson, p. 43)

Mills offered women the opportunity to make their own way in life. Becoming wage earners for the first time empowered these women with a new sense of confidence. Even the large numbers of women who worked in the mills to finance their brothers' education came away from the experience more confident and self-assured.

Working conditions. By today's standards, work in the mills during Robinson's time was demanding and difficult. Workers began their day at 5:00 in the morning and worked until 7:00 in the evening, with only two half-hour meal breaks in between. Robinson wrote that though she did not mind such a schedule, the worst part of it was having to get up so early:

> I do not recall any particular hardship connected with this life, except getting up so early in the morning, and to this habit, I never was, and never shall be, reconciled, for it has taken nearly a lifetime for me to make up the sleep lost at that early age. (Robinson, p. 20)

Inside the mills, the noise of so much machinery—pounding levers and grinding gears—could be deafening. As a drawing-in girl, Robinson worked in small rooms away from the busiest and noisiest part of the mill. In the early days of the mills, mill operators let workers progress at their own pace and did not force them to take on any more work than they could handle. As Robinson wrote, "We were not hurried any more than was for our good, and no more work was required of us than we were able easily to do" (Robinson, p. 20). As the years passed, however, and textile manufacturing became more competitive, workers were forced to labor at a quick pace, churning out products as fast as was humanly possible.

"The mill girl's alma mater." One of the most fascinating aspects of mill life was the urgency with which many girls went about educating themselves. Mill life, where books and ideas were shared and discussed on a daily basis, offered many mill girls their first opportunity at real learning. Many had come from faraway villages and farms where the only book available was the family Bible. Robinson recalled one boarder in her mother's boarding house who had traveled from her farm in Maine to work in the mills "for the express purpose of getting books" (Robinson, p. 26). This boarder read from two to four books per week, renting them for about six cents each at the local lending library. In exchange for running to the library and back, the boarder let Harriet and her siblings read the books, too.

With work consuming fourteen hours of each day, mill girls had precious little free time, yet many spent their free hours reading, writing, and learning. It was not uncommon for mill girls to spend their evening hours participating in reading groups, attending night school, and going to lectures. One lecturer, A. P. Peabody, gave a stirring picture of mill girls listening to a lecture:

> The Lowell Hall was always crowded, and four-fifths of the audience were factory-girls. When the lecturer entered, almost every girl had a book in her hand, and was intent upon it. When he rose, the book was laid aside, and paper and pencil taken instead ... I have never seen anywhere so assiduous note-taking. No, not even in a college class ... as in that assembly of young women, laboring for their subsistence. (Robinson, pp. 45-46)

The Lowell Offering. In October 1840, some of the mill girls got together to produce and publish, in the words of editor Abel C. Thomas, "the first magazine or journal written exclusively by women in the whole world" (Dunwell, p. 48). The sixteen-page *Offering,* which sold for about six cents a copy, published poems, articles, and stories written by mill girls. Robinson contributed several poems to the journal and later became its historian. The *Offering* received praise from literary circles around the country and even the world. English novelist Charles Dickens claimed that it would "compare advantageously with a great many English annals" (Dunwell, p. 48). In France, female writer George Sands hailed the work.

Strikes. In spite of the educational advantages, the spirited fellowship, and the income that the mills offered, workers were not always happy with the treatment they received. Robinson witnessed two strikes during her younger years, and participated in one of them. In 1834, when she was nine, workers left their posts at 11:00 on a Saturday morning, turning out to the streets to protest a 15 percent wage cut. The mill owners were surprised by this show of female resistance and called the striking workers "Amazons." This strike was one of the first cases of organized protest in the history of the textile industry and did considerable damage. Some rooms in the mills were left completely empty and the town's banks were drained as fired workers withdrew their savings and returned home.

Two years later, when Robinson was eleven and working as a doffer, workers struck because of a proposed pay cut that would allow mill owners to pay more to the boardinghouse managers. This time, Robinson was directly involved in the strike, leading a room full of girls into the march. She wrote: "I, who began to think they would not go out, after all their talk, became impatient, and started on ahead, saying, with childish bravado, 'I don't care what you do, *I* am going to turn out,' and was followed by the others" (Bushman, p. 26). This time, thousands—one-quarter of Lowell's working population—marched in the streets. This turnout, which lasted a month, produced some effects; several of the mills reversed the wage cut. Only later did Robinson realize that her action hurt her mother, who, as a boardinghouse matron, could have used the extra income.

Worsening conditions. As early as 1841, when Robinson still worked in the mills, workers were complaining about the inhuman conditions, claiming they were treated like machines. The piece below, titled "The Spirit of Discontent," was published in *The Offering:*

> I am going home, where I shall not be obliged to rise so early in the morning, nor be dragged about by the factory bell, nor confined in a close noisy room from morning to night. I shall not stay here.... Up before day, at the clang of the bell,—and out of the mill by the clang of the bell—into the mill, and at work in obedience to that ding-dong of a bell—just as though we were so many living machines. (Dunwell, p. 49)

As years passed, mills sped up production and gave workers increased work loads. Wages dropped and working conditions worsened. Reporters described mill hands as working endlessly and "when they can toil no longer, they go home to die" (Dunwell, p. 91). Housing became cramped as more and more workers moved to mill towns. In one home, reported the Lowell *Courier,* 120 people lived under the same roof; in another case, 22 people made their home in a basement.

Now, workers, with the support of the public, fought for a shorter working day (ten hours) and better wages. By the mid- to late 1800s, mill girls were replaced by immigrants—Irish, Italian, and Portuguese—who were willing to work for lower wages. As the twentieth-century approached, mill towns like Lowell, Lawrence, and Holyoke teemed with mill workers, many of them immigrant men. Housing became scarce and overcrowded. Cramped conditions, improper air circulation, and unclean surroundings caused outbreaks of tuberculosis, cholera, and typhoid. One out of every three spinners, many under the age of twenty-five, would die before completing ten years in the factory. It was a far cry from the dismal round of life in these mill towns to the pleasant, spirited days that Robinson wrote about.

One Mill Owner's Attitude Toward His Workers

As for myself, I regard my work people just as I regard my machinery. So long as they can do my work for what I choose to pay them, I keep them, getting out of them all I can. What they do or how they fare outside my walls, I don't know, nor do I consider it my business to know. They must look out for themselves as I do for myself. When my machines get old and useless, I reject them and get new, and these people are part of my machinery. (Steve Dunwell, *The Run of the Mill* [Boston: David R. Godine, 1978], p. 101)

Aftermath

Marriage and family. Harriet's marriage on Thanksgiving Day of 1848 to William Robinson ended her work in the mills. Her husband, who for a time published an antislavery newspaper, was politically active and his liberal views made him many enemies. The couple eventually moved to Malden, outside of Boston, and had four children, one of whom died in infancy. Robinson was content to live as a housewife while her husband worked. Later, however, after William's death, Robinson devoted much of her time to fighting for women's rights. She hoped to, but did not, see women get the vote in her own lifetime.

Suffragette. With her elder daughter, Hattie, Robinson joined the National Woman Suffrage Association, which promoted a woman's right to vote as well as her rights in the workplace and in the home. In 1881, Robinson published a book, *Massachusetts in the Woman Suffrage Movement.* At one point she testified before Congress on the subject of suffrage. Robinson and Hattie also formed a women's club in Malden.

In her later years, Robinson often was asked to lecture about her life as a mill girl. At these lectures she met women who were working in the mills of the late 1800s and soon learned that the conditions they labored under were far worse than anything she remembered. She wrote:

> The wages of these operatives are much lower, and although the hours of labor are less, they are obliged to do a far greater amount of work in a given time. They tend so many looms and frames that they have no time to think. They are always on the jump. (Selden, p. 112)

Robinson spent the last years of her life keeping active with her family, reading, writing, and sewing. She died on December 22, 1911, at the age of eighty-six. Death notices praised her contributions as a champion of women's rights. Years later, during the bicentennial celebration of the United States in 1976, Robinson's home in Malden was declared a landmark.

For More Information

Bushman, Claudia. *"A Good Poor Man's Wife"; Being a Chronicle of Harriet Hanson Robinson and Her Family in Nineteenth-Century New England.* Hanover, New Hampshire: University Press of New England, 1981.

Dunwell, Steve. *The Run of the Mill: A Pictorial Narrative of the Expansion, Dominion, Decline and Enduring Impact of the New England Textile Industry.* Boston: David R. Godine, 1978.

Robinson, Harriet Hanson. *Loom and Spindle, or Life Among the Early Mill Girls.* Originally published, 1898; reprint: Hawaii: Press Pacifica, 1976.

Selden, Bernice. *The Mill Girls: Lucy Larcom, Harriet Hanson Robinson, Sarah G. Bagley.* New York: Atheneum, 1983.

Women and Reform

- **1835** — **Angelina Grimké Weld** writes article supporting abolition movement.
- **1837–1838** — Angelina and **Sarah Grimké** write pamphlets linking women's rights to slaves' rights.
- **1848** — Seneca Falls Convention for women's rights is organized by Elizabeth Cady Stanton and Lucretia Mott.
- **1849** — **Amelia Bloomer** publishes *The Lily*, the first woman-owned newspaper in the United States.
- **1851** — The Bloomer costume comes into fashion.
- **1852** — **Susan B. Anthony** founds Women's State Temperence Society.
- **1860** — New York State grants married women property rights.
- **1869** — Anthony founds the National Woman's Suffrage Association, for women to gain the vote.
- **1870** — The Grimkés attempt to vote in Boston election.
- **1872** — Anthony votes in New York and is arrested.
- **1920** — Nineteenth Amendment is ratified; American women gain the right to vote.

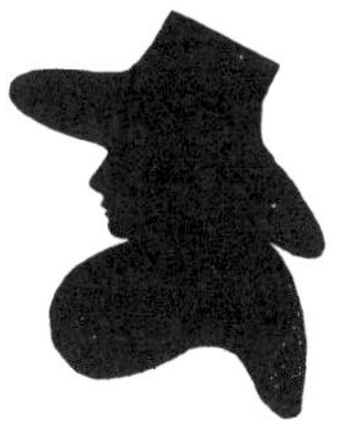

WOMEN AND REFORM

Early America regarded women as the moral conscience of society, superior in values to the nation's men. Yet it would not grant property or child-custody rights to women, and they were not allowed to vote and had few job opportunities. Women who needed to work could become teachers or midwives. In the South, a woman might manage a plantation household. In the North, she might find a job as a mill girl in a textile factory. But if she were married, her husband had the legal right to her earnings.

Society divided women and men into separate spheres of activity. Home and family were considered proper arenas for the women; business and politics were reserved for the men. Most men and women of the time accepted these roles. There were some, like the writer and social reformer Catherine Beecher (sister to the author Harriet Beecher Stowe), who openly supported them. In Beecher's view, having a separate role actually gave women power in society.

Raising a family was regarded as a woman's primary duty. But because women were considered the moral guardians of society, was it acceptable for them to move outside the home to establish orphanages, Sunday schools, and the like. Female volunteer groups began springing up in the early 1800s to encourage charity or religion. Soon some of the women became active in controversial issues, such as the movements to outlaw liquor and to

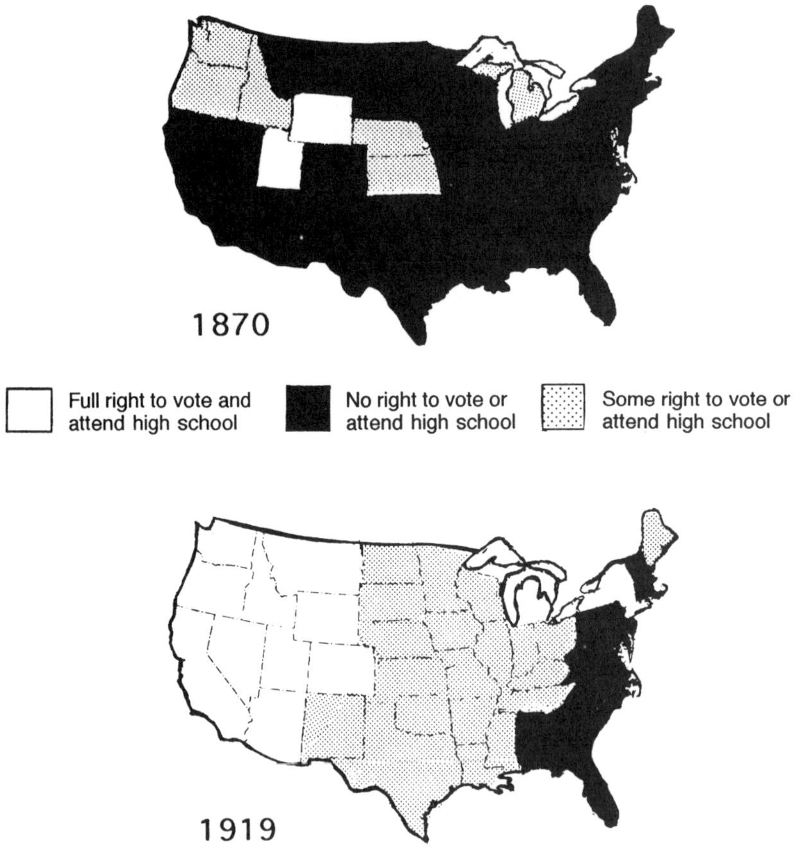

▲ **Winning equal rights for women was a slow process**

abolish slavery. This, in time, led women to work directly for equal rights with men.

In 1835, **Angelina Grimké Weld** wrote an article in support of abolition. Her essay was published in William Lloyd Garrison's newspaper, *The Liberator,* and immediately thrust Angelina and her sister **Sarah Grimké** into the public eye. The sisters, raised in the South, began to lecture and write on the major social issues of the day, temperance (the movement to abstain from drinking and outlaw selling alcohol), and abolition.

As the Grimkés and other women became more involved in organizations devoted to the improvement of society, they began to realize the need for a movement of their own. Women lacked rights in almost every area of life, from property ownership to education and job opportunity to voting rights. Involvement in the abolition movement especially led many women to draw sharp parallels between their situation and that of slaves. Women reformers called for their own equal treatment.

Females of all ages and backgrounds came to support the movement for women's rights. Married and single, from the North and from the South, women banded together to promote change. The first attempt by women to organize on their own behalf occurred in the North. Lucretia Mott and Elizabeth Cady Stanton organized the Women's Rights Convention in 1848 in Seneca Falls, New York. Antislavery activists, they had been discriminated against by male abolition leaders who refused to let women participate in a world antislavery meeting. The revolutionary Seneca Falls convention officially launched the women's rights movement as a cause of its own, separate from the abolition and temperance movements.

At the convention, sixty-eight women and thirty-two men passed a Declaration of Sentiments, similar to the Declaration of Independence. The declaration's writers listed sixteen forms of discrimination against women, including unequal wages and lack of property rights. A resolution calling for a woman's right to vote passed in the convention but was not supported by Lucretia Mott, who considered it too radical. Like many women and most men of the day, Mott believed the time had not yet come for women to gain the vote. She insisted that through men, women could influence elections. But others argued that until women could vote for change, and even hold office themselves, they were slaves under men's control. Among these reformers was **Amelia Bloomer,** the first woman to own and operate a newspaper in America. For several years after the Seneca Falls Convention, Bloomer wrote editorials in her newspaper calling for Americans to grant women the right to vote.

For the next few decades, women continued to lobby for equal rights, most fervently for property and voting rights. **Susan B. Anthony** emerged as the leading spokeswoman for granting women the vote. Canvassing the Northeast, she addressed anyone

▲ **Women protest at the voting booths**

who would listen to her on the subject. Anthony spoke to state legislatures and at conventions. In 1860, she was rewarded for her efforts when the New York State Legislature granted property rights to married women. The grant gave them complete ownership of their property and guardianship of their children in the event of the death of their husband or divorce. Up until this time, a woman was entitled only to one-third of the property (even if she had owned it entirely before marriage) and had no rights over her children. This was a huge victory for the women's movement, but Anthony and other women pressed for more. They pursued their struggle for the vote, believing it was the only way to ensure that women could effect social change.

Women would continue to participate in national causes, as they had since the 1820s. Anthony and Stanton would, for example, muster support in the 1860s for a constitutional amendment to abolish slavery altogether. Afterward, gaining the vote for women became their main crusade. Still popular in society, however, was the idea of women as the social conscience of America whose main responsibility was the home. Shared by political leaders of the time, this attitude would drag the women's struggle for the vote into the next century.

Sarah Grimké

1792-1873

Angelina Grimké Weld

1805-1879

Personal Background

Family. Sarah Moore Grimké was born on November 26, 1792, in Charleston, South Carolina. Her sister, Angelina Emily, was born thirteen years later on November 26, 1805. Despite their age difference (perhaps even because of it), Sarah and Angelina were from the beginning as close as any two sisters can be. More than best friends, Sarah and Angelina lived with each other all of their lives, with Sarah acting as a sort of substitute mother to Angelina during their childhood. Each sister possessed a strong mind and kind soul and, in spite of growing up in a male-dominated, slave-holding southern family, the two shared the belief that all people are created equal.

Unlikely abolitionists. Sarah and Angelina grew up in a prominent Charleston family. Their father, Judge John Faucheraud Grimké, fought in the Revolutionary War, served in the South Carolina state legislature as well as on the state's highest court, and operated a thriving cotton plantation. Their mother, Mary Smith Grimké, came from a wealthy, upper-class Charleston family. The Grimkés lived alternately between a fashionable townhouse in Charleston and the sprawling Beaufort plantation in the country. Like other large plantation owners, they kept scores of slaves, who did all the labor at Beaufort, from cotton picking to cooking to car-

▲ Sarah Grimké

Event: Antislavery and women's rights movements, 1837 to 1873.

Role: Daughters of a South Carolina slave-holding family, the Grimké sisters helped pioneer the antislavery and women's rights movements in the United States. As southern women, they played a key role in the attempt to gain the support of southerners for these movements. The sisters spread their opinions to the public through pamphlets, books, and lectures, using legal and Biblical evidence to support their views.

ing for the children. Slaves worked as nursemaids to the Grimkés' fourteen children and, in addition, each child was assigned a "constant companion," a slave child of about the same age who catered to his or her needs.

Even as a child, Sarah was uneasy about her family owning slaves and she never considered her "companion" anything less than her equal. The slave girl died suddenly when both were about eight, and a heartbroken Sarah refused to accept another in her place.

Sarah's childhood. Until Angelina came along, Sarah grew up lonely. She said of those days: "We had many outdoor enjoyments ... I, however, always had one terrible drawback. Slavery was a millstone about my neck, and marred my comfort from the time I can remember myself" (Lerner, p. 28). Not only was Sarah upset by the suffering of the slaves she saw all around her, but she was virtually alone in her views on the subject. Further, she felt cheated intellectually. Her father, a very well-educated lawyer, taught Sarah, along with her brother Thomas, much about the law. Sarah learned to debate along with her brothers at home and secretly studied Thomas's school lessons at night. But girls were not allowed a secondary education in those days and when Thomas went off to law school at Yale, Sarah had to remain at home. Her father remarked that if Sarah had only been a boy, "she would have made the greatest jurist in the country" (Lerner, p. 25). Disappointed that she could not pursue an education, at age twelve Sarah turned her attentions to home and church.

Sisters in suffering. The Grimkés were a very religious family and attended Episcopal services every Sunday. Several days a week Sarah and her sisters also taught Bible classes, in which they read Biblical stories to slave children. But the young women were not allowed to teach the slaves to read the stories themselves, for this was against the law in 1805. Sarah continually questioned why the slaves should have to learn the Gospel second hand and saw no reason that she should not teach her students to read the Bible for themselves.

While Sarah dared not break the law in public, she admittedly took great pleasure in secretly teaching her waiting-maid to read at night. She said proudly, "The light was put out, the keyhole screened, and flat on our stomachs, before the fire, with the

▲ **Angelina Grimké Weld**

spelling-book under our eyes, we defied the laws of South Carolina" (Lerner, p. 32).However, Judge Grimké caught Sarah and her maid one night and severely punished the two for their actions. Though he spared the maid from being whipped, he delivered to Sarah a stern lecture on the laws of the land. The episode broke Sarah's spirit for a time. She remained very quiet and somber until the birth of Angelina some months later.

Angelina's birth. Just turning thirteen and feeling rejected by the outside world, Sarah welcomed the arrival of her youngest sister. She saw in Angelina—"Nina" as she called her—the opportunity to be useful, to be needed. Her mother was worn out from the demands of her huge household and from bearing fourteen children (three of whom had died in infancy, leaving her quite grief stricken). Sarah begged to become Angelina's godmother. Her parents agreed, and from that day forward, Sarah assumed a responsibility for her youngest sibling that she would never give up.

Angelina grows up. As Angelina grew older under the watchful eye and loving influence of Sarah, she too struggled with the issue of slavery. During her early childhood, she attended a seminary for daughters of wealthy landowners. One day, Angelina fainted in class and Sarah was called in to retrieve her. When Angelina recovered, she told her sister that the sight of a slave child at the school had made her faint. About the same age as Angelina, the little slave boy had come to open a window but could barely walk to the front of the room. Staggering, he finally reached it and when he turned, Angelina saw that his small body was covered with whip marks. The wounds on his legs and back still bled. In retelling the story, Angelina wept.

Sarah tried to comfort Angelina but not much could be said; Sarah did not understand the cruel treatment of slaves either. She had merely learned that, as a young woman, she was basically powerless to change conditions in the South.

Father dies. By 1818, as Sarah turned twenty-six and Angelina entered her teens, their father had become deathly ill. Sarah was sent alone to accompany her father to Philadelphia, Pennsylvania, in search of a cure. In June 1919, the two left Philadelphia for the Atlantic coast in hopes that the sea air would do the ailing man some good. But it was too late—Judge Grimké died in Bordentown, New Jersey, by his daughter's side.

During the months that Judge Grimké hovered between life and death, he leaned on Sarah heavily and drew upon her strength. The two grew so close that they "became fast friends indeed" and Sarah regarded this "as the greatest blessing ... that I have ever received from God" (Lerner, p. 62). She was also on her own for the first time in the big city of Philadelphia, and the trip was a major turning point in Sarah's life. It opened her eyes to life in the North, outside of slavery. It also introduced her to the Quaker religion.

Quaker conversion. Sarah remained in Philadelphia for a few months after her father's death and, while waiting for a ship back to Charleston, she met some members of the city's Quaker Society of Friends. The Friends introduced Sarah to the works of Quaker leader John Woolman, and she was immediately inspired by his message. In his writings, Woolman strongly condemned slavery as evil and encouraged action against it. He, like Sarah, believed all people to be equal and was among the first to link the discrimination blacks faced in the North to the slavery of the South. Sarah identified with his message and began considering joining the church. Drawn to its antislavery doctrine, Sarah also was attracted to the fact that Quakers allowed women to become leaders within the church. Female preachers were common and Sarah thought that could be her calling. She did not convert immediately, however, but rather returned home to weigh her decision.

Upon her return, Sarah found the South unbearable. Having spent nearly a year in the North, she realized she could no longer live in the presence of slavery, even if it meant she had to move away from her family. "After being gone for many months in Pennsylvania," she wrote, "when I went back it seemed as if the sight of [the slaves'] condition was insupportable, it burst my mind with new horror" (Lerner, p. 72).

Within a month of her return and against her mother's wishes, Sarah packed her bags and moved permanently to Philadelphia, joining the Quaker Society of Friends.

Angelina's conversion. When Sarah made her exit, Angelina became the leader of the Charleston household. With their father deceased and the Grimké sons married or off at school, Angelina was left to look out for her mother and sisters and manage daily operations of the cotton plantation. However, she continually clashed with her mother over the issue of slavery. Angelina begged her mother to set her servants free—especially after the death of her father—but her pleas were unsuccessful. Her mother, deeply rooted in southern culture, saw nothing wrong with the practice of keeping slaves.

Angelina considered joining her sister in the North. When Sarah returned to Charleston for a visit in 1827, Angelina was impressed by the simplicity of her sister's Quaker dress and lifestyle. She was also taken with the Quaker philosophy of nonviolence; they refused to act violently, even in self-defense. As Sarah prepared to return to Philadelphia, Angelina decided she also would convert to the Quaker religion. But she felt that staying in the South might help persuade other southerners to see the evils of slavery. Angelina remained in Charleston for a few more months, attempting to convert friends and family members. But the time finally came when she could no longer tolerate living with slavery and, in November 1829, she joined her sister in the North.

Participation: Abolition and Women's Rights

Quaker sisters. In Philadelphia, Sarah and Angelina became active in the Quaker church and the abolitionist cause, teaching weekly prayer meetings and doing local charity work. Sarah studied to become a member of the clergy and Angelina attempted to further her education. The church, however, did not prove to be entirely in favor of either effort.

Angelina decided to become a teacher and traveled to Hartford, Connecticut, to apply to attend Catherine Beecher's famous female seminary. Upon acceptance to the school, she returned to Philadelphia to get permission from the church to move. But the Quakers disapproved and denied her permission to go. Instead they offered her a teaching position in a Quaker infant school in Philadelphia. Angelina agreed but was not satisfied. Similarly, Sarah's dream of becoming a preacher was crushed. She was continually discouraged by the men of the Philadelphia Society of Friends and finally gave up when one church elder rudely interrupted one of her prayer meetings. The sisters were beginning to realize that belonging to the church was not the way to satisfy their dreams.

Meanwhile, in the country at large, explosive events were taking place. Antislavery speakers were flooding the East Coast with their messages, which included emancipation, or freedom for the slaves; abolition, or the end of slavery altogether; and recolonization, or sending the nation's black population back to Africa.

By 1832, both sisters had become very discouraged by their limited roles within the Philadelphia branch of the Quaker church. The women longed to be more involved in the slavery issue; after all, that was why they moved north in the first place. Three events gave them freedom from some responsibilities and allowed them to more actively fight slavery. First, Sarah refused to marry the Quaker man who had been instrumental in her conversion, fearing she would become more of a slave than a partner in marriage. Next, Angelina's fiancé died suddenly in an epidemic. And finally, their dear brother Thomas, who also had been working for emancipation, died. With marriage possibilities and family ties cut, Sarah and Angelina felt they had nothing to prevent them from joining the abolitionists and putting all their efforts into working for the abolition of slavery.

The letter. Reading in William Lloyd Garrison's newspaper, *The Liberator,* of the formation of the American Anti-Slavery Society (AASS) in 1833, Angelina rushed to support his efforts (see **William Lloyd Garrison**). The Garrison-led AASS was the first interracial society that supported immediate emancipation of slaves, boldly declaring that "the Negro, free or slave, was a human being and a citizen and was to be considered as such" (Lerner, p. 160). Angelina attended AASS meetings in Philadelphia and became a member of the society's committee for the improvement of people of color.

As race riots began erupting throughout East Coast cities, Angelina felt compelled to become more deeply involved in Garrison's movement. On August 30, 1835, with a stroke of her pen, Angelina changed the sisters' lives forever. Though she had never met Garrison, Angelina wrote him a letter, that began, "I can hardly express to thee the deep and solemn interest with which I have viewed the violent proceedings of the last few weeks." She told Garrison to keep up the fight and volunteered to join him, saying, "This is a cause worth dying for" (Lerner, p. 174).

Without Angelina's permission, Garrison reprinted her moving letter in *The Liberator,* saying that he "could not, dared not suppress it" (Lerner, p. 174). The response to Angelina's letter was overwhelming, and at once Angelina and Sarah were thrust to the front lines of the fight against slavery. The Philadelphia Quakers were outraged by Angelina's act (Quakers were supposed to receive permission from the church before doing anything on their own), but the antislavery community embraced the sisters. At last they had found their calling.

Antislavery activities. Angelina's letter was reprinted in all the major reform newspapers of the day and was printed with Garrison's *Appeal to the Citizens of Boston* and the Quaker abolitionist poet John Greenleaf Whittier's antislavery poem *Stanzas for the Time* in a widely circulated pamphlet. Angelina stepped up her efforts in the AASS, participating in its antislavery conventions. Sarah supported more moderate activities such as the "Free Produce" movement—a call to boycott, or stop buying, products made by slaves—which began with her Quaker mentor, John Woolman. As a result of their new-found friends and activities, the sisters moved from Philadelphia to Providence, Rhode Island, to be with a looser, more liberal group of Quakers.

Power of the pen. In early 1836, from their new home in Rhode Island, Sarah and Angelina began to write a series of antislavery pamphlets and books. Angelina wrote *An Appeal to the Christian Women of the South* and Sarah produced *An Epistle to the Clergy of the Southern States,* followed by *An Address to Free Colored Americans.* These powerful works, which for the first time were written by southerners for southerners, had a huge impact. Because the women had grown up in the South and came from such a respectable family, southern folk at least considered reading what the sisters had to say. Angelina's *Clergy,* for example, declared that slavery was "opposed to Christian principles and to everything Jesus had taught" (Lacy, p. 74). The sisters also spoke out in favor of women working for abolition, saying that throughout the Bible there are examples of women taking public stands on important issues.

Following publication of their work, Sarah and Angelina were invited to speak throughout the Northeast. They addressed Anti-Slavery Society conventions in New York, Pennsylvania, Rhode Island, and Massachusetts and met all the famous abolitionists of the day, including Theodore Weld, who later married Angelina. Weld helped polish the sisters' public-speaking skills and in 1837 Sarah and Angelina began a twenty-three week lecture tour for the abolition movement.

The tour. Financing the trip themselves, the sisters visited sixty-seven cities, breaking new ground for women as public speakers. Up to this time, it was virtually unheard of for women to address audiences with both men and women in attendance and even fewer were so outspoken on the most controversial issues of the day. While they received praise from many for their courageous stand against slavery, the sisters also suffered countless attacks on their character. Congregational ministers blasted the Grimkés in a public letter, saying that a woman becomes "unnatural" when she "assumes the place and tone of a man" (Cooper, p. 59). Even Catherine Beecher, who herself ran a groundbreaking women's school, criticized the sisters' lecture tour. Like others, she felt it was not a "woman's place" to speak in public.

Because of the controversy their tour created, the sisters became aware of the overwhelming parallels between women's and slaves' role in society. Both were denied the right to vote and the right to a secondary education, and both were treated as second-class citizens. Sarah soon became convinced that until women were themselves completely free, they could not effectively work for the rights of others. Thus, Sarah was prompted to write *Equality of the Sexes,* the first document to link slavery to the unequal treatment of women.

Sarah did not wish to suggest "that the condition of free women can be compared to that of slaves in suffering or degradation" (Cooper, p. 62); rather, women faced the same limitations as slaves in education and work opportunity and so had a special duty to fight against slavery.

Sarah further insisted that women's domestic duties did not weaken their ability to succeed in the public arena and suggested to women that the claim to stand on perfect equality with men could only be proven by "scrupulous attention to our domestic duties" (Cooper, p. 61). Sarah realized women would have to play dual roles in society in order to be accepted in the public arena.

Angelina addresses the Massachusetts legislature. Angelina finished the year-long speaking tour with an address to the Massachusetts state legislature, becoming the first woman in U.S. history to speak to a legislative body. Afterward, both sisters returned to Providence for a much-deserved rest.

Aftermath

After the grueling tour, Angelina was physically exhausted, but she also was in love. She and Theodore were married in a very simple ceremony, with Theodore renouncing all claims to Angelina's property and Angelina omitting the line "to obey" from her wedding vows. Both black and white Americans attended the ceremony, including William Lloyd Garrison and black schoolteacher and abolitionist Sarah Mapps Douglass. The Philadelphia Society of Friends officially expelled Angelina for marrying a non-Quaker and Sarah for attending the wedding.

Angelina Grimké on Freedom of Speech for Women

The right of petition [protest] is the only political right that women have. The fact that women are denied the right of voting … is but a poor reason why they should also be deprived of the right of petition … the *very least* that can be done is to give them the right of petition…. If not, they are mere slaves, known only through their masters. (Lerner, p. 268)

Within the next two years, Theodore, Angelina, and Sarah all moved to a farm in New Jersey. The sisters were determined to pay "scrupulous attention to domestic duties" and show that active women could be good mothers and efficient housekeepers without the help of slaves. After 1839, the sisters concentrated on raising Angelina's children and tending their farm and home. Sarah and Angelina tried to stay as active as they had been in civil rights causes before the marriage, but Angelina's ill health prevented it. The tour and subsequent bearing of children had severely weakened her. So instead of touring and lecturing, the sisters wrote articles and speeches for others to recite at antislavery and women's rights conventions. They also took as boarders a great many abolitionists who toured the East Coast, including Elizabeth Cady Stanton and her husband, Henry.

During the Civil War, the sisters wrote articles supporting the Union. In March 1863, they penned "An Appeal to the Women of the Republic," which urged women to rally to the cause of the Union and hold a convention to support the war effort. Angelina, now much stronger physically, addressed the convention, which was presided over by Lucy Stone, Stanton, and Susan B. Anthony.

After the war the sisters and Theodore relocated to Hyde Park, a part of Boston, where they opened a coeducational school and continued to fight for minority rights. On March 7, 1870, when Sarah was seventy-nine and Angelina sixty-six, the sisters boldly declared a woman's right to vote under the fourteenth Amendment by depositing ballots in the local election. Along with forty-two women, Sarah and Angelina marched in procession in a driving snowstorm to the polling place. They were jeered by many onlookers but, because of their age, were not arrested. The gesture did not change the law against women voting, but it did receive a lot of publicity and was for the sisters a final "act of faith" (Lerner, p. 535).

Three years later, on December 23, 1873, Sarah died. Angelina suffered several strokes after Sarah's death, which left her paralyzed for the last six years of her life. She died on October 26, 1879. Theodore survived his wife by six years and died in 1885.

The Grimké sisters had spent their years promoting equality and free speech. They did not seek special treatment for women or African Americans, but simply the equal opportunity to succeed. In the words of Sarah Grimké: "All I ask of our bretheren is that they will take their feet from off our necks and permit us to stand upright on the ground which God intended us to occupy" (Cooper, p. 62).

For More Information

Ceplair, Larry. *The Public Years of Sarah and Angelina Grimké.* New York: Columbia University Press, 1989.

Cooper, James L., and Sheila McIsaac. *The Roots of American Feminist Thought.* Boston: Allyn and Bacon, 1973.

Lacy, Dan. *The Abolitionists.* New York: McGraw-Hill Book Company, 1978.

Susan B. Anthony

1820-1906

Personal Background

Susan B. Anthony was born on February 15, 1820, in Adams, Massachusetts. Named for an aunt, Susan Anthony Brownell, Susan was the second of six children. Susan's father, Daniel, operated a prosperous cotton mill at the family farm on Tophet Brook. Her mother, Lucy Read Anthony, did all the domestic work for her growing family as well as for eleven factory hands who boarded with the Anthonys. Both very hard workers, Susan's parents were charitable people who instilled in their children a strong work ethic and sense of goodwill toward others.

Quaker influence. Throughout Susan's childhood, the Anthony family was active in a liberal branch of the Quaker church known as the "Hicksite Friends." The Friends allowed women to be leaders in the church. Susan grew up listening to her aunt, Hannah Anthony, preach at local services and also watched her grandmother lead her congregation. At a time in history when women usually were expected to be seen and not heard, the sight of women as public speakers was highly unusual and surely had a profound impact on young Susan.

During Susan's early childhood, her father's business flourished. When she turned six, his mill was so successful he received an offer to expand. The family moved forty-four miles west to Bat-

▲ Susan B. Anthony

Event: Equal rights movement, 1848 to 1906.

Role: Throughout her lifetime, Susan B. Anthony worked for women's rights, the abolition of slavery, and temperance. Among her lengthy list of accomplishments, she helped secure women's property rights in 1860, founded the National Woman Suffrage Association in 1869, and challenged the fourteenth Amendment, paving the way for women to gain the vote.

tenville, New York, where her father set up three more factories and opened a general store. There the Anthonys became very active in the temperance movement, which promoted limiting the sale and consumption of alcohol. Her father organized a temperance society, which included all of his employees, and held meetings in his house in the evenings. His children participated in them.

Susan's first job. Susan was a hard worker. She helped her parents with both home and factory chores. With a dozen or so factory hands boarding with the Anthonys, a great deal of help was needed with the cooking, cleaning, laundry, and other chores around the house. There was also an assortment of tasks to be done at the fabric mill. She became a very good cook and an excellent seamstress.

By age twelve, Susan wanted to work outside the home. She and her younger sister, Hannah, spent much of their time watching the "factory girls" at their jobs, spooling cotton cloth and thread. When one of the spoolers fell ill, the two girls begged to replace her. Susan's mother objected to the girls' working in the factory, but her father wanted his daughters to become independent. He let them draw straws to see who could have the job. Susan won the draw and worked every day for two weeks until the spooler returned. She was thrilled to earn full wages ($3), which she split with Hannah. Susan spent her share on a set of dishes for her mother.

Susan learns at home. Susan learned to read and write at an early age and had an excellent memory. She was educated at public schools and then tutored at home. Learning subjects that ranged from arithmetic to sewing, she received a much fuller education than most girls of her day.

Teacher. By age seventeen Susan had learned enough to become a teacher, and in the winter of 1837 she taught in Easton (a few miles from Battenville) for $1 a week plus room and board. The following summer she taught in Reid's Corners for $1.50 a week, a wage that made her very proud because it was considered an excellent salary for a woman. That fall, with her sister Guelma, Susan set off for Philadelphia, Pennsylvania to attend a "Seminary for Females"—a boarding school where she could further her education. This was Susan's farthest venture from home thus far and she became quite homesick. She began to write letters to family and friends and in the process discovered that she had a natural talent for writing.

Financial crash. In 1838, while Susan was away at school, Daniel Anthony's once-thriving business collapsed. A financial crash in American business leveled the fabric manufacturing trade; the Anthonys not only lost their factory but were forced to auction off their personal belongings. They were forced to pull both girls from boarding school. Susan returned home and went to work to help her family. She recorded the turning point in her journal: "I probably shall never go to school again, and all the advancement which I hereafter make must be by my own exertions" (Harper, p. 35). In March 1839, the Anthonys moved to Hardscrabble (the name of the town was later changed to Center Falls). Susan took a job as a teacher, moving to a boarding school in New Rochelle.

Participation: Equal Rights Movement

New Rochelle, new life. At the age of nineteen, Anthony was for the first time truly on her own. She had great responsibilities placed on her from the moment she arrived in New Rochelle because her employer had fallen ill and Anthony was put in charge of all school activities. Perhaps more crucial to her development at this time were frequent visits to New York City, where she was exposed firsthand to the reality of race- and gender-based discrimination. One day, while visiting the integrated Oneida school, Anthony met several young black women. She rejoiced at the sight of black and white students eating, walking, and talking together. More commonly, however, Anthony saw discrimination. At church services, blacks were not allowed to sit even in the back; she wrote home: "What a lack of Christianity this is!" (Harper, p. 39).

Anthony also attended temperance meetings while in New York, where women preachers spoke. Upon hearing Rachel Barker, Anthony wrote to her brother-in-law, who did not believe women should be public speakers, saying:

> If you could see her you would believe in a woman's preaching. What an absurd notion that women have not intellectual and

moral faculties sufficient for anything but domestic concerns! (Harper, p. 40)

During her stay in the city she also realized her pay was but one–fifth of what a man in a similar position would earn. After the fifteen-week school term ended, Anthony received her paycheck of $30—just enough to cover her expenses in New Rochelle and pay for her return trip home. Anthony had done far more work than was normally required of a teacher's assistant yet she received five times less than a man would have received. Suddenly the $1.50-a-week salary that she had once been so proud to earn seemed very unfair. These mixed experiences opened Anthony's eyes. Though she witnessed the unequal treatment of both women and blacks, she also saw evidence that change was possible.

Renewed prosperity for the Anthonys. From New Rochelle, Anthony returned to Center Falls and for the next five years taught school there and gave her earnings to her parents. The family moved to a farm near Rochester in 1845. On April 25, 1846, Anthony received an invitation from the Canajorie Academie to head the women's department there, which she readily accepted. She taught at the Academie for three years, during which she became involved in teachers and temperance associations and also attended the first women's rights convention in Seneca Falls (known as the Seneca Falls Convention) in 1848. There she was exposed to the most powerful leaders of the abolitionist and women's rights movements. Upon hearing these remarkable speakers, including Elizabeth Cady Stanton and Lucretia Mott, Anthony began to consider expanding her career beyond teaching. She joined the Daughters of Temperance and was made secretary of the organization.

A Happy Person's Outlook on Life

"I have made up my mind that we can expect only a certain amount of comfort wherever we may be, and that it is the disposition of a person, more than the surroundings, that creates happiness." ([Susan B. Anthony, age twenty-eight] Harper, p. 50)

Temperance Society, 1849. It was in this role that Anthony developed into a great leader. At a society meeting in March 1849, Anthony made her first public speech. She called on all women to join her in the effort to promote harmony and improve the social system in America. The next day the local newspapers described her as "the smartest woman who ever has been in Canajorie" (Harper, p. 55).

It was not only newspaper reporters who noticed Anthony. Several men attempted to woo her, but without success. Anthony chose not to marry, continuing to devote her time to promoting ideals she believed would improve society.

Writes for *The Lily*. Amelia Bloomer, who published the first woman-owned newspaper in the United States, was also a member of the Daughters of Temperance (see **Amelia Bloomer**). She and Anthony became friends and, upon hearing Anthony speak, Bloomer hired Anthony to write columns for *The Lily.* Anthony contributed columns on a regular basis while still in her teaching position at the Academie. However, she soon found the confines of the classroom too limiting, and when her three-year term ended, she returned to Rochester. During the next two years, between 1850 and 1851, she continued to write for *The Lily* and also held temperance meetings in her house, just as her father had done years earlier. At these meetings, Anthony learned the plight of women who were married to alcoholics. In nineteenth-century America, a woman could not divorce her alcoholic husband, even if he abused or abandoned his family. In addition, a woman was allowed to keep only one-third of her property in the event of her husband's death. Anthony saw many abused and desperately poor women as a result of these unjust laws and realized the need for a drastic change. She became an outspoken advocate of legalized divorce and women's property rights.

Cooking, Politics, or Both?

In 1850, the Anthony household was a gathering place for free-minded thinkers. During the weekly Sunday evening meetings, great reformers such as Frederick Douglass and William Lloyd Garrison often stopped in for dinner and conversation. These occasions posed a special problem to Anthony, a gourmet cook as well as a thinker. According to biographer Ida Harper: "She was divided between her anxiety to sustain her reputation as a superior cook and her desire not to lose a word of the conversation in the parlor." (Harper, p. 60)

Elizabeth Cady Stanton. After fifteen years of teaching, Anthony now devoted her time to working for temperance, abolition, and women's rights. She wrote, lectured, and attended conventions throughout New York. In 1850, while attending an antislavery conference in Seneca Falls, Anthony met a woman who would change her life forever. Amelia Bloomer introduced her to Elizabeth Cady Stanton, who also wrote for *The Lily.* Anthony had heard Stanton speak two years earlier and had read her editorials, but the two had never formally met. Stanton and Anthony made an immediate connection. The small, portly mother and the dignified, young Quaker (Anthony was thirty) may not have resembled each other physically, but spiritually they were as close a match as two people can get. Their moral and political philosophies were so similar that most of their friends could not distinguish one's ideas from the other's.

Stanton welcomed Anthony into her family and the two became like sisters. Under Stanton's influence, Anthony began working harder than ever for the cause of women's rights. The two began organizing conventions and writing speeches and pamphlets. Anthony emerged as the public speaker while Stanton planned and wrote the speeches. Later, a friend would aptly describe the two women as perfect partners: "this noise-making twain are the two sticks of a drum ... for keeping up the rub-a-dub of agitation" (Harper, p. 189).

Anthony bursts into public life. In April 1852, Stanton and Anthony organized the Woman's State Temperance Convention in Rochester, New York. At the convention, Anthony made a speech that called not only for temperance and divorce law reform, but argued in favor of women's property rights and encouraged all women to work for the equal rights cause.

For the next six years, Anthony continued to encourage women to take active roles in all reform movements of the day. The press, however, severely criticized her efforts. The editor of the *New York Tribune* wrote that woman is "by her nature, her sex, just as the negro is and always will be to the end of time, inferior to the white race and, therefore, doomed to subjection" (Harper, p. 78). These comments did not stop Anthony, however. Instead, they strengthened her resolve to establish legal rights for blacks and women. She founded a permanent Woman's Temperance Society and in 1852 organized the Women's Rights Convention, of which Stanton was president. She and Stanton worked hard on their speeches, with Stanton continuing to pen the lines while Anthony spoke them. Anthony's address at the convention rocked the country. Her expanding list of demands for women's rights included calling on women to "march straight to the ballot-box and deposit a vote equal to her highest ideals" (Harper, p. 71). By this time, Anthony had become thoroughly convinced that in order for women to gain equal rights and respect, they must be allowed to vote. She realized that without the vote women had little or no influence over lawmakers and had no power to change divorce laws, secure property rights, or accomplish abolition. Thus she began her great crusade for women's suffrage and embarked on an ambitious journey to gain the vote.

Canvassing the state. Anthony and fellow activists began traveling across New York State in 1852 and 1853, lecturing in every town where they could get an audience. For the first time in state history, a body of women, led by Anthony, appeared before the New York State Legislature. They spoke in favor of temperance and divorce law reform and brought with them a petition with 28,000 signatures, calling for the state to prohibit, or outlaw, the sale of hard liquor. But their reception was far from warm. As one legislator put it: "Who are these asking for a law? Nobody but women and children!" (Harper, p. 83). Such comments only strengthened Anthony's determination to make a woman's signature equal to that of a man.

In 1854, there was a rift in the Woman's State Temperance Society. Anthony and Stanton both left the organization because it refused to adopt their equal rights platform. As a result, Anthony spent the next eight years working almost exclusively for women's suffrage and for abolition.

She canvassed the New England countryside, speaking at each annual Women's Rights Convention. In 1854, she went to Washington, D.C., to address Congress, and while on the coast attended antislavery rallies. She worked with abolitionists and suffragettes (women struggling to gain the vote) as the nation sat poised on the brink of civil war in 1859. Anthony refused to tone down her message in the pre-Civil War days. The rights of women and blacks had become so entwined that freedom for one spawned hope of freedom for the other. But, as Stanton wrote in a letter to Anthony at the close of that year, freedom for either seemed a long way off:

> All conspire to make me regret more than ever my dwarfed and perverted womanhood. When I pass the gate of the celestials and good Peter asks me where I wish to sit, I will say: "anywhere so that I am neither a negro nor a woman. Confer on me, great angel, the glory of white manhood, so that henceforth I may feel unlimited freedom." (Harper, p. 182)

Property rights won. Just as the nation neared one of its darkest hours, the dawn broke. Anthony returned to the New York State Legislature in early 1860 to witness an historic vote. On March 19, 1860, after a decade of rigorous lobbying by Anthony and her fellow suffragettes, the legislature voted to amend the property laws and granted women property rights for the first time in U.S. history. Called a legal revolution, the measure allowed women to buy and sell their own property and hold onto rights over their children in the event of the death of their husband.

Anthony was grateful for the victory but was not wholly satisfied. Gaining property rights was just one in a long list of guarantees she hoped to secure for women.

Aftermath

During and after the Civil War, Anthony supported the Union, but achieving voting rights for women remained her primary goal. In 1868, she began publishing the *Revolution* newspaper and the following year she founded the National Woman Suffrage Association. In 1872, she challenged the Fourteenth Amendment to the Constitution, which guarantees all citizens the right to vote. Saying that women are indeed citizens, she entered the polls and voted on election day along with a small group of other courageous women. Anthony was arrested for breaking the law and a sham of a trial ensued, in which the judge pronounced Anthony guilty before he even heard the evidence. Anthony was fined $100, which she refused to pay. The charges were later dropped because of a public outcry against the unfair proceedings.

Anthony continued to work and speak throughout New England in favor of suffrage until she was well into her eighties. Near the turn of the century, she finally settled on her family farm in Rochester, and died there of natural causes on March 13, 1906.

Anthony did not live to see women gain the right to vote, but she herself never doubted her efforts:

> I do not look back upon a hard life. I have been continually at work because I enjoyed being busy ... I had my own thanks for retaining my self-respect [and I] never [gave up]. I knew that my cause was just, and I was always in good company. (Harper, p. 952)

For More Information

Anthony, Susan B. *History of Woman Suffrage.* New York: Fowler & Wells Publishers, 1881.

Harper, Ida Husted. *Life and Work of Susan B. Anthony.* New Hampshire: Ayer Company Publishers, Inc., 1898.

Read, Phyllis. *The Book of Women's Firsts.* New York: Random House, 1992.

Amelia Jenks Bloomer

1818-1894

Personal Background

Early years. Amelia Jenks Bloomer was born to Lucy and Ananias Jenks on May 27, 1818, in Homer, New York. The youngest of five children (she had two brothers and three sisters), she lived with her family in the rural setting of Homer until 1825, when they moved to Clyde, New York. There the family remained for the next ten years.

Educated at home. Like most girls of her day, Amelia was taught at home and her education was very limited. It was thought that girls needed to learn only the basics—reading, writing, and a little arithmetic—in order to run an efficient household. Professions other than teaching were denied to women and secondary education was unavailable. With no other paths open to her and not ready for marriage, Amelia planned to become a teacher.

Growing awareness of women's rights. While studying at home with her mother, Amelia also attended church regularly with her family and did charity work. She learned Christian values from her mother, who was very active in the Presbyterian church. Through her charity work with the church, Amelia also witnessed the tragedy of alcohol abuse. With few laws governing the sale and consumption of hard liquor, alcohol abuse was quite common in nineteenth-century America. Moreover, women who were married

▲ **Amelia Jenks Bloomer**

Event: Women's rights movement.

Role: In speech and writing, Amelia Bloomer helped pioneer the women's rights movement in the United States. She published and edited *The Lily,* the first newspaper owned and operated by women in America, to promote temperance and equal rights. With her husband, Dexter, she carried her message to the untamed West beyond the Missouri River. Bloomer also was one of the first women to wear the daring and less binding "Bloomer costume" when it came into fashion, and its name is forever linked to hers.

to abusive alcoholics had no legal right to get a divorce. Churches often were the only refuge for such women. Seeing the horrors suffered by wives and children of alcoholics, Amelia joined her mother in becoming an avid supporter of the movement to control the sale and use of alcohol (the temperance movement).

As a teenager, Amelia also saw firsthand that property laws for women were unjust. A dear family friend lost her home when her husband died because, according to English common law in effect at the time, a wife was entitled only to one-third of her husband's property—even if it had all belonged to the woman before the marriage. Though the family friend had worked jointly with her husband to build their fortune, she was forced into poverty while a male third cousin inherited two-thirds of the estate. Later, Amelia wrote that this event made her "familiar with the cruelty of the law towards women" and prompted her in future years "to join ... in demanding for women such change in the laws as would give her a right to her earnings" (Bloomer, p. 48).

At age seventeen, with her schooling complete, Amelia secured a teaching job with the Clyde district school. She taught there for one year and then moved to Waterloo, New York, to help her sister Elvira with her new family. She remained with Elvira until 1837, when she accepted a job in the neighboring Chamberlain household as a tutor/governess for their three small children.

During the three years she worked for the Chamberlains, Amelia met a young law student from nearby Seneca Falls. A relative of the Chamberlains, Dexter Chamberlain Bloomer edited and partially owned the *Seneca County Courier* newspaper. He was a politically active and free-thinking young man and Amelia was immediately attracted to him. He too advocated temperance and, because of his Quaker background, thought it perfectly natural for women to actively participate in public life. Dexter and Amelia began working together in local temperance societies and soon became good friends. Within a year, their friendship blossomed into love and on April 15, 1840, the two were married. In the tradition of Angelina Grimké and Theodore Weld, Dexter and Amelia omitted the line "to obey" from the bride's wedding vows (see **Sarah Grimké and Angelina Grimké Weld**). They wanted a marriage of equals. True to her strong support of the temperance movement, Amelia refused to toast with alcohol at her wedding reception.

Participation: Women's Rights Movement

Married life in Seneca Falls. Amelia Bloomer was greatly influenced by her husband, Dexter, as well as by the activity in Seneca Falls. Home to some of the great thinkers of the era, Seneca Falls was alive with political debate. Elizabeth Cady Stanton lived there, along with a wide group of other intellectuals who gathered nightly to discuss politics and organize meetings.

Dexter himself was well educated and very well read. Before editing the *Courier,* he had worked as a teacher. Though Bloomer at twenty-two was more shy than her twenty-four-year-old husband, her great intelligence was apparent to him from the moment they met. They had corresponded during their courtship and, in the process, he learned that she possessed a natural talent for writing. Dexter continually encouraged Bloomer to write for the *Courier* and when they were married, she began to contribute to the paper. She wrote editorials on the temperance movement, signing them, because of her modesty, with a pen name (usually Gloriana or Eugene).

> **Anthony Comments on Bloomer's Marriage**
>
> "Your celebration of your 50th wedding day is one of the strongest proofs of the falseness of the charge brought against our movement for the franchisement of women, that ... equal rights for the wife will cause inharmony or disruption of the marriage bond. To the contrary, such conditions of perfect equality are the best helps to make for peace and harmony" (Bloomer, pp. 312-13).

As Bloomer continued to write, however, she steadily became more self-assured and outgoing. She soon dropped the use of pen names and proudly attached her name to her essays. She became very involved in local temperance societies and also started writing for the temperance society newspaper, the *Water Bucket.* With the encouragement of her husband, she widened her circle of friends and interests. She began attending meetings concerning women's property rights. An outgrowth of the temperance movement, the question of a woman's right to divorce while still maintaining her children and property was coming to the political forefront. By 1845, some property rights had been given to married women in New York State, thanks in large part to the efforts of the activists in Seneca Falls. Property rights for women on a national level, however, were still years off.

Seneca Falls Convention. During the next few years, from 1845 to 1848, Bloomer attended meetings, wrote editorials, and became increasingly involved in the women's rights movement. In July 1848, Elizabeth Cady Stanton and Lucretia Mott called the world's attention to the cause of women's rights and held the first women's rights convention in Seneca Falls (Seneca Falls Convention). Bloomer attended a July 19, 1848, meeting and another convention two weeks later in Rochester.

Twenty-One Reasons Why Women Should Vote

In one of her most famous letters, Bloomer responded to an article by the editor of the Des Moines *Register* listing twenty-one reasons why women should not be allowed to vote. She countered each reason with humor, as shown in this reply to reason number four: "Because woman is superior to man and she owes her superiority to the fact that she has never waded in the dirty pool of politics.' Dear me! How worried this man is about the 'dirty,' 'miserable' politics ... Really, if the place is so muddy it is high time that woman come in, with all the purity and goodness he gives her credit for, and sweep out the dirt." (Bloomer, pp. 165–66)

Bloomer returned from the meetings with renewed vigor for the temperance and women's rights movements and became more active than ever in the Daughters of Temperance organization. She wrote for its newspaper, the *Temperance Star,* and met Susan B. Anthony, an important leader of the group (see **Susan B. Anthony**). After attending the Seneca Falls Convention, Anthony and Bloomer both began to see the severe limitations of an all-woman group. Women were allowed to speak and work only within "female societies" but remained virtually unheard outside of them. Thus, it was very easy for their demands to be ignored by the general public. "But as the years rolled on," Bloomer noted, "women became more earnest and self-reliant, and were not satisfied with these secret doings. They wanted their light to be seen" (Bloomer, p. 37).

The Lily. That light shone through in *The Lily,* a newspaper that provided a voice for women on national issues. Bloomer founded *The Lily* on January 1, 1849. The monthly publication was the first newspaper owned and operated by women in the United States. It was dedicated to publicizing women's positions on temperance and to promoting women's writing. In her opening editorial, Bloomer announced:

> It is woman that speaks through *The Lily*.... Like the beautiful flower from which it derives its name, we shall strive to make *The Lily* the emblem of sweetness and purity ... to advocate the great cause of temperance reform! (Bloomer, pp. 42-43)

Bloomer served as editor and publisher of *The Lily* and hired Anthony and Stanton to write columns for her. Despite skeptical comments of men—even her husband, who said women could not run a newspaper—Bloomer took charge editorially and financially and made a success of it. She worked hard at making her newspaper as reliable as any of the day. As a result, the number of subscribers steadily increased, going from several hundred to more than 6,000 in just a few years.

Bloomer hired women to work at all phases of production, even as typesetters, jobs usually held by men. This set a great pattern for women working outside the home. In addition, Bloomer not only published *The Lily* but was made deputy postmaster of Seneca Falls when her husband was appointed head postmaster. She accepted the position, saying she "had determined to give a practical demonstration of woman's right to fill any place for which she had capacity" (Bloomer, p. 48).

Stanton and Anthony introduced by Bloomer. Stanton and Anthony both contributed to *The Lily*. However, the two did not meet until 1850, when Bloomer introduced them at the Seneca Falls Convention. Bloomer was always pleased that she had a part in bringing two such powerful personalities together.

***The Lily* expands.** With the help of Stanton's and Anthony's columns, *The Lily* began to broaden its scope. From 1850 to 1853, it turned its attention to the issue of women's suffrage (women's right to vote) and became increasingly political. Bloomer wrote editorials calling for the vote to be given to women. She accurately foresaw that gaining this right was a good distance off, though. Still, she insisted that women should remain active and vocal on all social issues:

> We cannot consent to have woman remain silent on the Temperance question till she obtain her right of suffrage. Great as is our

> faith in the speedy triumph of temperance principles ... we feel that the day is too far distant for her to rest all her hopes and labors on that issue. (Bloomer, p. 60)

As *The Lily* broadened its content, Bloomer strengthened her arguments in favor of women's rights. Taking cues from the Grimké sisters, she used legal and Biblical evidence to support her views in favor of a woman's right to receive equal opportunity in education and employment and to vote and hold political office. It is man, not God, she wrote, who considers woman inferior:

> He has brought the Bible to prove that he is her lord and master, and taught her that resistance to his authority is to resist God's will. I deny that the Bible teaches any such doctrine. God made them different in sex, but equal in intellect. (Bloomer, p. 62)

She claimed that "it is the fault of education that women are intellectually inferior" and boldly challenged men to treat women as equals:

> Show her that you regard her as an equal and that her opinions are entitled to consideration, in short, treat her as an intelligent, accountable being and ... if she prove herself not man's equal in intellect I will yield the point and admit her inferiority. (Bloomer, p. 63)

Bloomer costume comes and goes. In 1851, *The Lily* printed an article about the new "Bloomer costume" being worn by women who suffered from shortness of breath due to the tightly laced corsets and heavy, restrictive dresses that were the fashion of the day. The new costume consisted of a blousy tunic over Turkish-style pants. The article caused such a stir that letters poured in asking Bloomer for sewing patterns. Women reading about the comfort of the new styles demanded to know more about them and how to make their own. Subscriptions to *The Lily* increased to an all-time high. Bloomer herself began wearing the pant suits because they were "well adapted to the needs of my busy life" (Bloomer, p. 69). As the style spread, however, so did the controversy. Though very modest, the "Bloomer costume" was considered indecent by many men and women. Hecklers would attend lectures given by Bloomer and others wearing the pant suits to harass or gawk at them. News-

▲ **Bloomer styles**

paper reporters, rather than focusing on the content of the lectures, devoted their lines to describing the outfit and ridiculing the women who wore it. Thus after a few years, Bloomer stopped wearing the outfit because she was "not willing to sacrifice greater questions to it" (Bloomer, p. 70).

In addition to publishing *The Lily,* Bloomer lectured throughout New York State in 1853, drawing crowds as large as 5,000. More than a few remained violently opposed to her views. After listening to a speech in which she demanded equal rights, the Utica *Telegraph* openly accused her of hating men. Bloomer responded good-naturedly, with a sense of humor that so many of her critics insisted she did not possess:

> Bless your soul, Mr. *Telegraph!* we dearly love them all [men].... You must have had a ... lecture before going to the meeting that night ... which soured your feelings toward all womankind so that you ... heard through a cracked ear tube. (Bloomer, p. 114)

Aftermath

The Bloomers relocate. At the close of 1853, Dexter Bloomer bought the *Western Home Visitor* in Mount Vernon, Ohio, and he and his wife packed up and headed west. Amelia Bloomer continued publishing *The Lily* from her new home and, in fact, improved its appearance. She now produced it twice a month and personally wrote one to three pages per week for it. In addition, Dexter made her the assistant editor of the *Visitor.* She worked very hard at both jobs but devoted most of her attention to *The Lily.*

The Bloomers hoped to carry their message of equal rights and alcohol control to the new states forming in the West, where conditions were still untamed and state constitutions were yet to be written. The Bloomers intended to influence the formation of the states' constitutions. With this goal in mind, the Bloomers decided to venture beyond Ohio. After two years in Mount Vernon, Dexter sold his share of the *Visitor* and Amelia sold *The Lily* and the couple packed their bags for Council Bluffs, Iowa—then 300 miles beyond the nearest railroad line. Though sad at the thought of turning over *The Lily* to someone else, Bloomer realized that its publication had been a great accomplishment and that "it had done its work, it had scattered seed that sprung up and borne fruit a thousandfold" (Bloomer, p. 188). She saw that many other publications had sprung up as well and realized that she could now safely turn her attention to influencing settlers in the West. Bloomer continued to contribute to *The Lily* for a year or so, but the distance and difficulty of communication finally made her stop.

In her last years, Bloomer organized a Good Templars Society in Council Bluffs, in which women and men worked together for the control of alcohol. But she spent most of her time speaking in favor of women's suffrage and equal rights and became president of Iowa's first Women's Suffrage Society in 1871.

By 1879, Bloomer's health began to fail. She visited Colorado in order to receive medical treatment but gradually became weaker as the years progressed. She lived to celebrate her fiftieth wedding anniversary with Dexter on April 15, 1890. Four years later, on December 30, 1894, she died of heart failure at age seventy-six.

For More Information

Bloomer, D. C. *Life and Writings of Amelia Bloomer.* Boston: Arena Publishing, 1895.

Gattey, Charles Neilson. *The Bloomer Girls.* London: Femina Books, 1967.

James, Edward T. *Notable American Women.* Cambridge: Belknap Press of Harvard University Press, 1971.

Plantation System

1619 — Majority of colonial laborers are white; first Africans imported to Virginia for slave labor.

1670s — Slave labor starts to increase. Large-scale plantations develop.

1730s — Black slaves outnumber white indentured servants in the fields.

1793 — Cotton gin invented. New England shippers increase amount of slaves imported.

1808 — Congress outlaws importing slaves; slave trade within the United States increases.

1820 — The South becomes the world's largest producer of cotton.

1830-1860 — Mass movement of slaves from Virginia and Maryland southward. **James Henry Hammond** writes manual on how to run a plantation.

1842 — Hammond becomes governor of South Carolina. **Harriet A. Jacobs** escapes to the North.

1863 — All slaves are freed after January 1 by Emancipation Proclamation.

1865 — Civil War ends; sharecropping replaces slavery on plantations.

1905 — Diary of a plantation owner's wife, **Mary Chesnut,** is published.

1911 — Supreme Court decision in *Bailey v. Alabama* helps end the sharecropping system.

PLANTATION SYSTEM

The plantation, a large farm that grew mainly one type of crop, first appeared in America's colonial period. In 1612, John Rolfe began experimenting with raising tobacco in Virginia. The next fifty years saw the growth of tobacco farms of various sizes. They were worked mostly by white planters and servants until the 1670s, when planters turned to slave labor because of the dwindling supply of white indentured servants and a drop in the cost of African slaves. By 1700, colonists were also raising rice on large plantations in South Carolina and, after 1750, indigo was raised on Carolina plantations too. Both crops were raised with slave labor. The rice grew in humid, swamp areas, where gangs of slaves worked knee-deep in mud, catching malaria and other deadly fevers.

The American Revolution interrupted the growth of plantation agriculture and slavery in the South. For a short while after 1776, laws were relaxed, making it easier to grant slaves their freedom. Then a series of inventions in the production of cotton lowered its price and created a high demand for the crop. One of these inventions, the cotton gin developed by Eli Whitney in 1793, allowed more southern farmers to raise cotton than ever before (*see* **Eli Whitney**). The cotton gin separated the hard seeds from the lint in short-staple cotton, a kind that could be grown inland on a wide belt stretching from Georgia and South Carolina to Texas.

Meanwhile, the number of free blacks was growing. By 1810,

they owned property in the South and had begun to set up churches and schools. Southern whites moved to stop the growth. They tightened the laws again, making it harder to free slaves. At the same time, cotton was beginning to make more money than rice or tobacco for the region. In 1820, the South became the largest cotton producer in the world. Greater amounts of cotton would be produced in the years to come, until production reached its peak in 1860.

Cotton became "king" from 1820 to 1860, reshaping southern society. Raising the crop demanded a large labor force. To meet the demand, Southerners imported slaves in great numbers until the overseas slave trade was outlawed. Afterward, slaves were moved from Virginia and Maryland southward to cotton farms and then southwestward to grow more cotton. Thousands of slaves were smuggled into the country after the trade was outlawed. But the birth of slave babies in America contributed most to the rise in slave population.

Farmers in the South Who Owned Slaves, 1860

The percentage of whites in the South who owned slaves, by number of slaves owned:

More than 100 slaves	0.1%
10-99 slaves	6.6%
1-9 slaves	17.2%

76.1 percent of white farmers in the South did not own slaves in 1860. (Gary B. Nash, *The American People.* [New York: Harper & Row, 1986], p. 378)

Only a fraction of the cotton farms grew into large plantations. Located mainly in South Carolina and Louisiana, the largest plantations had labor forces of 100 slaves. Planters with more slaves usually owned several plantations. Most of the slaves in the South, however, did not work on large plantations, but on smaller farms. In fact, the majority of white farmers in the South did not own any slaves, and only a fraction owned over 100 slaves.

Economically slaves were profitable for their owners. In 1859 the average slave produced $78 yearly in cotton earnings but cost only $32 to feed, clothe, and house. The investment was somewhat risky. Slaves could fall ill and die due to the dismal conditions they typically endured—hard labor, crowded shacks for living quarters, too little clothing, and an endless diet of corn and salt pork. Yet slaves rose in value over the years. A field hand who sold for $600

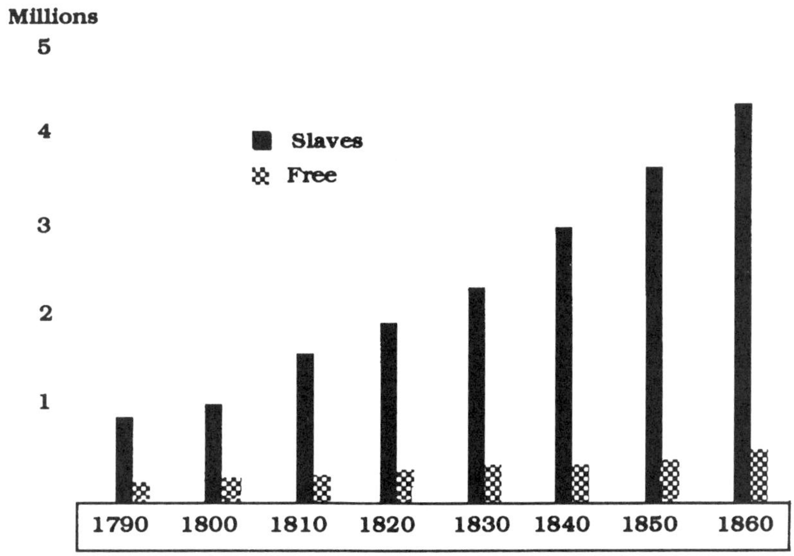

▲ **The status of blacks in the United States, 1790-1860**

in 1844 brought $1,800 by 1860. After earning a profit, planters would reinvest in more slaves to earn higher profits. The small minority of large slave owners came to dominate society in the South, and slaveholding served as the most common path to wealth and power. From success on the plantation, southern whites moved to positions in Congress. Society associated successful planters with authority, and most had more free time than the average southern farmer.

The black population of the South consisted of different groups, just as the white population did. There were black freemen, town slaves hired out on contract to work at shipyards, house servants, and field slaves. Large cotton plantations divided their field hands into gangs of twenty to twenty-five slaves, who worked their way along the cotton rows under the eye of a slave driver. Each slave was expected to pick 130 pounds of cotton a day. In the mid-1800s, a slave's life span averaged about twenty-one years. (The life span for whites was only slightly longer: twenty-five years.)

Women on both sides of the system suffered hardships. In the fields slave women labored to fill their cotton-picking quota, and at

▲ **Slaves toiling in the fields**

home they labored to care for their family, which could be torn apart at any moment if one of them was sold. Female slaves also were often viewed as sex objects by their master. The more children they bore, the more property he owned. Moreover, a master often considered it his right to have relations with his slave women. There were slaves such as **Harriet A. Jacobs** who refused such advances and therefore had to suffer the consequences. Meanwhile, plantation wives such as Catherine Hammond were expected to tolerate their husband's misbehavior but act properly themselves. **Mary Chesnut,** another plantation wife, grew to hate slavery. She thought of it as a curse that endangered the moral well-being of the southern white male.

Few adult slaves escaped being lashed by a whip as punishment for some offense or other. Yet many slaveholders were not considered cruel men. Like **James Henry Hammond,** they did what they felt was possible within the system to provide decent care for their human property. Their view of slave labor, on which their own fortunes depended, changed over the years. Slavery was first considered a necessary evil, then seen as a positive good. Abolitionists argued that owning slaves was morally wrong. In response, plantation owners pointed out that ancient Egypt and Rome had used slave labor, that it existed in the Bible, and that the United States Constitution did not forbid it. The South meanwhile plowed its wealth back into cotton and slave labor, without building cities or industry. A few wealthy planters held power in the region and, as long as they earned money by farming with slave labor, they felt no need for change.

James Henry Hammond

1807-1864

Personal Background

Family history. The Hammond family could trace its history back seven generations from James Henry Hammond's father, Elisha, to the first American member of the family who arrived in Massachusetts in 1634. Elisha Hammond was always restless—moving from one teaching position to another. The year 1806 found him in Columbia, South Carolina, where he wooed and wed Catherine Fox Spann. Still unsettled, the couple soon moved the short distance to Mount Bethel Academy. There, on November 15, 1807, James Henry Hammond was born, the first of four children. Hammond later wrote that from the day he was born, his father lived through him. An excellent teacher, Elisha took on the task of the boy's early education.

Teaching and law. James proved to be a bright student. At age sixteen, he was ready to enter South Carolina College—as a junior. He graduated two years later and grudgingly took up his father's profession. Hammond disliked teaching, however, and soon began to prepare himself for a career in law. He was not any fonder of law than of teaching but saw it as a way to become wealthy. By the age of twenty-one, he had begun practicing law in Columbia with some success.

Politics. Soon Hammond's restlessness and ambition for wealth and power directed him toward politics. As a stepping-stone

▲ **James Henry Hammond**

Event: The growth of the plantation system and the defense of slavery.

Role: Born poor, James Henry Hammond married into a wealthy family and became owner of a 7,500-acre plantation. By capable management, he expanded his landholdings until his plantations included 14,000 acres on which 330 slaves were worked. He championed slavery as a "positive good."

▲ **A plantation owner's mansion**

to this career, he became in 1830 editor of the *Southern Times,* a Columbia newspaper. In this position, he began to make a name for himself as an advocate of states' rights, which in the South meant believing that the states had the right to govern their own slavery-based economy.

Marriage. Hammond saw marriage as another way to advance his ambitions. A letter he wrote to his own son much later reveals Hammond's views on marriage. He confessed that his primary objective in marrying was to attain wealth. Hammond claimed he had never been able to become interested in a woman of a poor family no matter how lovely she might be. He advised his son to look for a wealthy wife and not be concerned about beauty or about partnership. "Women were made to breed—men to do the work of this world," Hammond wrote (Bleser, *The Hammonds of Redcliffe,* p. 5).

Hammond found his ideal partner in a submissive, rather plain young woman from a well-to-do family. In 1831, he married seventeen-year-old Catherine Elizabeth Fitzsimmons, the daughter of a wealthy plantation owner who had died some five years earlier and left her with a large inheritance. The two lived together the rest of their lives and had eight children.

Plantation owner. To Hammond, the most important part of this union was Catherine's inheritance, which now became his: the 7,500 acre plantation called Silver Bluff and its 147 slaves. The plantation was located a short distance from Augusta, Georgia, across the Savannah River. Hammond plunged into the work of reviving the plantation and expanding it. In a short time, he had increased the value of the plantation and its products.

Politics. Now financially secure, Hammond turned his attention once again to politics. Opportunity came in 1832, when South Carolina nullified, or cancelled out, the tariff (or tax) laws enacted by the federal government. President Andrew Jackson threatened to enforce the tariff with military action and the governor of South Carolina prepared to defend the state's actions. A champion of states' rights, Hammond was quick to offer his services. The governor gave him a military commission, but in the end a compromise was reached and no military action was necessary.

Two years later Hammond was elected to Congress. His term there was marked mainly by his advocacy of the death penalty for abolitionists. When the northern American Anti-Slavery Society began a mail campaign in Charleston in 1835, Hammond responded vehemently. "These men can be silenced in but one way—Terror—death.... This is the only remedy," he wrote in a letter to friend (Faust, p. 161). He denied that slavery was evil and defended it as "the greatest of all blessings which a kind Providence has bestowed upon our glorious region" (Faust, p. 176).

Troubled by ill health, Hammond resigned his post in Congress and returned to the plantation. In 1836, he decided to travel to Europe to seek a cure for his ailment. His wife was five-months pregnant when they sailed with their oldest son to live in Italy. The baby was born and died there, and a year later the Hammonds returned to Silver Bluff.

Political figure. Hammond continued to pursue his interest in politics. He lost a close campaign for governor in 1840 and was appointed brigadier general of the South Carolina militia in 1841. The next year he became governor of the state. His tenure in office was uneventful except for the founding of a military training institution for South Carolina, The Citadel.

By 1846, Hammond had been forced out of politics by a powerful brother-in-law who suspected that his own four daughters were receiving undue attention from Hammond. He would not return to political office until eleven years later, when he became a United States senator.

Except for his political strength in South Carolina and his ambition to expand his wealth, Hammond was not an unusual plantation owner. His overriding goal was to make more money. Hammond showed little concern for other people and, in fact, treated his own wife as property and nearly destroyed the spirits of his sons with his overbearing manner.

Expanding the plantation. His political career temporarily over, Hammond focused his attention on increasing his acreage at Silver Bluff. He cleared the nearby swamps and bought land from his less prosperous neighbors. In this way he nearly doubled the size of his plantation, which became so large that it had to be broken into several plots managed by overseers. Slaves did the work on the plantation year round, so acquiring additional slaves and keeping them healthy became important to Silver Bluff's growth. Hammond faced the same problems and concerns as other plantation owners of his day. He was unusual, however, in that he kept a record of events in his life as a plantation owner.

Participation: The Plantation System and Slavery

Owners and slaves. In the early 1800s, the federal government and various state governments outlawed the importation of any more slaves from Africa. South Carolina had been among the last states to comply with this law. Hammond could only expand his work force by buying from other owners or breeding his slaves and training the young to work as soon as they were able. Taking care of slave children who were too young to work was a financial burden on plantation owners, some of whom thought it more economical to abandon their slaves and hire the necessary workers. Hammond, however, believed in the slavery system. By careful management, he was able to make his plantation grow and prosper. Even when he assigned parts of it to his sons, whom he felt were incapable of management, Hammond earned a profit of about $35,000 a year, a very large sum in the 1800s. Part of this profitability came from keeping the cost of caring for his slaves low. He was able to provide for them over the years at the cost of about $18 per slave per year.

Slave work schedules. After Hammond took over at Silver Bluff, work schedules changed drastically. In the past a slave had been given a specific job for the day; when finished with the job, the slave was finished for the day. Hammond required his slaves to work all day, dawn to dusk. He felt the long hours increased the slaves' productivity, especially since they were worked in gangs and were required to keep up with the other workers. The long hours kept by his busy slaves also prevented them from meeting with other members of society. Hammond discouraged his slaves from trading in local stores or selling the produce from their small garden plots to neighbors. Instead, he controlled the food supply.

Believing that rich foods damaged his slaves, Hammond allowed them only small portions of cornmeal, pork, and molasses for their meals. Each slave at Silver Bluff received three pounds of meat and a peck of corn meal each week. This poor diet, combined with working under the unhealthy conditions in the swamp, took a toll on the slave population. In the first ten years of Hammond's management at Silver Bluff, 72 percent of the children born to slaves died before the age of five. A total of eighty-two slaves died in this decade; only seventy-three slave babies were born.

Each morning, the slaves were roused an hour before dawn by the sound of a horn. They then had an hour to prepare food for the day before being called by the horn to be at their work assignments. When it was too dark to work they were allowed to return to their huts. The slaves were not always cooperative and found many ways to disrupt the work schedule. A few months after he had moved to Silver Bluff, Hammond had written in his diary that all was still in

▲ **Slaves huts**

confusion because his slaves had not yet been brought under control. He felt that the first order of business was to gain control, and that could be done best by fear.

Fear. Hammond determined that he would either firmly manage or be overrun by his slaves. He felt he must "subdue" them, and took over complete control of the slave force until they were "broken in." He imagined himself to be a kind master, but believed that the past masters of the plantation had been so lax that the slaves had taken great advantage of the situation.

Hammond's "breaking in" meant controlling every aspect of the slaves' lives. He instilled fear in the slaves at Silver Bluff in several ways. Hammond hired overseers, who recruited boss slaves; this way a person of authority was always within sight. Infractions of work orders were treated with the lash, although this was to be avoided whenever possible. Slaves were valuable property. A good slave might be worth as much as $1,000. Too many signs of the lash indicated a difficult-to-manage slave, whose value dropped on the slave market. Even so, slaves at Silver Bluff were sentenced to as many as 100 lashes at a time for a variety of "crimes."

A manual for the plantation. By the early 1840s, Hammond had written what amounted to a manual for the control of his slave force and for management of the plantations. The manual was the product of his own first few years as a strict master and describes his efforts to balance the need to control slaves with the desirability of keeping them as contented as possible.

The manual carefully outlined the care of slaves. Each slave received his or her portion of food each week. In addition, each male slave received a blanket, a pair of shoes, four shirts, three pair of pants, and a jacket each year. Women, who were supposed to sew for themselves, received fourteen yards of cloth along with needles and thread. Children received one-third the allowance of adults and were placed under the charge of a nurse, who was given a pan and spoon for each of her charges. Workers labored from dawn to sunset, but at midday were allowed a break, which varied from one hour to three-and-one-half hours depending on the heat of the day. No work was permitted after dark. Slaves were required to be in their houses by about nine o'clock.

The manual also defined punishment. Public lashings were decreed for workers who did not perform their quota of work, left the plantation without permission, or in any way acted against the master's wishes. Visits to other plantations were forbidden, except for arranged visits between husbands and wives serving different masters. Married slaves who applied for and gained a divorce were to be given the 100 lashes, the highest number of lashes permitted for any break with the rules. Fifteen to twenty lashes was defined as "sufficient flogging" in most cases. During the beatings, the slave's hands were bound with a cord. In general, Hammond felt that flogging was a last resort. In fact, he told new overseers that he would judge their merit by "their success in promoting industry without flogging" (Faust, p. 100). In time, Hammond installed a system of rewards for slaves as encouragement for good behavior. Slaves traditionally had their only days off around Christmas time. But one

Christmas, when eight of Hammond's slaves were slow to return to work after the holiday, they were whipped by an overseer. When the slaves appealed to Hammond, they received a second flogging. And though Hammond thought organized religion was unnecessary and even dangerous if practiced by slaves and consequently forbade religious meetings, he permitted singing and praying to satisfy the slaves' spiritual needs.

Slave families. Under South Carolina law, marriages between slaves were not recognized. Consequently, slaves suffered from a reputation for loose living even though many lived together as husband and wife for most of their lives. Still, family life for slaves was shaky. A husband or wife could be sold to new owners individually or together at the will of the master. Children could be sold with their parents or siblings or alone. Hammond both encouraged and controlled slave families. He devised his own marriage ceremony, which he conducted during the Christmas season, but only after the couple had received his permission to marry.

At Silver Bluff, all families were strictly controlled by a sort of plantation court. In one log, Hammond recorded:

> Had a trial of Divorce and Adultery cases. Flogged Joe Goodwyn and ordered him to go back to his wife. Ditto Gabriel and Molly and ordered them to come together again. Separated Moses and Anny finally. And flogged Tom Kollock. He had never been flogged before. Gave him 30 with my own hand for interfering with Maggy Campbell, Sullivan's wife. (Faust, p. 85)

Owners, slaves, and sex. Hammond behaved in a manner not unlike many other slave owners of his day when it came to the control of his slaves. His case is unique only in that he kept a record of his activities. Though he encouraged—even forced—his slaves at Silver Bluff and later at Redcliffe to uphold their marriage vows, he did not apply the rule to himself.

In 1839, Hammond bought a new slave woman for 900 dollars; she came with a young daughter. Though the slave, Sally, was purchased for her skill as a seamstress, she soon was placed in the role of mistress to her master. Ten years later Hammond took Sally's daughter, Louisa, for a mistress as well.

This last action finally provoked his wife and, in 1849, she left him, taking their children. Catherine swore she would not come back until Hammond had sent Louisa away. Hammond finally did send his young mistress to live with his sister-in-law on the condition that she become a personal housemaid. True to her word, Catherine returned. And shortly thereafter, so did Louisa. Later, in a letter to his son about the disposal of the estate after his death, Hammond left instructions that Louisa should be cared for and always remain on the family estate. He felt it would be a dishonor to the Hammond name to have someone so intimately part of the family serve as a slave to another family.

The reactions of slaves. Throughout the South and throughout slavery, slaves passively and actively rebelled. One owner complained that his slaves would not work unless he was in sight. Clever slaves used a variety of methods to establish their own work quotas. For example, a slave might carry cotton back to the fields at night in order to have some on hand to meet the next day's quota. Frequently, slaves broke pieces of equipment in order to slow down the work schedule, and often slaves used the time-honored excuse of playing too-sick-to-work. (Some slaves who had seemed too sickly to accomplish much came to be very capable farmers of their own land after the Civil War.) In spite of making large sums of money from his plantation, Hammond wrote in his diary, "I find [slaves] chopping up cotton dreadfully and begin to think that my stand has every year been ruined in that way" (Stampp, p. 102). Hammond was, at times, so disturbed by his slaves that he thought it not worthwhile to acquire any more. There was, however, the matter of swampland to be cleared.

Health care. Work conditions in the swamplands were difficult; insects and decaying vegetation brought disease to the workers. To protect his investment, Hammond arranged for a nearby doctor to regularly visit the plantation and prescribe for the ill. For this he paid the doctor $2.50 per visit on the condition that he treat as many as needed help at each visit. Conditions grew worse, however, and more and more slaves became sick. Finally, Hammond built a hospital on one of the extensions of his plantation. It was said to be the best facility of its kind anywhere.

Education of slaves. Like most southern states, South Carolina had laws against teaching slaves to read and write. Lawmakers believed if slaves learned to read the news, it would stir discontent among them. If they learned to write, they could forge their own passes, or permits to leave the plantation.

Hammond, however, encouraged slave education by neglecting to enforce the law. He reported that he never interfered with slave efforts to educate one another and, as a result, owned a dozen slaves who read as well as he did. The master respected these slaves and the agricultural knowledge of some of his "drivers," or the black men who led the work parties. He instructed one overseer (men who parceled out jobs and rations and administered punishment) never to begin an agricultural project without consulting one wise driver, Tom Kollock. (Later, Hammond learned that Kollock actually undermined him by training his crews to work more slowly.)

Aftermath

Return to politics. After expanding his plantation system and building a large home called Redcliffe on newly acquired land, Hammond returned to politics in 1858 as a United States senator. He continued to be a strong supporter of the plantation system of the South and of slavery as he had always been. He declared in one Senate speech that cotton was king in the development of the American economy and that slaves were the mudsills (foundations) on which the American economy and society could be built. He also believed that slavery was sanctioned by the Bible and produced the best organization of society that ever existed.

As a senator, Hammond also supported the rights of states to make their own rules without federal intervention. He upheld the right of South Carolina to ignore, or nullify, federal acts that would give the central government greater authority over it. He particularly objected to the embargo, or ban on, trade with other countries, which robbed southerners of major markets for plantation products. Thus, he supported John C. Calhoun in his efforts to create a separate southern nation.

Beginning doubts about the Union. Toward the end of his service as a senator, Hammond revealed a conflict in his own thinking. Though he continued to support the institution of slavery in the

South and forecast that the South could raise a larger army than the North because of its social organization, he opposed extending slavery to the new territory of Kansas. He felt that the South held enough slave-holding territory to become the ruling power of the nation.

Support of slavery was losing ground, however, as shown by the election of President Abraham Lincoln. After Lincoln's victory, Hammond resigned from the Senate and returned to his home at Redcliffe. He now favored the idea of South Carolina seceding, or breaking away, from the Union.

Civil War. Hammond returned to the management of his slave-operated plantation. In his last years, he came to realize that his slaves had little affection for him, even though he had grown over the years to be a kinder owner. He continued to provide for their living needs and to help them with better-than-average health care even as the war between North and South erupted in 1861.

Hammond's own son, Harry, served as a southern officer in the war, which was fought largely over the rights of states to set their own policies. A loss by the South would mean outlawing slavery as the northern states had done. Hammond, however, did not live to learn the final outcome of the war. He died on November 13, 1864.

The next year, America's Civil War ended with the defeat of the South and the abolition of slavery. For many slaves, this was at first a mixed blessing. Though they were free, they had no education and nowhere to go. Hammond's own slaves, for the most part, remained on the plantation after they were freed, much to the dismay of his widow. Catherine Hammond was now faced with providing support for a large number of slaves, only some of whom she could afford to hire as workers on the plantation.

For More Information

Bleser, Carol. *The Hammonds of Redcliffe.* New York: Oxford University Press, 1981.

Bleser, Carol. *Secret and Sacred: The Diaries of James Henry Hammond, a Southern Slaveholder.* New York: Oxford University Press, 1988.

Faust, Drew Gilpin. *James Henry Hammond and the Old South.* Baton Rouge: Louisiana State University Press, 1982.

Stampp, Kenneth M. *The Peculiar Institution: Slavery in Ante-Bellum South.* New York: Vintage Books, 1964.

Harriet A. Jacobs

1813-1897

Personal Background

Born a slave. Delilah Horniblow was a slave to Margaret Horniblow in the town of Edenton, North Carolina, just as Delilah's mother, Molly, had been for much of her life. In the early 1800s, slaves could not be officially married without the permission of their masters, so the marriage of Delilah to the carpenter Daniel Jacobs, a slave on a neighboring plantation owned by Dr. Andrew Knox, is not recorded. Nevertheless, Daniel and Delilah had two children together. In the autumn of 1813, Harriet Ann was born, followed two years later by John.

Harriet was just six years old when her mother died. There must have been no thought of sending her to live with her father; he was, after all, the property of another master. So Harriet went to live in the home of her late mother's (and therefore her own) master. Margaret Horniblow was a kind master—so kind that Harriet did not realize until her mother died that she herself had been born into slavery. For a few years, Harriet stayed with Horniblow, who taught her to sew, read, and spell.

Property of the Norcoms. In 1825, twelve-year-old Harriet's life took a turn for the worse. Margaret Horniblow died and left Harriet and her brother to her niece, Mary Norcom. Because Mary was a child and still lived at home, this essentially made Harriet the

▲ **Harriet A. Jacobs**

Event: The growth of slavery and the plantation system.

Role: Born into slavery, Harriet A. Jacobs worked as a house servant in a southern city, then as a house servant on a plantation. She ran away and hid in an attic for seven years before escaping to the North, where slave hunters searched for her.

property of Mary's father, Dr. James Norcom. Harriet and her brother became house slaves for the doctor.

Grandmother Molly. Harriet's grandmother, Molly, was more fortunate. When her owner, Elizabeth Horniblow, died, Molly, along with her son Mark, was sold to Hannah Pritchard, an aunt of the Horniblows. Just four months later, Mrs. Pritchard gave Molly her freedom. In a short time, Jacobs's grandmother had earned enough from her cooking to buy the freedom of her son. Fortunately for Jacobs and her brother, the two free relatives moved into a house not far from that of the Norcoms. Jacobs could sometimes visit her grandmother, and the family remained in contact.

Unwanted advances. The Norcom house was not a pleasant one. Mrs. Norcom distrusted her husband, and for good reason. Dr. Norcom pursued other women, and soon began to make advances toward Jacobs. Suspicious, Mrs. Norcom took out her fears in threats and abuses on the innocent slaves. By the time Jacobs was sixteen, Norcom's advances and the abuse from his wife had become unbearable. Perhaps thinking that Norcom would leave her alone if she began having an affair with another man, Jacobs took up with one of the doctor's white neighbors, Samuel Sawyer, and became pregnant. When the suspicious Mrs. Norcom learned the news, she threatened Jacobs, prompting the doctor to send her off to live with her grandmother. It was there that Jacobs's son, Joseph, was born.

The Nat Turner affair. Jacobs and her son were living with Molly when the Nat Turner incident took place in Virginia in 1831 (see **Nat Turner**). Turner and some other slaves had staged a rebellion in which white slave owners and their families were killed. More than fifty slaves joined the rampage. By the time white farmers could gather a militia to stop the uprising, the rebels had killed fifty-five whites.

The event alarmed the white southerners, who armed themselves and proceeded to terrorize blacks, free or slave. The news of the Nat Turner Rebellion reached Edenton early in 1832, just after white men had held their annual muster, a yearly show of the militia to demonstrate its strength. Now it was announced that a second muster would be held and men came into town from all over the territory. Poor whites who were hired to search for signs of rebellion among the blacks tore through black family homes looking for weapons or signs that the blacks might join Turner's Rebellion. A band broke into Molly's house, threatened Jacobs and the others, and tore up everything in the house in search of any sign that the residents should be punished.

For two weeks whites roved the streets and spread into the farmland outside the town. Blacks suspected of plotting to join the rebellion were whipped and otherwise tortured. A black minister was taken off to be shot after a few bits of gunshot were found in his house. Black men from the farmlands were bound and tied to the saddles of horsemen who forced them to run to the jail yard in town. Black homes and black churches were destroyed. Eventually, calmer whites restored peace and innocent blacks who had been held in prison were released. Black slaves were returned to their owners, and the black community began to recover.

Participation: Plantation Life

"Breaking" Jacobs. In 1833, Jacobs was still carrying on an affair with Samuel Sawyer and her daughter Louisa was born. Soon after, Dr. Norcom again began making sexual demands on Jacobs. By 1835, the doctor had become so aggravated by her refusals that he sent her to be a slave on his nearby plantation. Forced to leave her son with her grandmother so that he could recover from an illness, Jacobs joined about fifty other slaves on the estate. Norcom planned to send her son to the plantation as soon as possible. In the meantime, however, Jacobs was to be punished for her failure to submit to his advances. Norcom's son, who was master at the new plantation, would "break her" and train her son and daughter to be slaves worthy of being sold. In Jacobs's words:

> I heard Mr. [Norcom] say to a neighbor, "I've got her down here, and I'll soon take the town notions out of her head. My father is partly to blame for her nonsense. He ought to have broke her in long ago." (Jacobs, p. 86)

Plantation slavery. Jacobs was committed to making the best of the situation. Assigned the task of getting the house ready for young Mr. Norcom's new bride, she performed her assignments faithfully even when daughter Louisa had to remain unattended in the kitchen for long periods of time. Still, Jacobs worried about Louisa each time she saw a child of one of the slaves knocked out of the way or beaten for being too near the master. She worried also about her own well being when she saw that the mothers of these children had been so thoroughly whipped, physically and in spirit, that they raised no protest over the brutality to their children.

Louisa. One day about noon, Louisa, who was feeling ill, disappeared from her place near a window of the room in which her mother was working. Jacobs went in search of the child and found her sound asleep in the cool space below the house, where earlier that day a large snake had been seen. The worried mother decided to send her child away for safe keeping. The next day, Louisa was put in a cart carrying shingles to town. She would remain with her great-grandmother until she was strong again. Norcom protested that he should have been asked for permission to do this, but he allowed Louisa to leave. At two years old, she was of no use to him.

The treatment of slaves. Jacobs was treated differently from most slaves on the plantation. During the first six weeks of her stay, as she prepared every room and every bit of furniture for the coming of the new Mrs. Norcom, she saw other slaves being treated much more harshly than she. In the fields, men, women, and children frequently were beaten for the slightest offense—beaten until, as Jacobs described it, pools of blood surrounded their feet. Because permanently scarred slaves brought lower prices on the trading block, brine, or salted water, often would be poured over the open flesh to make the wounds heal more rapidly.

Slave managers controlled every action on the plantation. On the Norcom plantation these overseers gave each male slave a weekly allotment of three pounds of meat, a peck (about eight quarts) of corn, and some herring. Women received half as much meat, and children over twelve and a half received half the allowance of the women.

Jacobs did not sleep in the huts arranged for the slaves, but rather, in the "great house." The young Mr. Norcom was beginning to have ideas like those of his father. Mrs. Norcom agreed to have

Jacobs in the house but refused to allow her a bed. Instead, Jacobs had to sleep on the floor. She was willing to endure this treatment for the safety of her children. But when she learned that the owners were planning to bring her children back to the plantation to be "broken in" with the idea of selling them, Jacobs realized she had to take action. Her own children were being used to force her to submit to Norcom and his son. She felt she had no choice but to run away.

Jacobs knew the risks she would encounter as a runaway slave. Her uncle Joseph had been so mistreated by his owner that he had knocked the man down and run away. Upon his capture, he was chained, jailed for six months, and then sold to an owner in far-off New York. Other runaways who had been captured had not fared so well as her uncle. Yet Jacobs reasoned that her children would be of less interest to the Norcoms if she was not there. So one dark night in 1835, she fled from the plantation and hid in the home of a friend.

The search begins. When the Norcoms learned of Jacobs's disappearance, they started a search. Unable to find her, Dr. Norcom took his anger out on Jacobs's relatives. Jacobs's Aunt Berry, her brother, and her children were all put in jail. Samuel Sawyer, perhaps troubled by the thought of his young children chained up in jail, arranged through a slave trader to buy the children and John. Sawyer then sent the children to live with Jacobs's grandmother, Molly.

Meanwhile, the Norcoms continued searching through the homes of Jacobs's friends. Her hiding place became unsafe for her and for the friend who sheltered her, so Jacobs's uncle arranged for her to steal out of the house at night and hide in a swamp. It was infested with mosquitos and snakes, but Jacobs judged it the better of two evils and bravely stayed there. For the moment, she was free of the Norcoms.

Her freedom was threatened, however, when a snake bit her. With her leg swollen and infected and with no way to treat the bite, it became necessary for Jacobs to move to another hiding place. Fortunately, Harriet's uncle Mark had been preparing for this. He had cut a carefully hidden hole in the ceiling of Molly's pantry. Above the hole was a small space between the pantry ceiling and the shingles of the roof.

▲ **An 1850 photograph of a slave on the run**

Jacobs's family waited until dark one night to help Jacobs escape the swamp and take up permanent residence in the attic of Molly's house. Equipped with only a blanket and water, Jacobs settled into the cramped space, which allowed for neither sitting nor standing, nor for stretching out and rolling over comfortably.

The seven-year exile. Jacobs remained in this small space below the roof for seven years. Mark and Molly brought her food and talked with her at night when everyone else was asleep. On a few occasions Jacobs was lowered to sit with them in the dark pantry for brief moments, but all the while, the air was tense with the fear that Norcom would discover her hiding place. His home was just around the corner and his office a short distance away in the next block. He often passed by Molly's house on his way to work.

Jacobs sometimes saw Norcom through a small hole she had carved out between the rafters with a piece of metal. This tiny opening to the outside world brought a little air into the sometimes hot, sometimes cold and damp space. She could see a little of the street and Molly's yard through this hole. To make matters worse, she could see Joseph and Louisa playing in the yard and hear the grumblings and threats of the doctor as he passed them. Jacobs did not dare let her children know where she was; if she did, the truth might be forced out of them and everyone would suffer. (Later, Joseph remarked that he knew that she was there but did not dare tell anyone about it.)

Years passed with Jacobs stuck in her prison. Conditions in the small cell were nearly unbearable. Mosquitos pestered her, mice scurried around her, and rain drenched her, but Mark was afraid to fix the holes in the roof lest she be seen from the street. Cramped into her small cell, she began to lose strength in her legs. Still she felt that she was better off here than living as Dr. Norcom's slave. Finally, in 1842, after seven years, an opportunity came to leave her hiding place. One of her uncle's friends found a sea captain who was willing, for a fee, to take Jacobs to New York.

Runaway. Although Molly knew the conditions were gradually taking her granddaughter's health and strength, she urged Jacobs not to go. North Carolina runaways were subject to severe punishment if caught—chains, whippings (as many as 100 lashes or more), and even branding. One North Carolina owner ran an advertisement for his runaway, describing her as "burnt ... with a hot iron on the left side of her face; I tried to make the letter M" (Stampp, p. 188). Some disgruntled owners offered a reward for the capture of a runaway, and would add more to that reward if the slave was returned dead. It was not uncommon to track runaways with dogs, which were sometimes not restrained from mauling the slave when he or she was found.

Jacobs knew that Norcom had already hired slave hunters to search for her in the North. While in the attic, Jacobs had written

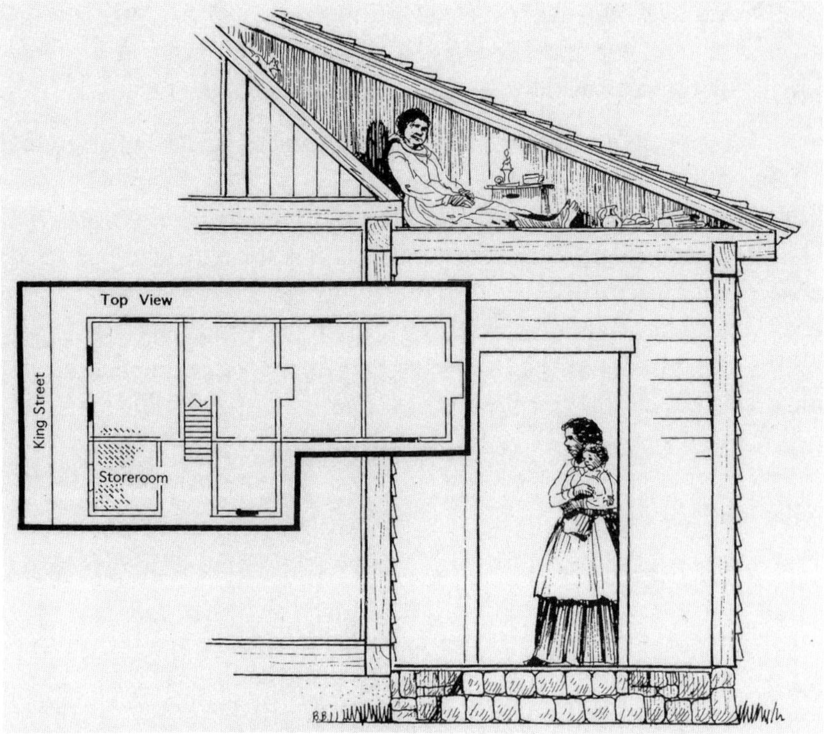

▲ **Cross-section of Jacobs's grandmother's house**

some letters to Norcom, and the family arranged for their delivery from New York. Her purpose was to distract the doctor from too close a search of the Horniblow house. Norcom had followed up on these letters at least once with a trip to New York to find her. If she really fled to the North, she would face the threat of slave hunters as well. Besides the constant threat of being caught, she would have to figure out a way to earn a living there. Knowing that she would be hunted, Jacobs still decided to go, convinced that her children would be better off if she could be free of Dr. Norcom. At the last minute she disguised herself and went with her new friend to meet the boat.

Northward bound. Just before she left, Jacobs finally spoke to Joseph and Louisa, whom she had peeped at and heard below her for those long years but had not dared to involve in her criminal act of running away from slavery. It was during their brief meeting that

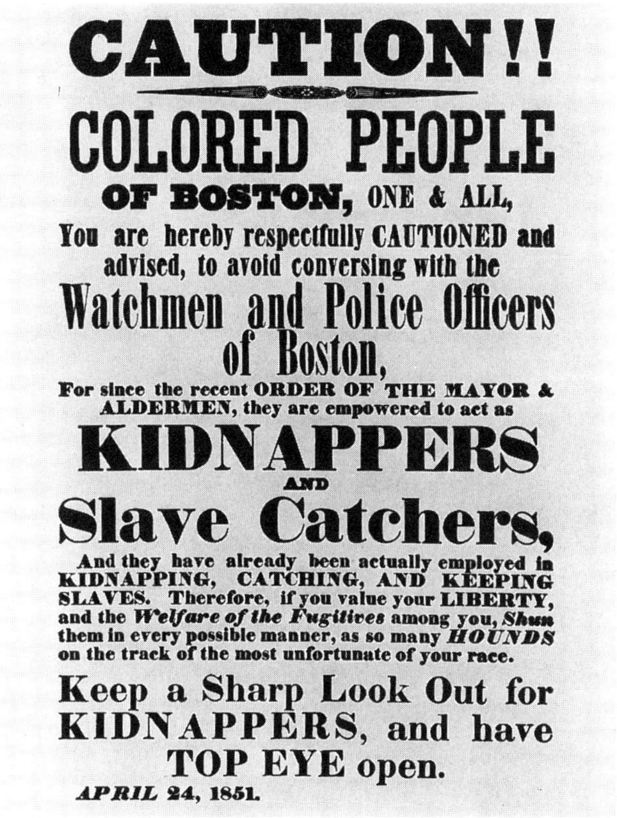

CAUTION!!
COLORED PEOPLE
OF BOSTON, ONE & ALL,
You are hereby respectfully CAUTIONED and advised, to avoid conversing with the
Watchmen and Police Officers of Boston,
For since the recent ORDER OF THE MAYOR & ALDERMEN, they are empowered to act as
KIDNAPPERS
AND
Slave Catchers,
And they have already been actually employed in KIDNAPPING, CATCHING, AND KEEPING SLAVES. Therefore, if you value your LIBERTY, and the Welfare of the Fugitives among you, Shun them in every possible manner, as so many HOUNDS on the track of the most unfortunate of your race.
Keep a Sharp Look Out for KIDNAPPERS, and have TOP EYE open.
APRIL 24, 1851.

▲ **Runaway slaves were warned to avoid the authorities in Northern cities**

she learned that Joseph had known her whereabouts for several years. He had heard her cough but had carefully kept the secret, often leading visitors away from his mother's corner of the house for fear that another cough would expose her hiding place.

New York. Jacobs arrived in New York in 1842 and was fortunate in her search for a job. She found work with the Willis family as nurse to their new baby daughter. She continued even after the death of Mary Willis and traveled with the family to England as caretaker of the Willises young daughter. All the while, Jacobs was sure that Sawyer, the father of her children, would free them now that he was their owner. He never did. John gained his freedom by running away, but her own children remained slaves.

Meanwhile, the younger Norcom died and his wife remarried. She wanted the slave property she believed she owned and made repeated attempts to capture Jacobs and her children, who had by that time joined her in New York. Whenever she heard a rumor about slave hunters or one of Mrs. Norcom's visits to New York, Jacobs would move to Boston, Massachusetts or some other distant place until the crisis passed. She was always on her guard.

Hunted or freed? The year 1850 was an eventful one. The new Fugitive Slave Law encouraged bounty hunters to search northern cities for runaways, so it was more dangerous than ever for an escaped slave in the North. Meanwhile, Jacobs's family support was fading. She had not dared to contact her grandmother or John, and Joseph had headed out to the California gold mines. John and Joseph left her life forever, later moving to Australia to pursue their search for gold. Fortunately, her former employer, Mr. Willis, remarried and now he and his wife, Cornelia, wanted Jacobs to care for their baby. Cornelia proved to be as kind as the first Mrs. Willis.

At the end of the year, old Dr. Norcom died. His daughter, Mary Matilda, now had official legal ownership of Jacobs and the two children. She and her husband, Daniel Messmore, made several attempts to capture the family. In 1852, Messmore again returned to New York to find Jacobs, but without success. Cornelia had arranged for her to escape to Massachusetts once again. Frustrated, Messmore put the capture and disposal of Jacobs into the hands of a slave hunter.

Cornelia had often spoken of buying Jacobs's freedom, and Jacobs had as often protested being bought. But, with a slave hunter on the chase, Cornelia felt she had to act. She offered the slave hunter $300 for Jacobs and her two children. It was a small sum, but better than nothing, and the slave hunter grudgingly accepted. In late 1852, Jacobs and her children were finally set free.

Aftermath

Antislavery work. For the rest of her life, Jacobs and Louisa worked actively in the antislavery movement. This work resulted in Jacobs writing her autobiography, which was published in England under the title *The Deeper Wrong.* In 1862 and 1863 Jacobs was in Washington, D.C., to help with relief work for runaway slaves.

When the Emancipation Act was passed in 1863, Jacobs and Louisa were living in Alexandria, Virginia, where they were distributing clothing and teaching health care. Then, with the surrender of General Robert E. Lee in 1865, Jacobs at last was free to return to Edenton, carrying relief supplies to the place where she had been imprisoned in a house that was now her own.

After a trip to England to raise money for an orphanage in Savannah, Georgia, Jacobs settled in Cambridge, Massachusetts, to operate a boarding house. She lived to see Louisa help organize the National Association of Colored Women in Washington. There, on March 7, 1897, Harriet Jacobs died.

For More Information

Holland, Patricia G., and Milton Meltzer, editors. *The Collected Correspondence of Lydia Maria Child, 1817-1880.* Millwood, New York: Kraus Microform, 1980.

Jacobs, Harriet A. *Incidents in the Life of a Slave Girl Written by Herself.* Self-published, 1862. Cambridge: Harvard University Press, 1987.

Stampp, Kenneth M. *The Peculiar Institution: Slavery in Ante-Bellum South.* New York: Vintage Books, 1964.

Mary Boykin Chesnut

1823-1886

Personal Background

Plantation life. In the early days of settlement, South Carolina landowners established plantations along the bays and major rivers near the coast. These plantations often had their own shipping facilities for trade with Europe and the northern colonies. As time passed, plantation owners were forced to farm fresh soil a distance away from the rivers, and it became more convenient to band together for trading purposes. Small trading centers were set up by the rivers to serve several nearby plantations. One of these small trading centers, Camden on the Wateree River, served plantations such as Mount Pleasant, the home of Mary Boykin Miller and Stephen Decatur Miller. The couple lived with Stephen's parents, who actually owned the property. Their daughter (the future Mary Boykin Chesnut) was born on her grandparent's estate on March 31, 1823.

Mary's father, Stephen Miller, was trained in law and active in politics. By the time she was born, he was a member of the state legislature and, by the time she was five years old, he had become governor of South Carolina. After that, Miller served in the United States Senate, which took him away from home for long periods of time. Unhappy with the long periods of separation, Miller resigned from the Senate to return to Mount Pleasant.

Early plantation experiences. Mary learned early about the

▲ **Mary Boykin Chesnut**

Event: The rise and fall of the plantation system and slavery.

Role: Born into a plantation-owning family, Mary Boykin Chesnut learned the duties of a plantation wife from her grandmother. She married at age seventeen and went to live on the plantation of her husband's family, an estate worked by more than 400 slaves. Even though she enjoyed the ease and comfort of plantation life, Chesnut came to wonder about and eventually express hatred for slavery.

workings of a plantation by observing her grandmother. Grandmother Miller rose early to assign the cleaning and cooking duties for her servants. Besides keeping the mansion clean and prepared for the frequent guests, Mary's grandmother also took charge of making and mending clothing for the slaves on the plantation. She spent whole days cutting out clothing for the children and assigning sewing to her nine seamstresses. Her grandmother worked with the servants and sewing crew so easily and effectively that Mary was nearly nine years old before she became aware that her grandmother's coworkers were slaves. Having learned to respect these workers, she thought of them as near equals.

Mary learned to read at an early age, probably from her grandmother also. Soon she was using this new-found ability to teach a favorite servant to read. It was illegal in South Carolina to teach a slave to read or write, but Mary was a favored grandchild and her grandmother was proud of her ability. In 1831, however, Mary's grandmother died.

Mary was twelve years old when the entire family moved to Mississippi, where they owned some other plantations. Most of the family fell ill, however, and within a year the family had returned to the South Carolina plantation to resume their lives there. Shortly after their return, the family was visited by Mr. Chesnut, owner of a nearby plantation, and his son James. James was twenty-one and had just graduated from Princeton.

Courtship and marriage. James and Mary began a courtship that ended with James proposing to Mary when she was fifteen years old. Her mother and father did not approve of such an early marriage and forced Mary to write a letter of refusal to James. At the time of the proposal and refusal, James was in Europe with his ailing brother. (It was the custom of wealthy Americans to sail to Europe for the best medical care if they fell very ill.) Despite the setback, Mary and James kept up their romance. Two years later Mary's mother, now a widow, relented. Mary wed James in 1840, beginning her days as Mary Boykin Chesnut.

Participation: The Plantation System

Mulberry plantation. The newlyweds remained in South

Carolina, moving to Mulberry, the plantation of the Chesnut family. It was owned by James's grandparents, who lived there along with his parents and two of his sisters. With this many women in the family, the newlywed Mary had little to do.

Mulberry was a beautiful place to live. It stood above the Wateree River a few miles from the town of Camden (population less than 1,000). A mile-long, oak-tree-lined road led from the river dock to the large plantation house. The house had been built some twenty years earlier, but the owner had intended it to survive for a long time. Bricks made and fired on the estate formed walls two-feet thick. Three stories high and filled with large rooms, the house centered on a grand hall and spiral staircase. The drawing room, dining room, and library, along with Grandmother's bedroom and a nursery, were on the ground floor. Below was a full cellar. The second and third floors contained six bedrooms each. A two-story brick building behind the main building housed the kitchen and laundry rooms. A hydraulic pump forced water from outside through pipes to tanks in the attic of the house to be used in the several bathrooms and basins. There were also storerooms, pantries, and a wine cellar. Behind the house lay the brick cottages for the house servants along with an icehouse and a smokehouse. The whole settlement was surrounded by giant trees shading the house and a great parklike lawn. Elsewhere there was a small village of huts for the slaves who worked in the field.

Such an arrangement was common to many plantations, which were virtually independent communities. As such, the plantation had to provide for the many and varied needs of its family and workers. Food for the household was grown, processed, and stored on the plantation. Clothing for the family and slaves was made there also. Plantations had stores to meet the needs of the slaves and doled out medical aid as necessary. Visits to town were mostly for social events or to trade plantation products.

As a farm-based factory system, the plantation handled all phases of crop production and distribution. The one main crop—which at Mulberry was cotton—had to be processed, packaged, sold, and transported to market. In addition, the several hundred slaves who worked the plantation had to be managed and kept in good health. The owner's wife oversaw the maintenance of the mansion. Due to the steady stream of visitors paying business or social calls, it had to be cleaned from top to bottom every day. One would think there would be enough work to keep everyone busy.

An idle role. At Mulberry, however, Colonel James Chesnut and his wife, Mary Cox Chesnut, had been in charge of the estate for twenty-two years before his son James arrived with his new wife, Mary. Every detail of the daily management of the house already had been laid out. Consequently, the new Mrs. Chesnut found herself with little to do. She even had her own personal maid who answered to her smallest needs. Chesnut described her role at Mulberry:

> My dear old maid is as good as gold ... [in the morning] she brings water and builds a fire ... says sternly "Aint you gwine to git up—and fust bell for breakwus done ring."
>
> Which mandate, if I disregard—she lets me sleep as long as I please—and brings me—Oh! such a nice breakfast to my bedside. While I loiter over my breakfast she gets my room in what she calls "apple pie" order—When I am in my dressing room and bath she sweeps and dusts. It all seems cleaning and getting to rights by magic. (Muhlenfeld, p. 46)

For an educated and energetic young woman, this life of ease soon turned from a joy to a bore. Chesnut spent many hours at the window of her room observing the comings and goings below and the beautiful scenery. She also spent hours reading books from Mulberry's library as well as books she and her husband collected. She continued to teach the slaves to read and write, which was still against the law but was secretly applauded by her new family.

Entertainment and gossip. Mostly, however, Chesnut's life, like the lives of most plantation women, was filled with entertaining the many visitors and with gossip. Later, as the Civil War swelled around her, Chesnut began a diary in which she wrote down bits of gossip about the neighbors as well as comments on the people she met, including Jefferson Davis, the future president of the Confederacy, and his wife, Varina, as well as many local politicians and plantation owners. Typical of the tidbits that helped to liven her days on the too-peaceful plantation is this 1861 entry:

> Tom River has a horn blown every morning before day to wake up his people. Dr. Tom and Sally have no clock, so when they hear the horn, they get up and prepare breakfast. Some time ago ... they heard the horn, got up and cooked their breakfast and ate it, and still had to wait for day. You can imagine those two sitting by the fire, with little to say, waiting and waiting! The horn had blown at ten o'clock at night for a Negro to take a dose of medicine. (Chesnut, p. 4)

Politics. Chesnut's contact with the outside world was mostly through her sister and through her own husband. She supported James in his political ambitions as he became a state legislator and later a United States senator. When in 1860 James resigned following the election of President Abraham Lincoln and returned home, Chesnut joined her husband in support of Jefferson Davis and the Confederacy.

Chestnut and slavery. By this time, Chesnut had seen much that made her question the wisdom of slavery. She had objected to an advertisement in the Camden paper selling a slave "so white as to be mistaken for a citizen" (Woodward, p. 215). And she had seen numbers of light-colored children around many of the neighbor homes. The sight led her to wonder about how having slave women, who were readily available and viewed as property, might tempt the male slave owners to behave in immoral ways. She had wondered also about the fate of slave women whom she had seen at auctions. Chesnut was strongly affected by these auctions, as shown in her later writing: "South Carolina slave holder as I am, my very soul sickens—it is too dreadful" (Woodward, p. 21). Seeing separate church services for blacks and whites made her question why all "Christians" did not talk to one another.

Other things strengthened Chesnut's hatred of slavery. A friend, Mary Whitherspoon, had returned home unexpectedly to find her slaves having a party and using the plantation silver. Threatened with floggings, the slaves had smothered Whitherspoon to death. At another household a mistreated maid had attempted to poison her master, a respected colonel. In yet another incident, Chesnut noted a slave woman so driven by her master that she took her own baby and waded into a raging river to end their lives and escape her woes.

In her diary, Chesnut wondered if it was a sin for a white southern woman to be opposed to slavery. Part of her dislike for slavery came from her belief that caring for the blacks was unprofitable. She wished the northerners "had the Negroes—we the cotton" (Woodward, p. 199). She also disliked slavery because she thought of slaves as "dirty Africans" and because she was disgusted with the treatment many slaves received.

Aftermath

Secession. Chesnut stayed at the plantation for a few weeks while her husband went directly from his post as a senator in Washington to Columbia, the seat of South Carolina government. Here he participated in the South Carolina Secession Convention and was appointed to a committee to prepare an Ordinance of Secession. An epidemic of smallpox interrupted the convention, however, and it was moved to Charleston, where Chesnut joined her husband. There she became caught up in the excitement of preparing for war: "Minutemen arming with immense blue cockades and red sashes soon with swords and gun marching and drilling" (Muhlenfeld, p. 97). Chesnut continued her diary during these hectic times, although some of the war years are not included in the records that remain. Chesnut wrote in longhand at least fifty volumes of her diary, which became a source of valuable information for future generations. (The diary was edited after the war, however, which led historians to question its accuracy.)

At the outset of the Civil War, Chesnut was still living at Mulberry even though her husband's political activities often took him away from home. While she entertained at home, she listened to the news of the war. Chesnut sat many hours in her private room sewing shirts for the Confederate soldiers. All the while, she wished that her own husband would become involved in the battles, but he was at first involved only in affairs of the state. For the next five years, the two spent little time at Mulberry.

James Chesnut was convinced that the southern states could form an independent Confederacy that could become a reality without bloodshed. When six other states joined South Carolina in this effort, he, with Chesnut, moved to Montgomery, Alabama, to attend a new convention of representatives of the seceded states. There Chesnut struck up a lifelong friendship with Jefferson Davis's wife, Varina.

Civil War. During the war, the Chesnuts moved frequently. From Montgomery, James would go back to South Carolina for another convention while Mary would travel to Florida to visit her sick sister, Kate. They were in Montgomery when the new Confederacy was formed with Jefferson Davis as president, in Charleston when war was declared, and in Richmond, Virginia, during many of the events there during the war. At Richmond, Chesnut showed her commitment to the Confederacy by urging her husband to volunteer for the fight. He, however, remained committed to the idea of a peaceful secession until the plans to take Fort Sumter in Charleston Harbor began to take shape. By that time, Chesnut had returned to Mulberry and her husband had enlisted. He became an aide to Jefferson Davis.

Mary Chesnut on Some Famous People of the Civil War

Robert E. Lee: "A man riding a beautiful horse joined us. He wore a hat with somehow a military look to it. He sat on his horse gracefully, and he was so distinguished at all points that I very much regretted not catching the name." (Chesnut, p. 155)

Jefferson Davis: "The President took a seat by me on the sofa where I sat. He talked for nearly an hour. He laughed at our faith in our own prowess." (Chesnut p. 108)

Abraham Lincoln: "Lincoln is a good humoured fellow such as usually sit on shop boxes and whittle sticks." (Woodward, p. 35)

Meanwhile, life at Mulberry had changed. Chesnut spent many hours at her diary and even more time sewing shirts for soldiers. She also set out many mornings with loads of provisions for the hospital operated by Louisa McCord and the Wayside Hospital of Jane Fisher. All the while she wrote about her frustration with her husband and other men who were not fighting: "Oh if I could put some of my reckless spirit into these discreet cautious lazy men"; "Beauregard is at Norfolk and if I was a man I should be there too!"; "If I was a man I would not doze and drink and drivel here until the fight is over in Virginia" (Muhlenfeld, p. 113).

The diaries tell of her excitement at sitting on the housetop to watch the bombardment of Fort Sumter. Mostly, however, Chesnut's writing documents divisions among southerners. Jefferson Davis was a hero to some, a tyrant to others. Some men clamored to join the fighting, others used every trick to avoid it. One gentleman from a plantation was drafted as a private and insisted on taking along his servant and a baggage cart. According to Chesnut, he got both wishes. Another entry in the diary tells of panic about the blacks at the beginning of the war. The slaves were a large force and white southerners feared they would join on the side of the North. Chesnut writes of the anxiety over a Union attack that resulted in blacks being lined up and shot by their masters, who did the deed as coldly as they might shoot birds. Over and over again, Chesnut writes of the many injustices against the blacks, injustices aggravated by the fears of the war.

Moving to Columbia, then Alabama, then Richmond, Chesnut visited her mother and continued to entertain whenever there was opportunity to get more news of the war. When her husband was made brigadier general and assigned to Chester, South Carolina, Chesnut joined him there. She was in Chester when Senator Clement Clay brought the news that General Robert E. Lee had surrendered.

Return to Mulberry. By the time James and Mary Chesnut returned to Mulberry, James's mother had died and his ninety-three-year-old father was blind and feeble. Mulberry was now in poor condition from being pillaged by Union raiding parties during the war. The plantation was deeply in debt. The Chesnuts found themselves in much the same situation as many of their plantation-owning friends. War had ravaged their holdings and freed their slaves. It had left many of the owners nearly penniless. Chesnut's chief source of funds was a milk and eggs business, which she and a former slave named Molly operated as a partnership. Fortunately for the Chesnuts, their 500 former slaves were as much at sea as they. The slaves were free, but with nowhere to go and no way to earn their own living. James offered to hire them to stay through the crop season of 1865 and most agreed.

Post-war plantation life. The plantation began to rebuild. James remained active in politics, leaving management of the planting and harvesting to his wife. She was such an effective manager that the Chesnuts were soon prosperous enough to build a second home in Camden. Still, the couple worried about Mary's future if her husband James should die before her. James's father had willed the property only to his own children. Should James die before

Mary, she would be left with nothing; Mulberry would belong to the direct descendants of the old man. In the 1870s, the couple arranged for Mary Chesnut's security by building a third home, Sarsfield, which was held directly in her name. In 1884, her mother and her husband died within three weeks of each other. Chesnut was left alone with only Sarsfield as a land possession.

In her last years, Chesnut began to think of writing as a means of earning money, so she began to organize her diary for publication. Much of her writing was corrected by her with publication in mind. It is, therefore, not easy to tell whether she really hated slavery or if she later changed her diary to make it seem so. In all, it appears that Chesnut had long felt the sentiment she had expressed in a question in 1861:

> I wonder if it be a sin to think slavery a curse to any land[?] Men and women are punished when their masters and mistresses are brutes, not when they do wrong.... God forgive us, but ours is a monstrous system, a wrong and an iniquity. (Chesnut, p. 21)

The diary of Chesnut, an interesting account of the Civil War from the viewpoint of an active southern woman, slave holder, and plantation owner, was published in 1905 under the title *A Diary from Dixie.*

For More Information

Chesnut, Mary Boykin. *A Diary from Dixie.* Edited by Ben Ames Williams. 1905. Reprinted: Boston: Houghton Mifflin, 1949.

Muhlenfeld, Elisabeth. *Mary Boykin Chesnut, A Biography.* Baton Rouge: Louisiana State University Press, 1981.

Woodward, C. Vann, and Elisabeth Muhlenfeld, et al. *The Private Mary Chesnut: The Unpublished Civil War Diaries.* New York: Oxford University Press, 1984.

Slave Resistance

1791

Slave revolt on West Indies island of St. Domingue (present-day Haiti and the Dominican Republic).

1800

Gabriel Prosser plans to arm 1,000 slaves for a revolt in Richmond, Virginia, but is stopped.

1820

Slave population in the South reaches 1.5 million and continues to rise.

1822

Denmark Vesey assembles army of several thousand to stage slave revolt in Charleston, South Carolina.

1831

Nat Turner leads slave revolt in Southampton County, Virginia.

1837

Gag rule is passed, preventing discussion of petitions against slavery in Congress.

1839

Slaves on board the *Amistad* mutiny; vessel lands in Connecticut.

1840

John Quincy Adams defends blacks who mutinied on the *Amistad* in the Supreme Court.

1844

Adams succeeds in having the gag rule removed from Congress.

SLAVE RESISTANCE

From the start, blacks resisted slavery in America. The mutiny was a form of resistance adopted on the voyage from Africa, and slave revolts broke out in New York (1712) and South Carolina (1739) in the early years after their arrival. Also from the start, punishment was severe. Rebels were tortured, hanged, and beheaded to squash all future thoughts of open revolt. Slaves reacted by inventing different forms of resistance. They dragged out jobs, faked illnesses, broke tools, or burned crops. Thousands of slaves in Virginia resisted slavery during the Revolution, siding with the British when they promised slaves freedom from bondage.

Slave resistance persisted after the Revolutionary War. In the cotton fields of the South, slaves continued to resist slyly. They sang work songs, for example, whose lyrics expressed their defiance. The slaves refused to be treated as property, forming their own institutions on the continent—the black church and close-knit slave families. Some slaves openly resisted by running away. Runaways called "maroons" formed their own communities in Florida and other swampy areas of the South. Slaves also escaped along the Underground Railroad. This was not, in fact, a railroad, but rather a network of safe houses and places where runaway slaves could rest on the pathway of escape to the North and Canada. Hunted by slave catchers and hound dogs, only a small fraction of these runaways ever reached freedom. The few who succeeded had help mostly from other blacks.

Slaves attempted also to resist by open revolt after the Revolutionary War. Outside the United States, slaves on the Caribbean island of St. Domingue (present-day Haiti and the Dominican Republic) won a bloody rebellion in 1791. Some of the island's white slaveowners escaped to North America, and panic spread that the rebels would be moving on to incite an uprising in the United States too. Whites in the South, where the slave population had been growing, became alarmed. They strengthened their "slave codes"—laws governing the behavior of slaves. Already in many areas it was against the law for slaves to carry weapons, own property, or leave their plantation without a pass, but stricter codes were adopted. Now slaves could not visit whites or black freemen. They could not hold a meeting among themselves unless a white man was present or strike a white person, even in self-defense. Slaves were subject to the death penalty for revolt.

Despite these obstacles, a few southern blacks managed to plan major uprisings against whites and one actually took place. In 1800, in Richmond, Virginia, Gabriel Prosser, a twenty-four-year-old free black man, plotted to arm 1,000 slaves to attack Richmond. During a delay caused by a drenching rainstorm, the plan was betrayed by some black house servants. In the end, Governor James Monroe ordered that twenty-five of the rebels, including Prosser, be hanged.

Twenty-two years later **Denmark Vesey,** a fifty-five-year-old free black, almost succeeded in staging another revolt, which promised to be much larger. One estimate suggests that 9,000 blacks were ready to participate in Vesey's uprising. The plan was to first seize weapons in and near Charleston, South Carolina, murdering all whites and any blacks who got in the way of the rebels. This plot, like Prosser's, was betrayed before the hour of the uprising. Afterward, there were hysterical reactions in the community, and a trial was held that exhibited a sharp split among whites in their opinions about the rights of blacks.

Each time news of a possible rebellion surfaced, southern states tightened their laws, trying to further restrict the behavior of their black inhabitants. Yet **Nat Turner** managed to plan and carry out a rebellion in Southampton County, Virginia, in 1831, killing white men, women, and children on local plantations. In the end the rebels were hanged and scores of other blacks were slaughtered by panic-stricken whites. But Turner's revolt left Southerners with a new realization. Whites who had persuaded themselves that slavery was a positive good could no longer deny the misery felt by blacks kept in bondage.

More slave revolts may have been planned than those discovered. Clearly there were some attempts at open rebellion, but in each case they were directly and rapidly squashed. Another avenue was political action through government channels. At the time, these were only indirectly open to blacks. Protesters sent Congress petitions to end slavery through white leaders such as **John Quincy Adams.** In the 1830s, Congressman Adams insisted on reading in the House of Representatives petitions to abolish slavery sent to him by whites as well as blacks. Congress grew tired of all his reading. The members tried to stop Adams by passing "gag rules," which stated that all petitions on slavery would not be discussed.

At the end of the 1830s, Adams more directly involved himself in the fight against slavery and the slave trade. He argued in the Supreme Court a case in defense of black captives who staged a mutiny on board a slave ship, the *Amistad.* The violence of this mutiny was followed by government action in the form of a court case, which would decide the fate of the black captives. The same two methods, violence and political action, would again affect the fate of blacks in the approaching Civil War.

Denmark Vesey

c. 1767-1822

Personal Background

Boyhood in the West Indies. The date of Denmark Vesey's birth remains uncertain, as does his past before 1781. He was either born in Africa or as a slave on St. Thomas, an island in the West Indies claimed by the European nation of Denmark. The island became a center for the slave trade and for the growing of sugar and cotton. Over 4,000 black people and under 400 whites lived there in the late 1700s.

In 1781, Joseph Vesey, the captain of an ocean-going vessel, stopped at St. Thomas and picked up 390 black slaves, including a fourteen-year-old boy. Won over by the boy's keen mind and fine looks, Captain Joseph Vesey took a liking to the youth. He named him Denmark and gave the boy some decent clothes before dropping him off on the island of St. Domingue to be the slave of a French planter. France controlled St. Domingue, then considered the richest colony in the new world. Considerably larger than St. Thomas, the island was populated by more than a half-million people: 480,000 slaves, 32,000 whites, and 24,000 free blacks.

Denmark stayed on St. Domingue for roughly three months, during which time he may have heard the grumblings of slaves, which, ten years later, would build into a bloody uprising. The planter who had purchased Denmark returned "the faulty merchan-

▲ **Denmark Vesey worked on a slave ship in his youth**

Event: Uprising of black slaves and freemen in Charleston, South Carolina.

Role: Denmark Vesey, a free black man, masterminded a plan for a black revolt in South Carolina in 1822. There has been disagreement over whether Vesey, in fact, had a detailed plan for a deadly uprising or whether whites blew the incident out of proportion. In either case, white leaders felt the threat of an uprising was real. Their reaction to the plot affected the course of American history. Responding to the Vesey revolt, South Carolina took its first steps toward separation from the Union.

dise" to Captain Vesey the next time he stopped at the island. The boy, he explained, had a fit of epilepsy on the job (probably an act rather than a genuine fit). Afterward, the captain took Denmark in as his own personal servant, and the boy experienced life at sea on a slaver, a vessel that transported slaves.

Teenage years in the slave trade. Slavers traveled to Africa, the Caribbean Islands, and North American ports (such as Charleston, South Carolina) in a triangular route. On the second leg of the voyage, called the Middle Passage, they journeyed from Africa to the Caribbean across the Atlantic Ocean. A crew of perhaps six men hauled a cargo of more than 100 slaves at a time. Packed like sardines, the slaves were chained together on a temporary deck three feet below the main deck. Their main food was boiled rice, which they ate with their hands while they sat on their heels.

It was not unusual for one-fourth of the slaves to die during the three-to-four month Middle Passage. Some suffocated. Others died of diseases. When the weather was stormy, the dead would remain chained to the living for days while the small crew spent all their time keeping the craft afloat. There were suicides, too; slaves jumped overboard rather than subjecting themselves to such beastly treatment.

What particular horrors Denmark may have witnessed on such voyages is unknown. It is likely, however, that Captain Vesey transported slaves from their homes in Africa to the Americas with Denmark on board. Certainly he saw the reshaping of free Africans into beasts of burden, and probably the boy identified with the slaves, whose ages generally ranged from ten to eighteen. His own sea years lasted until age sixteen.

Life in Charleston. In 1783, with the Revolutionary War over, Captain Vesey decided to settle down at one of his regular ports of call, Charleston, South Carolina. His slave Denmark, who by now had adopted the last name of his owner, settled there with him. For a time, the captain became a land-based slave merchant. Slaves were sold twice a week in Charleston "like bullocks [cattle] and horses.... They are exposed to sale on a sort of stage, turned about and exhibited from all sides, by the common cryer, put up and adjudged to the highest bidder" (Lofton, p. 29). After a year or so, Joseph Vesey changed to selling ships' supplies.

Charleston was the fourth-largest city in the United States at the time and South Carolina the foremost state in the South. Life centered around large plantations that grew rice and cotton on the flat lowlands of the Charleston district. Owned by a small group of planters, the plantations were worked by hundreds of slaves. Their white owners generally lived on the plantations for part of the year, but moved to townhouses during the winter and summer months.

More blacks than whites populated the city year round. Slaves specialized in certain occupations there, including marketing, fishing, and laboring as butchers, carpenters, bricklayers, tailors, shoemakers, and barbers. While some of them worked for their masters, other slaves were hired out to different employers for a profit.

Early slave revolts. Strict rules governed slave behavior in South Carolina, and the laws grew stricter as news of revolts filtered into the state. In 1791, the slaves on Denmark Vesey's one-time home island of St. Domingue staged a bloody uprising against their French plantation owners, burning more than 1,000 plantations and farms and slaughtering whites, including women and children. Survivors fled to the United States, with 500 of them settling in Charleston with their slaves. Some of these refugees called on Joseph Vesey, who had so often stopped at their island during his years at sea. They brought along their slaves, who might have shared with Denmark news of the successful uprising from which they had fled.

In 1798, people in South Carolina learned about a plan in their own state to burn Charleston, just as slaves had burned St. Domingue. The plan was smothered, but people in the city grew scared and decided to put stricter controls on slaves. The state already had a law against teaching slaves to read and write, and a new act in 1800 forbade them to assemble in a secret, locked place. That same year in Richmond, Virginia, the slave Gabriel Prosser planned an uprising, but news of his plan leaked out. Thirty-five blacks were hanged and others arrested. Altogether about 1,000 had gathered to stage an attack that never occurred.

Vesey wins his freedom. Meanwhile, something remarkable happened to Denmark Vesey. In 1800, after spending seventeen years in the city of Charleston as a slave, he won a lottery prize of $1,500. Now thirty-three years old, Vesey used $600 of the prize money to purchase his freedom. With the remainder, he set himself up in business as a carpenter, joining Charleston's free black community.

Sometime in the next twenty years, Vesey earned enough money—carpenters made $1.50 a day—to buy his own house at 20 Bull Street. During his years in Charleston, Vesey is known to have had at least seven wives (at some points more than one at a time), two sons, a daughter, and three stepchildren. His families lived in various parts of the city, and all of his children and some of his wives were slaves.

As the years passed, new events increased Charleston's fear of a slave revolt. The rebellion at nearby St. Domingue, after all, had ended with black slaves gaining their independence in 1804. In 1805, South Carolina passed a new law: any freeman or white citizen who joined a slave revolt would be sentenced to death. Then, in 1819, the United States was torn by a debate over whether to admit Missouri into the union as a free state or a slave state. A leader in the debate, Senator Rufus King, condemned the entire practice of slavery, his words having a powerful effect not only on whites but also on blacks such as Vesey. Fearing that King's words would lead to an uprising, South Carolina tightened its grip on slaves. In 1820, afraid that free blacks might stir the slaves to revolt, it forbade the entry of any more free blacks into the state. Also outlawed was the emancipation, or freeing, of any more South Carolina slaves except by the state legislature. Blacks, at the time, outnumbered whites in Charleston, which was populated by 12,652 slaves, 1,475 free blacks, and 11,654 whites.

Vesey, like other free blacks already living there, was allowed to stay in South Carolina. By 1822 he was fifty-five years old and had accumulated about $8,000 worth of property. He could read, write, and speak several languages, skills he had learned during his time as a slave. His work as a carpenter had earned him the respect of the Charleston citizenry. He seemed a religious man, too, which both pleased and concerned whites who frowned on his particular church. A Methodist, he and other blacks had a few years earlier broken with the white church in Charleston to form their own branch of the first all-black organization in the nation, the African Methodist Episcopal Church.

Participation: Denmark Vesey's Revolt

Vesey assembles his army. Little is known about what made Vesey decide to take action, but much is known about how he built his rebel army. Vesey used religious gatherings to share his views. Protesting that slavery was unjust, he referred to the Bible for proof that owning slaves was a sin. According to one report, Vesey spent nine years convincing blacks to adopt his views, not only at the African Church but also on the streets, in shops, and at his home.

By the end of 1821, Vesey talked about taking direct action. Time was at hand, he argued, for slaves to rise up and fight for freedom. To support his arguments, Vesey read to the mostly illiterate crowds from a variety of sources. From the Bible he read about how the children of Israel delivered themselves out of slavery in Egypt, urging the congregation to likewise deliver themselves from the bondage of whites. After all, he pointed out, blacks had already proven themselves equal to other Americans by fighting in the War of 1812 at the Battle of New Orleans. He also read Senator King's remarks against slavery as proof that Congress had already decided slavery was wrong. (According to reports, Vesey went so far as to claim the United States had already freed the slaves; South Carolina was keeping them in bondage against the supreme law of the land.) Vesey also read to them from antislavery pamphlets and from news reports about events in St. Domingue. If his listeners would only rise up in unison, he promised, they, like the slaves of St. Domingue, would overcome their white owners.

Organizing the army. Vesey had several lieutenants to help lead the uprising: Ned and Rolla Bennett, Jack Purcell, Peter Poyas, Monday Gell, and Gullah Jack. The Bennetts were well positioned, being servants to Thomas Bennett, the governor of South Carolina. Poyas, a ship carpenter who seemed fearless, could write; Gell, a harness maker, was both intelligent and dependable. Small with bushy whiskers, Purcell laid charms and curses on others and had a following among superstitious slaves. A few groups of blacks had already formed themselves into units ready for combat: the Gullah Society, the slaves from St. Domingue, and the plantation slaves. The final number of rebellious blacks remains unknown, but by some counts the total reached 9,000.

The plan. Vesey regularly met with others at Gell's harness shop or at his own home on Bull Street to plot the uprising. Typically, he read a passage from the Bible about slavery and then passed a hat around to collect money for weapons and for horses for the messengers who would, at the proper time, alert slaves in the country to join the rebels in the city. Though slave blacksmiths fashioned some of the weapons, the plan called for seizing others from the stockpile kept at nearby arsenals when the attack started. Vesey got hold of a pistol, Poyas and Gell found swords, and Rolla Bennett, a dagger. By summer 1822, about 350 more daggers had been fashioned for the fateful day, along with roughly 200 to 300 bayonets. Vesey also had some wigs and whiskers made from white men's hair for use as disguises.

The black army intended to strike at midnight in several locations at once. Poyas was to lead a party up a main street to seize the state arsenal and guardhouse, meanwhile attacking and distracting the whites. Another party, under Ned Bennett, would take control of a nearby national arsenal. A third party led by Rolla Bennett would kill the governor. Purcell planned to take his group to some local stores to seize more weapons. Meanwhile, Vesey would lead his party down to the main guardhouse, killing whites who interfered along the way. Once they had the weapons, the rebels would torch the city and begin a general massacre of whites, as well as of blacks who refused to join the rebellion. Vesey justified the killing of these blacks with a phrase from the Bible: "He that is not with me, is against me" (Luke 11:23). As in St. Domingue, Vesey ordered that even women and children must be killed. He assured his army that their cause was just, and that blacks from Africa and St. Domingue would later join in the fight. Many in the army, though, worried about what would happen after the uprising. After they struck, Vesey promised them they would sail to safety in St. Domingue.

The plot is betrayed. On Saturday, May 25, 1822, William Paul approached another slave, Peter Prioleau, and suggested he join in the upcoming revolt. Alarmed, Prioleau went home and informed his master's family of the plot. The master relayed the information to James Hamilton, a city official, who had Prioleau repeat the story to the city council. Paul was arrested. He at first denied the plot but later confessed after a time in solitary confinement.

Learning of the arrest, Vesey moved up the date of the attack from July 14 to June 16, 1822. This change was revealed to the whites by another slave, George Wilson. In a panic, city leaders moved quickly to make more arrests. Among the new prisoners were Peter Poyas and Ned and Rolla Bennett. Denmark Vesey remained at large. There was a pledge of secrecy among the rebels that at first was well kept. Vesey had burned all the books and papers connected to the uprising, and Poyas set an example for the other prisoners by refusing to talk. The authorities had gotten a few names of other conspirators from Paul, but Poyas refused to divulge any more names, despite being chained to the floor of a cell, threatened, and tortured. By then, however, the authorities had learned enough to suspect that Vesey was the leader of the revolt. They arrested him the night of June 22, bursting in on him at the home of one of his wives.

A Slave Reacts to the Vesey Conspiracy

Peter Prioleau described to the court his response when approached to join the Vesey uprising: "I was so much astonished and horror struck," Prioleau explained, "that it was a moment or two before I could ... tell him I would have nothing to do with this business, and that I was satisfied with my condition, that I was grateful to my master for his kindness and wished no change." (Starobin, p. 17)

The trials. Blacks in South Carolina were subject to different courts than whites. Copying Barbados, an island in the West Indies, the state had passed a special law saying slaves were unqualified to be governed by the laws of the state or nation. They set up ad hoc, or temporary, courts for black prisoners. Serving as judges in these courts were two justices of the peace and at least three freeholders, or estate holders. Three out of the five judges could convict the accused, who had no right to appeal, or question, the decision.

The defendants in Vesey's plot were tried one at a time. Highly irregular procedures were allowed. In some cases, the defendants were not allowed to see their accusers. Witnesses could give testimony without taking an oath, and hearsay testimony was admitted and considered. The Bennetts and Poyas showed no fear at their trials. Vesey, brought before the court on June 23, was at first confident, acting as if the law were on his side. He had a lawyer, George Warren Cross, and was permitted to question the witnesses. A slave, Frank Ferguson, gave the most damaging testimony:

> I know Denmark Vesey and have been to his house—I have heard him say that the negroe's situation was so bad he did not know how they could endure it ... he said ... he had spoken to Ned [Bennett] and Peter [Poyas] on this subject; and that they were to go about and tell the blacks that they were free, and must rise and fight for themselves—that they would take the Magazines and Guard-Houses, and the city and be free ... he said himself, Ned Bennett, Peter Poyas and Monday Gell were the principal men and himself the head man ... that they would kill all the whites ... and that he had spoken to 6,600 persons who had agreed to join. (Starobin, pp. 31-32)

In self-defense, Vesey argued that the charges against him had to be false. No free black man in his position had any reason to revolt. But the evidence against him was too damaging. The court found him guilty and passed the death sentence. Five others were to die with him on July 2 between 6:00 and 8:00 a.m. There were rumors of a rescue attempt, but it never occurred. The six went to the gallows, with Poyas giving orders: "Do not open your lips! Die silent, as you shall see me do" (Lofton, p. 169). Whites thought they saw a few tears trickling down Vesey's cheeks at the end of his trial, but he never did confess to anything.

The hearings, begun on June 19, had lasted for two months. Altogether seventy-one men were found guilty, including sixty-seven blacks and four whites. Thirty-five of them were hanged to death, and almost everyone else was banished. Afterward, the authorities rewarded Prioleau, who had reported the plot, and Wilson, who discovered the new date of the rebellion. These two slaves were freed, given $50 a year for life, and excused from paying state taxes. Slave owners whose human property had been hanged were awarded $122 for each slave lost (a new slave cost about $650).

▲ Executing Negroes in New York

Aftermath

A split in the white community. The trials were over, but the panic was as great in August as it had been in June. For a time the papers kept quiet about the incident, afraid of stirring blacks into a new revolt. There was a sharp split in the white community, though. Governor Thomas Bennett and his brother-in-law William Johnson, a justice of the United States Supreme Court, argued that the trials had been unfair. Most white residents in the city opposed the views of these two leaders. The governor published one version of the trial, and the city published another for the public to read. While the governor was convinced that the slaves had, in fact, planned a revolt, he was deeply disturbed by the city's overly harsh treatment of them. Rumor, he said, had made the conspiracy, or plot, seem larger than it ever was. He chided the judges for refusing to let the accused see their accusers, and he raised a question about the free blacks: Were they entitled to the same rights as slaves, or more? (In 1843, the U.S. government ruled that free blacks were entitled to the same rights as whites.)

Innocent Bystander Dies During Vesey Hangings

A great crowd turned out to witness the hangings that took place in Charleston on Friday, July 26, 1822. Caught in the rush, a small slave boy was trampled to death by horses.

Expressing similar opinions, Justice William Johnson wrote to John Quincy Adams, who was secretary of state at the time of the uprising and a known abolitionist: "I do not hesitate to express the opinion that the whole of the alarm of 1822 was founded in causes that were infinitely exaggerated" (Starobin, p. 85). He went into greater length in a letter to Thomas Jefferson:

> I … begin to feel lonely among the men of the present day … particularly so in this place.… I have lived to see what I really never believed it possible I should see—courts held with closed doors, and men dying by scores who had never seen the faces nor heard the voices of their accusers.… Incalculable are the evils which have resulted.… Our property is reduced to nothing—strangers are alarmed at coming near us; our slaves rendered uneasy. (Starobin, pp. 84-85)

William Johnson's daughter, Anna Hayes Johnson, heard the news and the rumors. She wrote of them in letters to her cousin, which show a panic more typical of the community. On June 23, 1822, she wrote: "It seems that the Governour[,] Intendant[,] and my poor father were to be the first three ... murdered ... we poor devils were to have been reserved to fill their Harams." On July 18, 1822, she wrote: "I never heard in my life more deep laid plots or plots more likely to succeed ... their intention was to ... carry us [girls] ... to St D there to be sold as slaves" (Starobin, pp. 72-73).

The backlash. After the trials, the panic resulted in harsher laws. The state passed the Negro Seaman Act on December 31, 1822, concerning any vessel coming to the state with free black workers on board. Such freemen could be seized and jailed, said the law, until the vessel left the state, whereupon its captain was bound to carry away the "free person of color" and pay for his stay in the jail. Pestered by the act, ships from Great Britain came and left South Carolina. Going to what they thought was a higher authority than the state, the British traders protested to the United States government. Justice Johnson declared the Negro Seaman Act unconstitutional, and other leaders agreed. But South Carolina enforced the act anyway. The state had begun to ignore the central government, taking its first stubborn steps along a bumpy road that would carry the South into the Civil War.

South Carolina After the Trials

Life in South Carolina grew increasingly strict after the Vesey trials. In 1836, postmasters burned an antislavery pamphlet by Angelina Grimké, a white citizen who had left the state. Police were ordered to arrest her if she returned.

For More Information

Lofton, John. *Denmark Vesey's Revolt.* Kent, Ohio: Kent State University Press, 1983.

Starobin, Robert S., ed. *Denmark Vesey: The Slave Conspiracy of 1822.* Englewood Cliffs, New Jersey: Prentice-Hall, 1970.

Nat Turner

1800-1831

Personal Background

Childhood. Nat Turner was born in Southampton County, Virginia, on October 2, 1800, the property of Benjamin Turner (it was common practice for slaves to take the last names of their owners). Little is known about Nat's father, who apparently escaped to freedom when Nat was still a child, but much has been written about his mother, a native of Africa called Nancy. According to one legendary account, she was the daughter of an African tribal chief; in another story she supposedly wanted to kill her infant son rather than allow him to live his life as a slave. Whatever the truth of these stories, it is clear that both parents were convinced that Nat was a special, talented child with an extraordinary mind. Nat himself insisted that at the age of three or four he could recall events that had happened before he was born. This talent, he claimed, greatly astonished others:

> [It] caused them to say ... I would surely be a prophet, as the Lord had shown me things that had happened before my birth. And my father and mother strengthened me in this my first impression, saying ... I was intended for some great purpose. (Clarke, p. 99)

His master, who noted Nat's unusual intelligence, observed that the boy had too much sense to be of much service to anyone as a slave.

Education. His permissive second owner, Samuel Turner,

▲ **Nat Turner**

Event: Slave uprising.

Role: Nat Turner, who was born a slave, led the bloodiest slave revolt in United States history. A highly appealing preacher, Turner believed he was chosen by God to lead his people to freedom through violent action. He began his rebellion on August 21, 1831, and, with a following never exceeding seventy, was responsible for the deaths of approximately sixty whites before his uprising was crushed.

allowed Nat to study white children's schoolbooks, and he undoubtedly escaped much of the hard work that was the usual lot of slave children. Nat later recalled that the other slaves developed confidence in his superior judgment, relying on him to help plan any mischief they intended to commit. Much influenced by others' belief in his special powers, Nat avoided mixing in society. He instead devoted himself to fasting and prayer.

Religion interested Nat the most. He attended religious meetings, where the slaves sang hymns that expressed their longing for a better life. He studied the scriptures, especially the Old Testament accounts of the Israelites escaping slavery in Egypt and an angry God punishing their tormentors. He believed the Holy Spirit spoke to him directly and that he "was ordained for some great purpose in the hands of the Almighty" (Clarke, p. 101).

Marriage. Although he lacked formal training for the ministry, Turner began to preach at black religious meetings. He soon became a popular speaker in slave churches. Like many other slave preachers, Turner recognized the hypocrisy of white slave owners who thought of themselves as Christians yet kept his people in chains. Slave owners in Southampton County bragged about their kind treatment of slaves but continued to break up families and prescribe brutal whippings for the slightest violations of the slave codes.

Turner himself married a young slave woman named Cherry, but when Samuel Turner died, she was sold to one master and he to another (Thomas Moore). Their masters lived close together and Turner and Cherry were sometimes able to see each other, but their forced separation was probably a great source of suffering for them. Turner was particularly pained at being separated from his children.

Visions. As the years passed, Turner grew more and more bitter about his own enslavement and that of his people. He began to develop a clearer sense of what he felt was his mission: he believed God wanted him to lead others to freedom. In fact, after running away from a new overseer and escaping capture for thirty days, Turner returned on his own so that he could fulfill his destiny. He fasted for long periods and prayed feverishly for divine guidance. He began to have bloody fantasies. In his visions he saw white and black spirits fighting each other and blood flowing in the streams. He prayed long for an explanation and experienced more visions. As Turner later described the visions, he saw Christ's hands, found blood on stalks of corn, and spotted pictures and numbers on leaves. He told others of his visions and gained greater renown among the slaves; some thought he could even control the weather and heal the sick.

Then on May 12, 1828, Turner "heard a loud noise in the heavens" and the Holy Spirit informed him that Christ had laid down the yoke he had borne for the sins of men and that Turner "should take it on and fight against the serpent" (Clarke, p. 104). He interpreted this vision to mean that he was to lead a violent revolt against slavery in which he should kill his enemies with their own weapons. God, Jehovah of the Old Testament, would tell him when to strike; until he received another sign, he was to keep his mission a secret.

Events leading to revolt. In 1828, before any further sign appeared to Turner, his master, Thomas Moore, died. Moore's widow married Joseph Travis, who in effect became Turner's step-master (legally, however, Turner belonged to Moore's nine-year-old son, Putnam). Turner later admitted being treated kindly by Travis, who would be the first victim in the bloody revolt that was taking shape in Turner's mind.

Turner's position as a preacher greatly aided his cause. He was allowed to travel more freely than most slaves, which gave him the opportunity to learn in great detail the roads, woods, dwellings, and general layout of the countryside where the uprising would take place. He also was able to recruit the men who were to be his most trusted lieutenants. He deliberately kept his plans secret to all but these few so the plot would not be leaked to the public beforehand. Because he was successful at keeping his plans hidden, the attack would come as a total surprise to the slave-holding class of Southampton County.

In February 1831, Turner received the sign he had prayed for, an eclipse of the sun. He gathered together four trusted men—Hark, Henry, Nelson, and Sam—and informed them that they would begin their revolt on July 4, a day whose historic and symbolic significance Turner clearly understood. Turner, however, beset by doubts, became sick and the uprising had to be postponed. The conspirators did not have to wait long for another sign. It appeared on August 13, when the fog apparently caused the sun to repeatedly change color. By late afternoon a black spot could be seen moving across the sun's surface, clear proof to Turner that God wanted him to begin his rebellion. By August 20, he and his men were ready to strike. They gathered in the woods and vowed to win liberty or die trying.

Participation: Nat Turner's Revolt

The plan. On Sunday, August 21, 1831, at a place in the woods called Cabin Pond (near the Travis farm, where Turner lived), the four chosen lieutenants awaited their leader's arrival. They were joined by two new recruits, a friend of Hark's named Jack and the powerful slave Will, who would prove invaluable in performing the bloody work that lay ahead. Always mindful of the need to maintain an air of mystery, Turner arrived late, after nightfall, suddenly appearing before his men by torchlight.

Now known as the "Prophet," Turner revealed his plans to his inner circle. The rising would begin that night, when many of the local militia were attending a religious camp meeting. Every white person they encountered would be killed, including women and children. The six men involved in Turner's plot wondered whether their revolt could possibly succeed when their numbers were so small. Turner assured them that other slaves and even free blacks would rise up and join them when they learned that an uprising had begun. He never explained what the long-range goal of his revolt was. He told his men only that they were headed to the city of Jerusalem, Virginia, where they would seize weapons, and that every white they met on this ten-mile trek was to be killed. In fact, Turner may not have had any long-range plans, for he believed "God would guide him after the revolt began, just as he had directed Gideon" (Oates, *The Fires of Jubilee,* p. 45).

The uprising. Turner and his band left the woods around 2:00 a.m. on August 22, 1831. They spared the farm of Giles Reese because that was where Cherry, Turner's wife, lived. Instead they made the Travis homestead their first target. They moved soundlessly across the yard, armed with axes (even after they acquired guns the rebels tried not to use them, fearing the sound of shots would raise the alarm). The men found the doors to the house locked, so Turner climbed up a ladder, entered the house through a second-story window, and let the other slaves in. His men wanted their leader to have the honor of drawing the first blood. Turner led them into Joseph Travis's bedroom, where he swung his axe at the sleeping slave master. The blow only bounced off Travis's head and set him screaming. So Will stepped forward and killed Travis with his axe. In a matter of a few minutes, Turner's men slaughtered four more whites, including Mrs. Travis and young Putnam Moore.

The rebels took four guns, several old muskets, and a pound or two of gunpowder from the Travis place. Gathering his men at the barn, Turner taught them the few military maneuvers he had learned: "We paraded; I formed them in a line as soldiers, and after carrying them through all the manoeuvres [that] I was master of marched them off" (Clarke, p. 106). The men had gone only a little distance when someone remembered an infant sleeping in a cradle back at the Travis house. Will and Henry were sent back to kill it.

The savagery and bloodshed at the Travis homestead was repeated over and over again that night as Turner and his band surprised farm after farm. At the home of Salathul Francis, only 600 yards from the Travis place, Mr. Francis, the only white there, was beaten to death when he answered a knock at the door. At the next farm, Piety Reese was murdered in her bed; "her son awoke, but it was only to sleep the sleep of death, he had only time to say 'who is that,' and he was no more" (Clarke, p. 106). At dawn, about a mile from the Reese farm, the slaves came upon the home of Elizabeth Turner, widow of Nat Turner's second master. Her neighbor, Mrs. Newsome, was there. Will hacked the terrified Mrs. Turner to death while Nat hit Mrs. Newsome on the head with his sword. But the blow did not kill her, so Will moved Nat aside and did away with her also. This marked the second time that Turner had attempted but had been unable to kill a victim.

As the sun rose that Monday morning, Turner, whose band was slowly increasing in number, sent a group on foot to one farm while he led a mounted force to Coty Whitehead's place. As they approached the house, they spotted Richard Whitehead standing in the cotton patch, called him over, and Will murdered him with his axe. At this point Turner broke away from the mounted party to chase a young servant girl, mistakenly thinking she was one of the family. Realizing his error, he returned to find the whole family murdered, except for Mrs. Whitehead and her daughter Margaret. He watched Will pull Mrs. Whitehead out of the house and onto the step where he practically chopped her head from her body with his broad axe. Turner himself flushed Margaret out of her hiding place and chased her; he confessed later that "after repeated blows with a sword, I killed her by a blow on the head, with a fence rail" (Clarke, p. 107). Margaret Whitehead was the only victim personally killed by Nat Turner.

Resistance. Turner encouraged his forces to continue after the massacre at Coty Whitehead's farm. They quickly found that they no longer had the element of surprise with them. The whites at Richard Porter's house had escaped, warned by their own slaves. Will led a mounted force to the home of his master, Nathaniel Francis, who was gone and whose pregnant wife escaped slaughter because a slave hid her in the attic. Quickly killing the farm's overseer and two of Francis's nephews, Will hurried to another farm, owned by John Barrow. The elderly Barrow, a veteran of the War of 1812, courageously fought the slaves, allowing his wife to escape into the woods. Barrow was eventually killed, his throat slit. The rebels, impressed with Barrow's courage, wrapped his body in a quilt and left a plug of tobacco on his chest.

Aware that the alarm was spreading among the white people, Turner, with some difficulty, managed to unite his divided forces. He sent his twenty most reliable men ahead to massacre as many whites as possible before every homestead could be forewarned. But by then they were mostly too late; many families had taken refuge in Jerusalem, and militia forces were gathering to put down the rebellion.

Levi Waller, another slave owner, heard of the slave uprising and sent for his children, who were at a nearby school. He hoped to flee with his family, but some of Turner's men rode into his yard before he could do so. They chased Waller into some tall woods, where he hid. From his hiding place he watched in horror as his

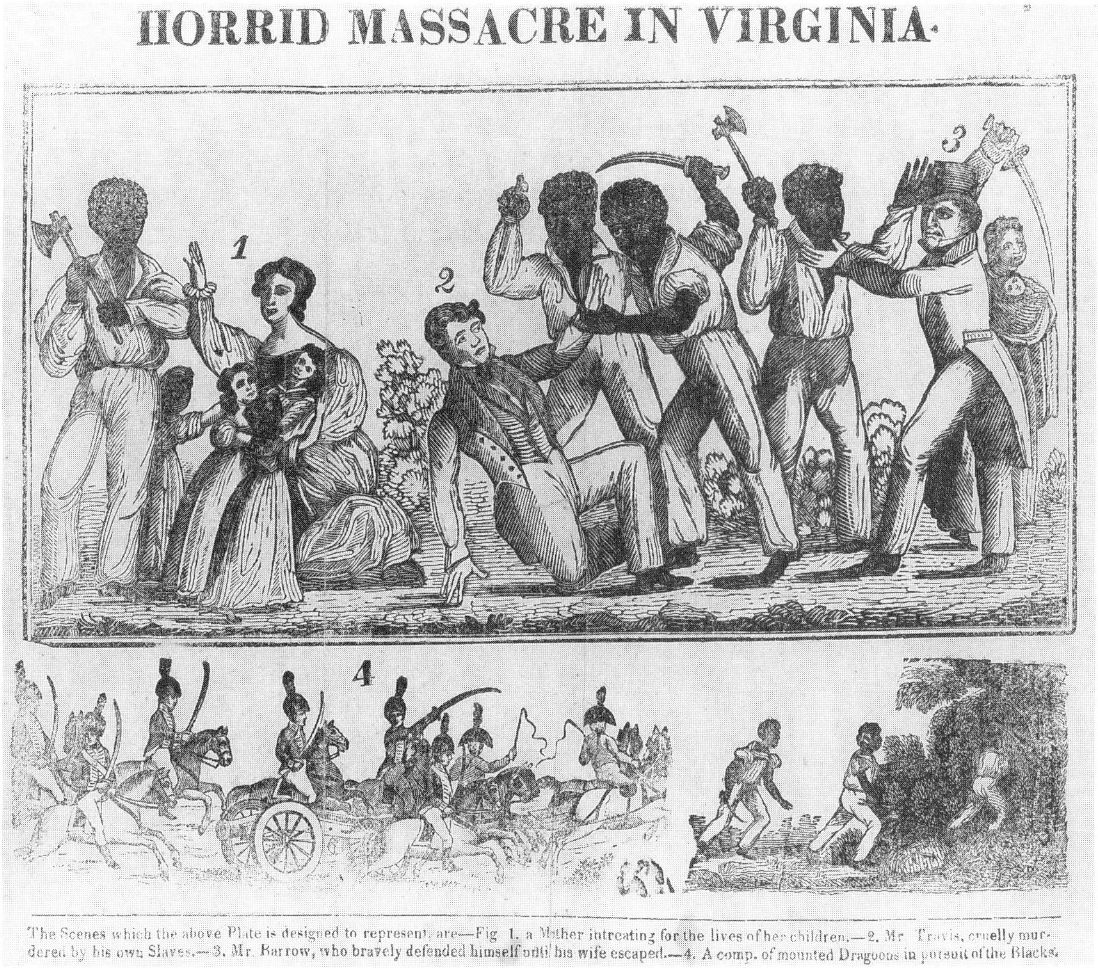
HORRID MASSACRE IN VIRGINIA.
1
2
3
4
The Scenes which the above Plate is designed to represent, are—Fig. 1. a Mother intreating for the lives of her children.—2. Mr. Travis, cruelly murdered by his own Slaves.—3. Mr. Barrow, who bravely defended himself until his wife escaped.—4. A comp. of mounted Dragoons in pursuit of the Blacks.

▲ **An artist's rendering of Turner's uprising**

wife and children were killed. One little girl survived by hiding in a chimney while all the other children, ten in all, were beheaded and piled in one bloody heap.

Battle of Parker's farm. Turner trailed behind his band and did not participate in these vicious killings. He had personally killed only Margaret Whitehead, apparently believing he had to kill at least once in order to maintain control over his men. He later said that he seldom saw the murders committed (especially after the events at the Whitehead farm), but sometimes arrived in time to see the results of the raids. In those instances he would view with satisfaction the mangled bodies as they lay, then take off in search of other victims.

Several other families were slaughtered by the rebel band after they left the Waller place. As they moved on, Turner felt that a crisis was near. He pushed his men on toward Jerusalem, but several of them wanted to stop at the plantation of James Parker, where they had relatives. This delay proved fatal for the rebels. At the Parker place, Turner's men encountered the white militia, eighteen men under the command of Captain Alexander Peete. Turner ordered his men into action and they forced the whites to flee. The slaves gave chase but then the retreating militiamen were joined by a larger force. The combined white army counterattacked and dealt Turner's men a sharp defeat. Some of the slave army's strongest men were wounded and a number of others fled, including Turner.

Capture and escape. Even after the disastrous battle at Parker's farm, Turner refused to quit. He was still determined to attack Jerusalem. He gathered what men he could and struck out down a back road, hoping to take the city from the rear. He and his small force found that the bridge they hoped to use to enter Jerusalem was heavily guarded. They retreated, hoping to find reinforcements. In the meantime, militia forces were swelling to great proportions, while Turner's force, never greater than seventy men, had dwindled to around twenty. The slaves raided Dr. Simon Blunt's farm, hoping to gain some new volunteers. Instead, Turner's band blundered into an ambush. Whites inside the house gunned down a number of the rebels and captured several, including Hark. Blunt's own slaves helped the whites defend the plantation and even assisted in the capture of a few rebels. Turner retreated but his dwindling band was overtaken by another militia force. In a final confrontation, Will was killed and the remaining rebels were driven off, scattering as they fled. Turner escaped and hid out in a hole he dug under some fence rails.

A great manhunt was undertaken to find Turner and the rest of the escaped rebels. Within a week almost all of Turner's men were captured or killed. One free black rebel killed himself to escape trial and certain execution. Taking the law into their own hands, outraged whites may have killed as many as 200 innocent slaves, in many cases mutilating and burning their bodies. Rumors swept through many southern states that other rebellions were about to erupt. These rumors proved to be unfounded, but the hysteria produced by Turner's revolt was difficult to calm down.

Capture and confession. In the meantime, Turner remained free. He eluded capture for more than two months, though a large reward was offered for him. His hiding place was near Cabin Pond, where his revolt had begun. He was finally taken by one Benjamin Phipps, who, armed with a shotgun, stumbled across Turner's hiding place in a hole under the top of a fallen tree.

Turner was paraded by a white guard to Jerusalem to stand trial. A lynch mob called for his blood every step along the way. He showed no fear and absolutely no sign of remorse. He admitted that he alone had plotted and led the revolt, talking of his visions and sense of mission. He was further questioned by Thomas Gray, to whom he dictated his *Confessions,* still the main source of information about the uprising.

Turner was open and direct in the testimony he gave Gray. He explained his motives and described the savage violence that occurred during the uprising in full detail. He said that women and children, who made up the bulk of the victims, would have been spared in later attacks if the revolt had continued. He also related that one farm had been spared because its white inhabitants were little better off than most slaves. He kept insisting that his movement was divinely inspired and that he was a prophet of God. When Gray asked, in light of the rebellion's failure, "Do you not find yourself mistaken now?" Turner answered curtly, "Was not Christ crucified?" (Clarke, p. 104). He denied knowledge of any wider uprising, but expressed his belief that others must feel as he did and might rise up under the right circumstances. Surely he knew he would be executed. Unafraid, he said he was willing to face whatever fate awaited him. Gray, although he thought Turner was a "gloomy fanatic," described him as having a "natural intelligence … surpassed by few men I have ever seen" (Clarke, p. 97). He also observed that Turner made a fearsome figure when he spoke of the bloodshed he had inspired, and raised his hands heavenward. The sight was enough to curdle Gray's blood in his veins.

On November 5, 1831, Nat Turner came to trial. He was found guilty of revolt against the government and sentenced to the gallows. He was executed on November 11. He showed no sign of fear and made no statement. The same court tried forty-eight other blacks, sentencing eighteen to death and deporting ten others.

Aftermath

Searching for causes. After the uprising, southern whites spoke of the train of alarming events leading up to Nat Turner's Revolt: Denmark Vesey's frightful slave conspiracy in 1822; David Walker's written *Appeal,* calling on slaves to use force to gain their freedom; and William Lloyd Garrison's antislavery newspaper, *The Liberator.* According to Turner, however, none of these events inspired his revolt. He claimed that it sprang from his visions, the heavenly voices he heard, and the cruelties he and others suffered as victims of the slave system.

Consequences. Nat Turner's Revolt had far-reaching consequences. Despite Turner's claim that he was not inspired by others, southerners blamed northern abolitionists, especially Garrison, for prompting Turner and his men to open rebellion. No evidence was ever produced to support this accusation. In fact, Garrison argued that he and his friends were dedicated to nonviolent methods; they were peace-loving Christians who intended to free the slaves through moral argument. Yet the end result of all the discussion was that in the South slave uprisings and abolitionism were forever linked. Southern support for abolitionism quickly died out.

A principal result of Turner's revolt was that the slave system was tightened to such a degree that further uprisings were nearly impossible. In the Virginia legislature in December 1831, the fate of slavery was debated. Some Virginians, mostly in the western part of the state, wanted to prevent further violence by abolishing slavery and colonizing the state's blacks somewhere out of the country. After a fierce debate and a close vote, the legislature rejected these proposals as being too complicated and expensive. Virginia, along with the rest of the South, decided instead to strengthen the slave codes, intending to so restrict the slaves that rebellion would be impossible.

The South's response to Nat Turner's Revolt (and to the rise of abolitionism) is known as the Great Reaction. What little freedom of action slaves had enjoyed was snatched away. Free blacks also saw their rights limited. Slave schools, slave churches, and slave preachers like Turner were forbidden. Slave patrols and militia systems were expanded. The South became a closed society; debate over slavery was eliminated. Slavery, once regarded as a "necessary evil," was now defended as a "positive good" as stated by Senator James Henry Hammond, who considered slavery the greatest of all blessings. (see **James Henry Hammond**). No abolitionist literature could be sent through the southern mail. Southern congressmen supported the "gag rule," which forbade any Congressional action on antislavery petitions (see **John Quincy Adams**).

Hero or fanatic? The terror created by his movement, and the savage killings that were carried out by his followers, made the name Nat Turner infamous throughout the South. He was regarded as a fanatic by some people and a hero by others. There were Americans who remained horror-stricken by the brutal actions of Turner's band, while others came to regard Turner as a champion who murdered whites because slavery had murdered blacks. In either case, the revolt succeeded in destroying an argument that was common among southern slave holders of the time: that their slaves were well-treated and content with their lives.

For More Information

Bisson, Terry. *Nat Turner.* New York: Chelsea House, 1988.

Clarke, John Henrik, ed. *William Styron's Confessions of Nat Turner: Ten Black Writers Respond.* Boston: Beacon Press, 1968.

Oates, Stephen B. "Children of Darkness." *American Heritage,* 1985, pp. 42-91.

Oates, Stephen B. *The Fires of Jubilee: Nat Turner's Fierce Rebellion.* New York: New American Library, 1975.

John Quincy Adams

1767-1848

Personal Background

Early life. If ever a person were groomed to become president of the United States, it was John Quincy Adams. The Adams family in America had begun humbly. Henry Adams had migrated from England just two years after the founding of Massachusetts Bay Colony. Henry and his fellow immigrants built homes just outside of Boston and named the community Braintree after the town in England from which they had come. From those poor but hard-working beginnings, the generations of Adams had grown and prospered, becoming leaders in the colony. Samuel Adams had led the citizens of Boston to revolution.

John Adams, an uncle of Samuel, had graduated from Harvard College in 1755, became a Latin master there, then studied law. By 1764, John Adams, who would later become the second president of the United States, was a prosperous businessman and lawyer. The next year he married a strong and bright young lady, Abigail Smith. Two years later, on July 11, 1767, the couple gave birth to their second child and first son, John Quincy Adams—named after his mother's grandfather.

Much was happening around Boston in those days to interest and educate young John Quincy. There was talk about revolution against Great Britain, and his cousin Samuel Adams was one of the

▲ **John Quincy Adams**

Event: The early American controversy over slavery.

Role: While never officially declaring himself to be in favor of abolishing slavery, John Quincy Adams became an outspoken champion of this movement in Congress. He defended the citizens' right to petition government, an important tool of abolitionists. Adams also played a major role in the most noted slave trial of his day—the case of the slave ship *Amistad*.

leaders of the dissent. When John Quincy was eight years old, he watched Americans fight the British for control of Boston in the struggle that became known as the Battle of Bunker Hill.

John Quincy would later say that from the date of his birth he represented the hopes and pride of his father. John Adams was often away on business, but that did not stop John Quincy from looking up to him. As early as the boy was able, he began to write letters to his father as often as possible.

Abigail's influence. Abigail took on much of the responsibility for raising the children in her husband's absence and shared her husband's hopes for their oldest son. Her leadership of the family showed early when danger struck Boston in the form of a smallpox epidemic. Abigail reacted quickly. In England, doctors had been experimenting with a new form of smallpox prevention. They infected a person with cowpox, which seemed to help him or her resist the more deadly disease of smallpox. Medicine in America was not as far advanced, but there were some doctors willing to try the new method. Abigail chose a doctor, but he had no cow with cowpox. Off she went to a hospital with her children and the family cow, which would provide the cowpox. John Quincy later developed only a slight case of cowpox, just a few pimples, and never came down with the dreaded disease of smallpox.

The strong-willed Abigail greatly influenced John Quincy. She too had high hopes for her oldest son. Certainly, the boy's education was not to be trusted to just any school or teacher. He was tutored personally by his father's law clerks and proved to be a quick and able student. In fact, he scarcely needed the tutors, becoming an eager reader and writer at an early age. This was fortunate, for his education would soon be interrupted. His father was becoming more and more involved in politics and in 1778 would travel to Europe on missions for the new United States. He was to help negotiate a settlement to the war and to establish friendship with France and Prussia. John Quincy, just ten years old, begged his father to take him along. His parents did not think much of this idea, but in the end agreed to let him go.

Europe. John Quincy was quick to prepare for his stay in Europe. He found a shipmate who spoke French and set about learning that language before the ship docked. His father, meanwhile, had no intention of relaxing his goal for educating his son. As soon as they arrived in Paris, John Quincy was hustled off to one of the finest schools in France, Passy Academy. There, complained his father, the boy learned more French each day than the older John could learn in a week. Soon, however, John Quincy's education was interrupted again. On October 12, 1779, father and son returned to Versailles, France to board a ship for Spanish territory. About this time John Quincy began to keep a journal of his adventures, which he would continue for many years.

Once in Spanish-held land, John Adams arranged to send his son to an academy in Amsterdam, the Netherlands. John Quincy thought the teachers there were stuffy and ill prepared. He became outspoken in his view that they were poor teachers, and it was not long before the headmaster and his own father agreed that he should leave the academy. John Quincy continued his studies through his reading. Soon a new opportunity for learning came when Francis Dana, America's minister to Berlin, the capital of Prussia (in present-day Germany), hired fourteen-year-old John Quincy as his private secretary.

The two set out in 1781 for Berlin and then St. Petersburg, Russia. From there, John Quincy traveled with a friend to the cities of Stockholm and Gothenberg in Sweden, Copenhagen, Denmark and Kiel, Denmark (which is now in Germany). Meanwhile, John Adams had become ill and physicians recommended that he go to the famous health spa in Bath, England, to recover. John Quincy accompanied his father there. In 1784, father and son returned to Massachusetts. John Quincy now felt he was ready for college. He entered Harvard intending to study law and graduated in 1787, second in his class of fifty-one.

Politics. Practicing law seemed to be a sure way to financial security, so Adams arranged to read for the law, or serve as a law clerk, under the successful attorney Theophilus Parsons. He (actually his father) would pay Parsons $100 when his training was completed. Although he studied earnestly as always, Adams discovered he disliked practicing law. Nevertheless, on August 9, 1790, he opened a law office on Court Street in Boston. Business was slow. Fortunately, his father's business grew so rapidly that he needed help in operating it. Adams took the job, managing the business when his father was out of town. The salary it provided allowed Adams to focus less on law and to write his own ideas about politics. So as not to upset his father's political plans, Adams wrote under the names of Publicola and Menander.

Minister in Europe. In 1794, George Washington was serving his second term as president of the United States and John Adams his second term as vice president. Agents for the new country were busy around the world trying to establish trade relations that would help pay for the large costs of the Revolutionary War. The president searched for someone to represent American interests in Holland. Adams had been there and spoke the languages most used in Europe. Also, he understood the goals of the president and vice president. At the age of twenty-seven, Adams was appointed Minister Resident to the Hague, the capital of the Netherlands.

Louisa Catherine Adams. The new minister's job at the Hague concerned trade and financial matters. Perhaps the most memorable part of the stay in Holland was a visit to Joshua Johnson, the American minister to Britain. There were several young ladies in the Johnson home, but one caught Adams's eye. After a series of visits, he and Louisa Catherine Johnson became engaged.

The wedding was delayed and delayed again as Adams was sent first to London to help John Jay arrange a peace treaty there, then to Portugal. Louisa grew more and more impatient. When his father became the new president of the United States, Adams was reassigned to be the United States minister to Berlin. Finally, in early July 1797, Adams asked Louisa to set a date for their marriage. Having been forced to wait nearly three years, Louisa chose July 26, 1797.

The stay in Berlin proved uneventful except for the arranging of a trade agreement with Prussia. Near the end of John Adams's term as president, it appeared that he and the Federalists might lose the election to Thomas Jefferson and the Republicans. Adams wondered how he should behave as minister for the new president if this happened. President Adams also had considered the awkward position his son would be in should Jefferson become president, so he recalled John Quincy from Berlin before leaving office in 1801.

State Legislator Adams. A year later, John Quincy resumed his political career as a member of the Massachusetts governing body, the General Court. A year after that, the Federalist party elected him United States senator from Massachusetts. Although a Federalist, Adams soon established himself as an independent voter in Congress. He took office just as the Louisiana Purchase was being considered. On his first vote as a senator, Adams joined the Republicans to approve this purchase. Four years later, he also supported President Jefferson in placing an embargo, or ban, on trade with Great Britain and France.

Adams was defeated in his bid for re-election to the Senate. Afterward he joined the Republican Party and became a professor of public speaking at Harvard.

United States Minister Adams. Jefferson served his two terms in the presidency and was replaced by James Madison. One of Madison's first moves was to send Adams to Russia as part of a commission to secure that country's help in settling America's differences with Great Britain. Adams was in Paris when the Treaty of Ghent ended the War of 1812 without a victory for either side.

At war's end Adams was assigned to London as representative to a convention concerning trade and navigation between America and Europe. While there, he was appointed as the new minister to Great Britain. This was a position his father had filled earlier and his own son, Charles, would fill later. In 1815, however, the British were still smarting from having to make peace with the upstart United States. Adams could accomplish little in London.

Secretary of State Adams. Succeeding Madison as president, James Monroe recalled Adams and appointed him secretary of state. His job now was to advance the Monroe Doctrine, which he largely wrote. It proclaimed that the United States would not interfere in affairs in Europe and that the United States had the sole right to participate in activities in the Americas. As secretary of state, Adams also arranged for the United States to acquire Florida from Spain.

President Adams. As President Monroe's term in office came to a close in 1824, the race for his replacement heated up. The Republicans had four strong men interested in the job: Secretary of State John Quincy Adams, Secretary of War John C. Calhoun, Secretary of the Treasury William Crawford, and Congressman Henry

Clay. The famous general of the recent War of 1812, Andrew Jackson, opposed them. Although Jackson drew the most popular votes, no one won a majority of the votes in the electoral college. It fell to the House of Representatives to choose the new president from among the top three contenders. Though Henry Clay had a great deal of influence in the House, he did not have enough electoral votes to be considered. He decided to use his influence to elect John Quincy Adams, who became the sixth president of the United States. Henry Clay was rewarded by assignment as secretary of state.

Now, in 1825, John Quincy Adams took the position his father had prepared him for all his life. He came to the presidency filled with ideas and plans: expand the country's roads and canals, build a national university, and create a standard system of weights and measures for American business. However, he was bitterly opposed by Jackson supporters inside and outside of Congress. In addition, the new states west of the Appalachian Mountains were beginning to feel their strength and were dividing the country into special-interest groups. Adams's term as president turned out to be perhaps his most unproductive years in politics. After a single term, the people's choice, Andrew Jackson, became president. Adams returned to a quiet private life.

Congressman Adams. The quiet life lasted only a year, however. Adams was asked to run for Congress as a representative from his district. Some wondered if that position would not be insulting to a former president, but Adams assured them that it would be an honor for anyone to serve his country in any position. He became a representative from Massachusetts in 1831 and held that office for seventeen years. It was in this period that Adams performed his greatest services to the nation in support of citizen's rights and those working to abolish slavery.

Participation: The Antislavery Movement

Position on slavery. Adams had established an early reputation for siding with any just cause regardless of his political party's position. By 1820, he had come to regard slavery as an institution that would destroy the United States. He correctly predicted that slavery would lead the nation into war unless it was curbed. Rather than promoting drastic changes, however, he proposed a gradual approach to abolition. He wanted to first deny the importation of slaves, then refuse to allow slavery in new states, and, by 1845, end slavery altogether. Although he was never an avowed abolitionist, he opposed in Congress any movement that supported slavery.

The right to petition. One consuming interest of the new congressman was the right declared in the Constitution of citizens to petition government for action on issues they considered important. In the 1830s, the growing movement to abolish slavery resulted in a great number of petitions to Congress each year. Congress wearied of these petitions, but Adams seemed receptive to them; in fact he received more petitions than any other member of Congress.

John Quincy Adams and the Right to Petition

February 14, 1838, was Adams's finest day for petitions. He read 350 petitions to Congress; 246 concerned slavery, including:

158 petitions to cancel the gag rule

65 for abolishing slavery in the District of Columbia

17 for prohibiting slave trade within the United States

4 for abolishing slavery in United States territories

2 opposing admission of any new state that allowed slavery

Adams felt responsible to the citizens and insisted on reading their petitions at each session of Congress. At one session, he read a petition supposedly signed by twenty-two slaves even though slaves had no legal rights as citizens. At another session he received more than 500 petitions to abolish slavery. This was too much even for Adams to read and he suggested to Congress that he read one and indicate receiving the 500 petitions. When some pro-slavery congressmen objected, Adams countered that he would then read each of the 500 petitions separately. By 1837, probably in response to Adams's endless reading of these petitions, Congress had developed a habit at the beginning of each session of enacting some form of "gag rule." The rules were patterned after what was known as the Pinckney Resolution: "All petitions, memorials, resolutions, propositions or papers, relating in any way to the subject of slavery or the abolition of slavery, shall without being printed or referred, be laid on the table, and that no further action whatever shall be had thereon" (Hecht, p. 545).

Each year, Adams would raise his objections to such a gag bill, pointing out that it could easily be extended to other subjects. And each year, he proceeded to read aloud the petitions sent to him even though they would be laid aside never to be discussed. In 1837, the first year of the gag rule, he managed to describe the contents of petitions from 228 women calling for immediate abolition of slavery in the District of Columbia. Adams was ordered to take his seat and stop talking about the petitions.

The next year the gag rule was renewed by a vote of 139 to 69. That same year Adams asked to read a petition seemingly from some slaves in South Carolina. Congress refused him. The joke was on Congress, however. Adams had tricked the House into embarrassing itself. He had asked to read a phony petition, written by a slave owner who pretended it came from some slaves, begging Congress not to abandon slavery. The following session a gag rule was again enacted by a vote of 163 to 18.

Impeachment. At another session of Congress, Adams read a petition not directly related to slavery but written by abolitionists calling for the immediate breakup of the United States government. For reading this, Adams was called up on impeachment charges. He then exercised his great powers as a speaker, asking, whenever he tired, the clerk of Congress to read the part of the Constitution that defined the right of citizens to petition. A weary Congress finally agreed to drop the impeachment charges if he would withdraw the petition. Adams refused and continued to defend himself until a worn-out Congress decided to drop the whole matter.

The *Amistad*. The *Amistad* incident of 1839, involving the fate of a ship and its human cargo, brought national focus to the plight of slaves. Even though in 1817 Britain and other European nations, including Spain, had agreed to make importing slaves illegal, a Spanish ship, the *Teçora,* had sailed to Sierra Leone, Africa and taken on a cargo of slaves bound for Cuba. Although illegal, the slave trade was still profitable in the Spanish islands because once a slave ship landed there, a quirk in the law made the slaves legal property. After the *Teçora* landed, two slave traders picked out 49 men and 3 young girls from the more than 1,000 Africans confined in a large holding barn. These slaves were put aboard a low, black coastal ship to be taken 200 miles to Port Principe. The ship, *Amistad,* was already loaded with trade goods, including pottery, copper plates, and silks. The slaves were put below in the cargo storage

▲ Joseph Cinqué

area, but were not shackled in any way. Since they needed to be kept healthy, a few at a time were brought on deck for exercise.

It may have been an incident during one of these exercise periods that began the uprising. As the story goes, one of the captives (none of whom spoke English or Spanish, only African languages) managed by signs to ask a crewman what would happen to them. The crewman, who was the vessel's cook, in jest signaled that the slaves were to be cut up and eaten by whites. Whatever the truth of this story, the captive, a man named Singbe, began to stir the blacks to riot. (All the captives had been given Spanish names, Singbe was called Joseph Cinquez, or Cinqué.) When a crewman flogged another captive for taking an extra drink of water, the riotous feelings on the ship grew.

The slaves rebelled, killing the captain and cook. Cinqué kept the two slave owners alive to serve as navigators on a voyage that would return them to Sierra Leone. However, the slave owners managed to direct the ship in a crisscross pattern along the American coast. Nearly starved, the blacks broke open the ship's cargo and helped themselves to raisins, medicines, and wine. Some became drunk, some sick, and some died.

The Case of Dorcas Allen

Dorcas Allen had been freed by her dying mistress fifteen years earlier. She had married a free black man and raised a family. Years later, a slave hunter named Rezen Orme discovered that the dying mistress had not completed a certificate giving Dorcas her freedom. He seized Dorcas and her children and sold them to a southern slave owner. Separated from her husband, Dorcas became temporarily insane. She cut the throats of two of her children and tried to commit suicide. John Quincy Adams became interested in her case. He visited Dorcas in prison, and counseled her husband, Nathan. Then he forced the slave owner to give back to her and her two other children their freedom for $475. Her husband raised the money, with the help of $50 donated by Adams.

An international incident. The ship became more worn and the sails tattered. As the *Amistad* floundered along the coast, several ships reported sighting the long black vessel. Some even came close enough to see if the ship needed help, but hastily withdrew after spotting armed blacks aboard. Finally a navy patrol boat under the command of Lieutenant Thomas R. Gedney took the *Amistad* in tow and brought it to New London, Connecticut.

Gedney claimed the ship and its cargo, including the captives, as salvage. The contents, he argued, should by rights be his. Spain demanded the immediate return of the ship and cargo to Cuba. One of these claims would have ended the case quietly except for an abolitionist leader, Lewis Tappan. He enlisted the aid of a New York paper, the *Emancipator,* in publicizing the event. After much delay, the complicated case was brought to court. Spain had outlawed the transport of slavery, but approved the sale of slaves once they arrived in Cuba. The *Amistad* was a Spanish ship. However, the captives had been taken illegally from Sierra Leone and were certainly not captive slaves at the time Gedney took them in his charge. They had freed themselves at sea. After much deliberation, Judge Andrew Judson ruled that the blacks were free to return to Africa. The United States had no right to try them for murdering the ship's captain and four-man crew at sea.

The case was not closed, however. Spain was still pressing its demand for the ship, and Gedney was still pressing his claim for salvage. Secretary of State John Forsyth, himself a Georgia slave owner, sided mostly with the Spanish. President Martin Van Buren did not want an international incident over the thirty-nine remaining blacks, so he prevailed on the appeals court to send the case to the Supreme Court. With the government involved in the prosecution, Ellis Grey Loring, an abolitionist attorney aiding the blacks, felt that he needed a nationally recognized authority to bolster his side. He asked John Quincy Adams to help.

Adams for the defense. Adams had always been quick to take up the challenge of a just cause. He accepted the offer and spent many hours discussing the legal points with the defense lawyers and many hours writing letters explaining the legal positions. Other lawyers presented the case in court (the chief defense attorney was Roger Baldwin). Finally, Adams presented his argument in a six-hour defense that focused on the meaning of the Constitution and on America's position as the champion of justice for all. He also accused the U.S. executive branch of unfair sympathy for the two Spanish slave holders over the black rebels.

The Supreme Court's decision was read by Justice William Story. The ship would be given to Gedney as legitimate salvage at sea. But at the time he took the ship, the blacks aboard were freemen, transported illegally under international law, and were free to return to Africa. Off the record, Story called Adams's defense an "extraordinary argument ... for its power, for its bitter sarcasm, and its dealing with topics far beyond the record and points of discussion" (Jones, p. 182). After much negotiation with the United States and England, abolitionists finally chartered a ship and returned Cinqué and his friends to Sierra Leone. (Cinqué later became an interpreter for the American Missionary Association among the African blacks.) Americans had for eighteen months used the *Amistad* affair as a vehicle to make public the evils of the

African slave trade and of slavery itself. No case involving slavery would attract as much attention for the next two decades.

Aftermath

In Congress. Adams returned to Congress, where he continued to champion the right of citizens to petition the government. During his last years, he helped secure approval for Texas to join the Union and saw the outbreak of the Mexican War. Adams collapsed on the floor of Congress in February 1848. He died on February 23.

The Adams family. Charles Adams served in the Massachusetts legislature as his father had done and later followed in the footsteps of his famous grandfather and father as a representative of Massachusetts in Congress. He was a member of Congress when the Civil War, long ago predicted by his father, began. After the war he served as minister to Great Britain at a time nearly as dismal as that in which his father and grandfather had served. All this service to his country was somewhat surprising given that Charles had once expressed his dislike of politics. At that time Adams had lectured his son: "I've never sought office but I have no dislike of it. In a Republican Government the Country has a right to the services of every Citizen. And each Citizen is bound in duty to perform the service" (Hecht, p. 463). Charles's son, John Quincy Adams II, served in the legislature between 1866 and 1877.

The Adams family was not without its woes. John Quincy's oldest son, George, drifted from one escapade to another, never able to direct his attention for long. As early as 1827 he was being cared for because of a nervous illness. He repeatedly got involved in losing ventures. Adams paid off his son's debts several times and tried to get him into some useful work. In the end, his parents refused to help him further. By 1828, George had apparently grown mentally ill and had given up hope; at age twenty-seven he killed himself by jumping off a ship. A third son, John, also died at a young age in 1833. Adams's wife, Louisa, died in 1852, having been in ill health much of her married life.

Adams legacy. Adams had fought hard for the citizen's right to petition and for the elimination of injustice and slavery. In 1844, four years before his death, he finally succeeded in having the gag rule that forbade petitions about slavery removed from the rules of Congress.

For More Information

Allen, David G. *Diary of John Quincy Adams.* Washington, D.C.: Howard University Press, 1982

Hecht, Marie B. *John Quincy Adams.* New York: Macmillan, 1972.

Jones, Howard. *Mutiny on the Amistad.* New York: Oxford University Press, 1987.

Antislavery Movement

1774–1804
States in the North free slaves or adopt laws to gradually free them.

1808
U.S. Congress bans slave trade.

1820
Missouri admitted to the union as a slave state; slavery barred in other areas of Louisiana Purchase.

1829
David Walker writes *Appeal,* calling for violent slave revolt.

1831
William Lloyd Garrison begins publishing *The Liberator;* Nat Turner executes rebellion.

1832
Race riot occurs in Philadelphia.

1839
Liberty Party formed to outlaw slavery through political action.

1845
Frederick Douglass publishes *Narrative of the Life of Frederick Douglass.*

1848
Free-Soil Party, formed in part by unhappy Democrats, promises to abolish slavery in District of Columbia.

1850
Sojourner Truth publishes *Narrative of Sojourner Truth.*

1852
Harriet Beecher Stowe publishes *Uncle Tom's Cabin.*

1860
Civil War begins.

1863
Emancipation Proclamation frees slaves in Confederate states.

1865
Thirteenth Amendment ends slavery in the United States.

ANTISLAVERY MOVEMENT

Some of America's colonists, Quakers in Pennsylvania, objected to slavery as early as 1688. Such talk increased in the Revolutionary period, with all its discussion of liberty and equality. In the North, state after state began to free its slave population, starting with Rhode Island in 1774 and ending with New Jersey with a plan adopted in 1804 to gradually free slaves. Meanwhile, in 1794, the first society was organized to outlaw slavery throughout the United States. It began a movement that would continue for the next seventy-one years. Members of the movement, both whites and blacks, were called abolitionists because they intended to abolish, or wipe out, the slave trade and slavery in America.

The abolitionists used several tactics in their struggle against slavery. Foremost among them was moral persuasion—that is, convincing whites that slavery was morally wrong. Other tactics involved political action: sending antislavery petitions to Congress and forming a third political party, that was against slavery. Some protesters boycotted, or refused to purchase, goods produced by slave labor. Rarer but more direct was the tactic of armed rebellion to end slavery.

Though armed revolts did occur from time to time, they were always quelled by the overwhelming force of the whites. In 1831, Nat Turner led a deadly revolt, creating widespread alarm in the South (see **Nat Turner**). Two years earlier, a free black named

David Walker had penned his Appeal, a passionate call for slaves throughout the South to take up arms and revolt. Many Southerners blamed Walker at least partly for inspiring Turner to stage his bloody revolt. After Walker's mysterious death in 1830, his *Appeal* was reprinted and circulated to the public several times.

The same year that Walker died, the American Colonization Society sent 259 free blacks to Liberia, a colony in Africa. Early reformers felt that blacks would never be able to join American society on an equal footing. Many of them recognized prejudices in the North, where blacks were free, and feared a race war if the entire population of blacks were to win liberty and remain in the United States. Such thinking led Thomas Jefferson and others to propose a program of gradually freeing the slaves and setting up colonies for them elsewhere, usually in Africa. The idea appealed to a few black leaders, but most free blacks scorned this approach. They considered the United States their home.

William Lloyd Garrison was a white reformer who also scorned this approach. In 1831, Garrison began publishing *The Liberator,* which became the most influential antislavery newspaper. He called for immediate freedom for all blacks, along with recognition of their rightful place as equal citizens who belonged in America if they wished to stay. At first Garrison enjoyed little support for immediate abolition, at least among whites. It was the free black community that kept *The Liberator* alive, buying subscriptions and offering donations. Slowly, Garrison's following grew.

By the late 1830s, abolitionism had become an organized movement with increasing support from whites. Theodore Weld helped found the American Anti-Slavery Society in 1834, two years after Garrison founded the New England Anti-Slavery Society. Weld brought the cause into the political arena, in contrast to Garrison, who stubbornly insisted that it was a moral problem, not a political one. Weld and his followers lobbied Congress for antislavery laws. He also took the cause to college campuses. Weld led students from Lane Theological Seminary in Cincinnati, Ohio, to the city's slums. Together they set up libraries and taught evening classes to blacks until college leaders declared there should be no direct ties between their campus and antislavery activities. In response, Weld left the college, as did many of the students. Some

▲ **An 1835 handbill published by the American Anti-Slavery Society**

of them went on to become traveling antislavery agents and were jeered at by crowds who threw rotten eggs and stones at them.

Abolitionists faced hostile audiences in the North. The English ended slavery in the British Empire in 1833, and it was believed they were stirring up the movement in America to create disharmony in the new nation. Anti-abolitionists thought of themselves as defenders of American liberty when they rioted in the 1830s, destroying abolitionist printing presses and attacking free blacks. Meanwhile, the campaign to sway public opinion continued. Anti-

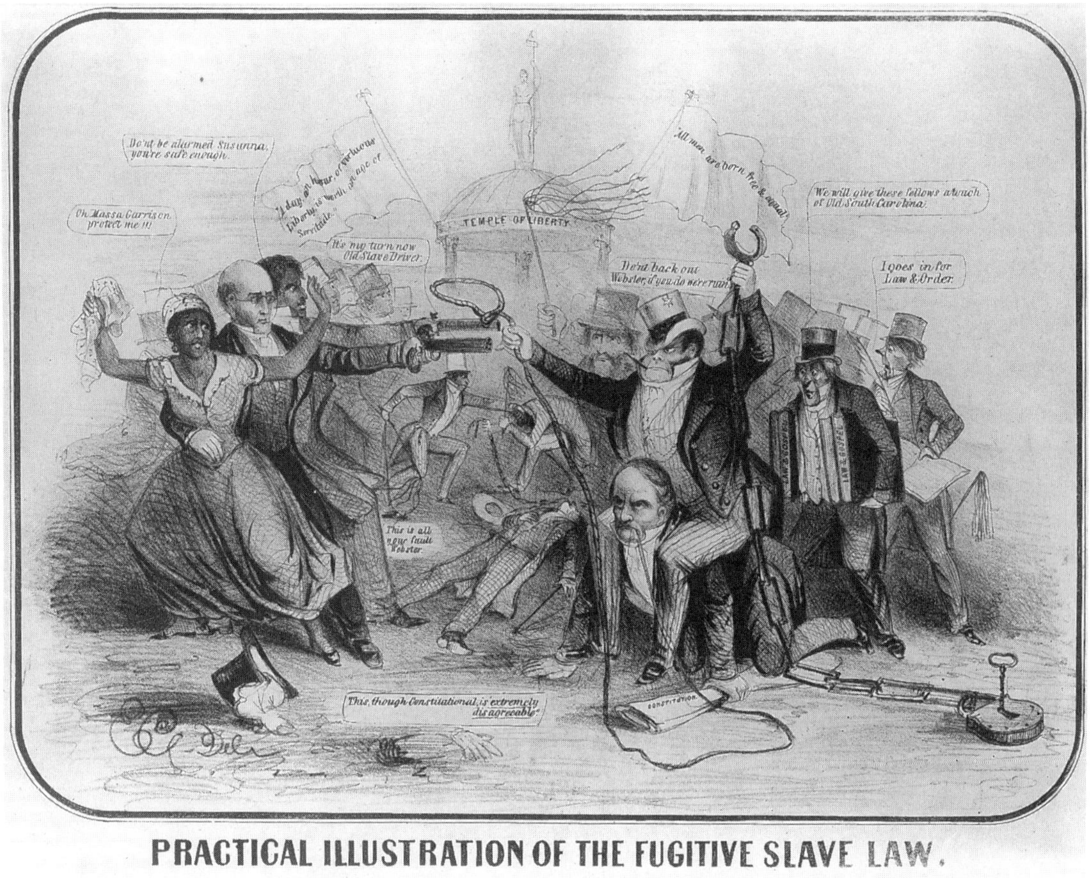

▲ **Both the abolitionists and slaveholders were lampooned in the press**

slavery speakers made appearance after public appearance. A million pieces of antislavery mail were sent out in 1835 alone. Antislavery bazaars raised funds for the movement. And propaganda was spread through posters, candy wrappers, songs, and children's readers that carried antislavery messages. But not all antislavery mail reached its destination. South Carolina destroyed all such mail sent into the state.

Frederick Douglass, an escaped slave whom Garrison invited to speak at a meeting in 1841, was a tall, powerful speaker for the cause. Also a writer, Douglass produced an autobiography that was read by many whites. His book became the model of a new literary form, the slave narrative. **Sojourner Truth,** another former slave turned public speaker, also carried the antislavery message to white audiences. Her balance of passionate conviction and earthy humor enlivened public gatherings to which she was invited on her travels in New England and the West.

The greatest single factor in changing public opinion, however, was the appearance in 1852 of *Uncle Tom's Cabin* by **Harriet Beecher Stowe.** Partly inspired by Douglass's autobiography, the novel tells the story of a gentle and religious slave, Tom, who is beaten to death by his evil master but forgives him just before dying. The story, read and discussed throughout the North and South, had a huge impact on the public's view of slavery as an evil. It came out in monthly chapters with dramatic endings, and the entire tale became a stage play attended by enthusiastic audiences. *Uncle's Tom Cabin* helped antislavery immensely. Mindful of the novel's huge impact, Abraham Lincoln quipped that it had brought on the Civil War.

Thus, the abolition movement was a mix of methods and personalities, and they all drew attention to the cause. Yet abolition never became popular in pre-Civil War America, even in the North. It would take the war to make the cause an urgent one, and the Emancipation Proclamation along with the Thirteenth Amendment to end slavery altogether in the nation.

David Walker

1785-1830

Personal Background

Very little is known about David Walker's childhood. He was born in Wilmington, North Carolina, on September 28, 1785, the son of a free black woman and a slave father. His father had died several months before his birth. In slave states, if a mother were free, so were her children. Technically, David was freeborn, but even so, he spent his early years in the midst of what his father had endured as a slave. In the South, where most free blacks lived, slavery was a constant presence, visible everywhere. Even in the North, where most states had outlawed slavery by the early 1800s, the practice of segregation, or separation of the races, and other civil rights restrictions reminded blacks that they were not accepted as equals in white society.

Education. Slaveholders usually discouraged education for the slaves, knowing that the slaves' ignorance made them easier to control. (Slaveholders lived in constant fear of revolt.) In some areas it was even illegal to teach slaves to read and write. Still, a few slaveholders permitted or even encouraged their slaves to learn and a few deliberately educated their slaves before setting them free.

Somehow, Walker, a free black, learned to read and write as a youth. Though some free black communities supported their own schools, often, education meant no more than informal lessons from

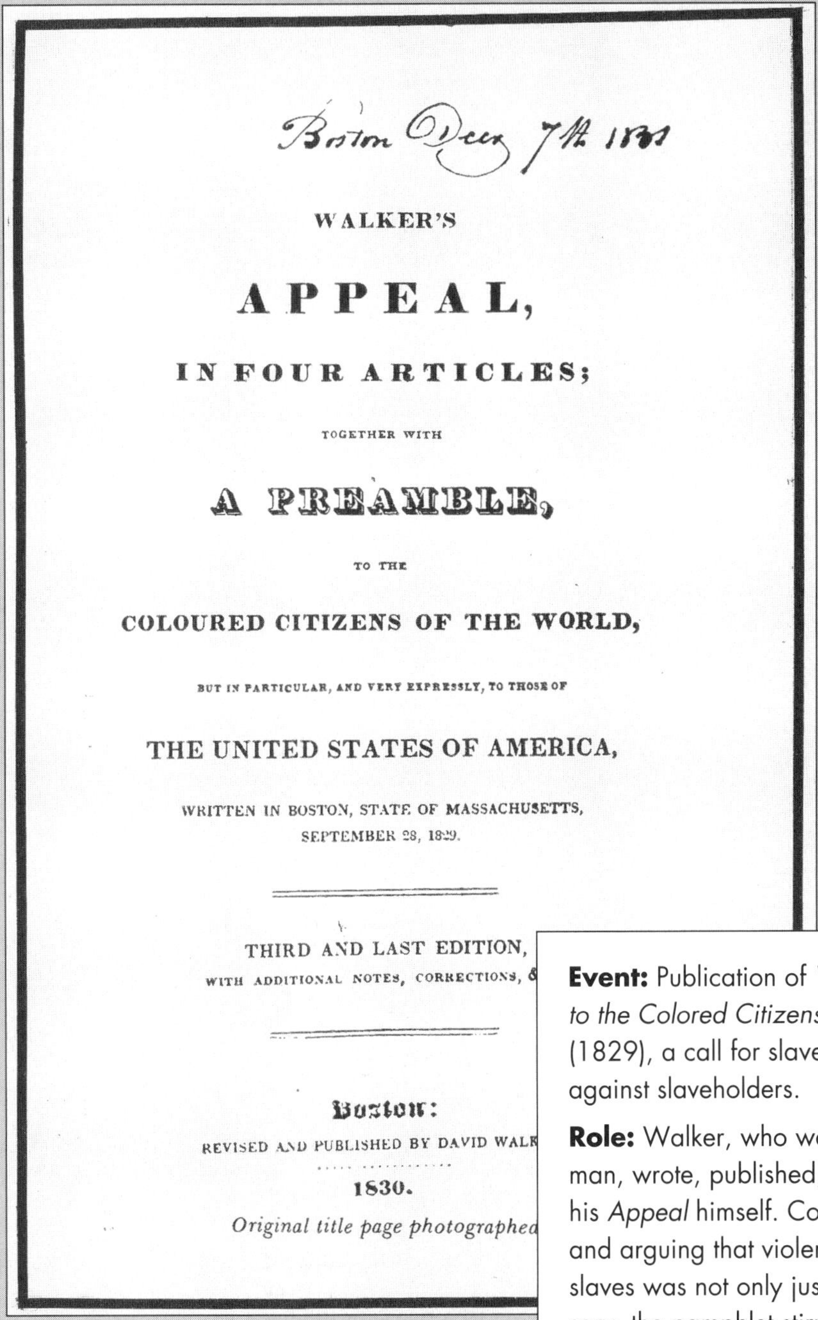

Boston Decr 7th 1831

WALKER'S

APPEAL,

IN FOUR ARTICLES;

TOGETHER WITH

A PREAMBLE,

TO THE

COLOURED CITIZENS OF THE WORLD,

BUT IN PARTICULAR, AND VERY EXPRESSLY, TO THOSE OF

THE UNITED STATES OF AMERICA,

WRITTEN IN BOSTON, STATE OF MASSACHUSETTS,
SEPTEMBER 28, 1829.

THIRD AND LAST EDITION,
WITH ADDITIONAL NOTES, CORRECTIONS, &

Boston:
REVISED AND PUBLISHED BY DAVID WALK

1830.

Original title page photographed

▲ ***Walker's Appeal***

Event: Publication of *Walker's Appeal to the Colored Citizens of the World* (1829), a call for slaves to rise up against slaveholders.

Role: Walker, who was a free black man, wrote, published, and distributed his *Appeal* himself. Condemning slavery and arguing that violent revolt by the slaves was not only justified but necessary, the pamphlet stirred the fears of whites, the pride of blacks, and the anger and outrage of both.

adults who had struggled for learning themselves. Regardless of how he learned, it is clear from the references in his later writing to ancient Greek and Roman, European, and American history that Walker spent long hours poring over many history books in his youth, despite the obstacles of poverty and discrimination.

Travels. From an early age, Walker held a deep hatred of slavery, which was probably passed on to him by his free mother. His feelings were strengthened by his travels around the South and, perhaps, in other parts of the United States. Slaves in the South generally lived and ate in a way comparable to that of the poorest nations today—except, of course, that they were forced to work hard all day long, from before dawn to after dark. Although conditions varied, working as a plantation slave was very much like spending your life in a prison camp with hard labor. Some slaveholders, however, looked after them well; Thomas Jefferson, for example, built apartments for his slaves that were better than the houses of most poor whites.

For the most part, however, huts were pieced together from a few scraps of wood, with dirt for floors. Slaves usually had no more furniture other than a few planks for a bed. Food amounted to a little corn and maybe some bacon or herring, rationed out in small amounts each month. Most men and women wore only a single piece of clothing: a pair of tattered pants, or a shirt, dress, or underwear. Children often wore no clothes at all.

Families were routinely broken up when a wife, husband, or child was sold to a new master, which often happened with no warning. The white male owners could and sometimes did force themselves sexually on slave women of any age at any time they pleased. Many slave children had white fathers because the master had raped their mothers. And there were constant whippings to punish even the smallest offense—or for no reason at all. European or northern visitors to the plantations reported that the cries of those being whipped could be heard all day long. Not used to viewing humans as pieces of property, the visitors were disturbed by the cries, which the slaveholders had long stopped hearing. In his own travels around the South, Walker faced constant reminders of how his people were being treated.

"Enlightened and Christian nation." Seeing the conditions under which the slaves lived and worked, Walker became convinced that no people anywhere had ever suffered more. As he later wrote in the *Appeal,* his condemnation of slavery, black slaves were "the most degraded, wretched, and abject set of beings that ever lived since the world began; and I pray God that none like us ever may live again until time shall be no more" (Aptheker, p. 63). Walker also grew scornful of the hypocrisy of white Americans who claimed to be Christians and to love freedom and liberty while either keeping slaves or allowing slavery to exist at all. In the first paragraph of the *Appeal,* for example, he sarcastically refers to the United States as "this enlightened and Christian nation" (Aptheker, p. 63). Though the tone is angry, Walker's *Appeal* is filled with entertaining sarcasm, showing that Walker was able to balance his bitterness with a lively sense of humor.

"Free" Blacks in America

By the 1820s, America's black population had reached nearly 2 million, of which about 250,000 were free and the rest slaves. Most of the free blacks, about 150,000, lived in the South, where they had virtually no rights or legal protection. In the North, too, "freedom" did not mean equality. Blacks could only vote in a few states, and most states had laws against blacks marrying whites, testifying against whites in court, or moving into a state in order to look for work or a home. Riots against black neighborhoods were common in northern cities.

North to Philadelphia. Disgusted by slavery, and by the treatment of free blacks in the South, Walker decided to move to the North sometime in the early 1820s. He went first to Philadelphia, Pennsylvania where he came under the influence of black leader Richard Allen, bishop and founder of the African Methodist Episcopalian (AME) Church. Allen's church was a major force among free black abolitionists. Allen led black opposition to "colonization," the idea that blacks should leave the United States and set up their own communities abroad. Based on the assumption that blacks could never live happily in white society, colonization had supporters among both black and white abolitionists. Those who opposed it, like Allen and William Lloyd Garrison, stressed the contributions that patriotic blacks had made to America and demanded that blacks be accepted on an equal basis with other Americans (see **William Lloyd Garrison**). Strong-willed and popular, Allen undoubtedly helped shape Walker's views during the time he stayed in Philadelphia.

Boston. By about 1825 Walker had moved to Boston, Massachusetts. In 1826, as soon as it was created, he joined the General Colored Association of Massachusetts, an organization of free black abolitionists who also strongly opposed colonization. He immediately took an active role in the association and in 1828 gave a speech calling for opposition not only to slavery but to slaveholders' attempts to track down escaped slaves in the North. Walker also acted as Boston agent for two black New York weeklies, *Freedom's Journal* and *Rights of All,* and helped collect money to purchase the freedom of a young black poet from North Carolina.

Kidnaping of Solomon Northup

During the early decades of the 1800s, southern slaveholders had the legal right to track down escaped slaves in the North, capture them without any trial, and bring them back to the South. The slaveholders began going North not only to catch escaped slaves, but to capture free blacks and make the false claim that they had escaped. A free black from New York named Solomon Northup spent twelve years as a slave in Louisiana after being taken this way in 1841. Only when he got word to friends in New York were the friends able to come South and prove that he had been wrongly seized. Hundreds of others were not so lucky. An educated man and a violinist, Northup wrote of his ordeal in a book called *Twelve Years a Slave.*

Clothing shop. In the meantime, Walker opened a clothing shop on Brattle Street, near the bustling wharves of Boston harbor. His shop was probably of a type common at the time, a sort of pawnshop for secondhand sailors' gear. The sailors could sell the shop their heavy sea clothes and equipment when they went ashore, then return to buy a new outfit on finding another job at sea. Segregation meant that being a sailor was one of the few jobs widely available to free black men. Consequently, many free blacks either were sailors or had work connected with sailing. For example, James Forten, a wealthy and well-known leader of Philadelphia's black community, had made his money as a sailmaker. Walker's vocal presence at meetings and his magnetic personality were making him better known in Boston's black community. His clothing shop became an informal meeting place, where sailors and others could gather to talk things over and exchange information.

Publication of the *Appeal*. Adding to Walker's growing reputation were the strength of his views and the flowing speech with which he presented them. In 1829, he gave those views full expression by writing and publishing *Walker's Appeal, in Four Articles; Together with A Preamble, to the Colored Citizens of the World, But in Particular, and Very Expressly, to those of the United States of America.* A pamphlet of seventy-six pages, the *Appeal* sent immediate shock waves throughout America, but especially through the South. In one year, Walker had printed and distributed three editions, the last of which was even more radical than the first two. The work was read and passed around among slaves, free blacks, and whites alike. Almost overnight, Walker became the most famous black man in America and, to some, the most hated.

Marriage and family. In 1828, the year before the publication of his *Appeal,* Walker married a woman named Eliza. Nothing is known about her or about their relationship, although a son was born shortly after Walker's death. Named Edwin G. Walker, their son was elected to the Massachusetts House of Representatives in 1866.

Sailors' pockets? Like so much else about his little-known life, how David Walker managed to distribute his *Appeal* so successfully remains a mystery. One sensible suggestion is that he cleverly used his clothing shop, both by handing out copies to black sailors and by stuffing them into the roomy pockets of heavy garments like jackets and pants. The copies would be found later by sailors—white or black—and read during idle hours at sea. When coming ashore, the sailors might bring a copy with them and leave it at a waterfront tavern. Shipping was heavy between North and South, and most copies seem to have found their way into southern states through port cities like Savannah, Georgia, Charleston, South Carolina, and New Orleans, Louisiana. It was certainly in such cities that southern reaction was quickest and strongest. The slaveholders, always fearful of uprisings, still had strong memories of Denmark Vesey's 1822 slave revolt.

Reaction. The *Appeal* was banned in the South, and most southern states also put a price on Walker's head. In Georgia, when a single copy was found, the state legislature rushed a law through the next day that set the death penalty for anyone found distributing it. Savannah's mayor called on Boston mayor Harrison Gray Otis to punish Walker. Otis, though condemning Walker's views, wrote back that Walker had done nothing illegal under Massachusetts law. Southerners were not the only ones who were outraged by *Walker's Appeal,* however. Moderate and liberal northern whites, some of them supporting abolition, also condemned its call for violence. Even William Lloyd Garrison, though he later changed his mind and supported the *Appeal,* at first criticized it for promoting bloodshed. The pamphlet scorned blacks for submitting to slavery and encouraged them to rise up against it.

From the *Appeal*

"If you can only get courage into the blacks, I do declare it, that one good black man can put to death six white men; and I give it as a fact, let twelve black men get well armed for battle, and they will kill and put to flight fifty whites." (Aptheker, p. 89)

Content of *Walker's Appeal.* In reading the *Appeal,* it is hard to avoid the conclusion that Walker's powerful, passionate arguments, clearly and logically presented, were as responsible for the heated reaction as his call for violent revolt. He showed not only that slavery itself was wrong, but that it rested on a racial distinction that was also wrong. He attacked colonization efforts on the same ground. The *Appeal* also measured slavery against the moral standard of Christianity, finding a cruel hypocrisy in slaveholders who claimed to be Christian. "How can the preachers and people of America believe the Bible?" Walker asked. "Does it teach them any distinction on account of man's color?" (Aptheker, p. 106).

Walker also discussed the contradictions of allowing slavery in the country. He pointed to America's revolutionary past, taking the example of Thomas Jefferson, author of the Declaration of Independence. Walker poked bitter fun at Jefferson's writings, which include the famous "suspicion ... that blacks ... are inferior to whites in the endowments both of body and mind" (Davis, p. 289). Jefferson, of course, had also written in the Declaration that "all men are created equal." "See your Declaration, Americans!!!" Walker demanded. "Do you understand your own words?" (Davis, p. 289). Finally, he pointed out that Americans had fought for their own freedom, and asked why blacks should not be allowed to do the same. It is on this basis that he justified his call for open and violent revolt. At the same time, he suggested that the black community should show forgiveness if the slaves were freed.

Mysterious death. Rumors reached Boston that huge sums

of money had been offered for Walker's death, or even more if he was captured and brought South. Friends pleaded with him to go to Canada, but he refused, staying in Boston to prepare the second and third editions of his *Appeal*. In the *Appeal* itself, he had referred to the likelihood of his being killed for publicizing his views. On June 28, 1830, shortly after finishing the third edition, David Walker was found dead near the doorway of his clothing shop. The cause of death remained unexplained, but friends were convinced that he had been poisoned.

Aftermath

Radical, brilliant, uncompromising. *Walker's Appeal* undoubtedly changed the way blacks approached the issue of slavery. If it did not directly inspire revolts such as Nat Turner's in 1831, it certainly helped set the stage for them in popularizing the idea of rebellion. But more important perhaps, Walker's was the first black voice to use elements of white culture—Christianity and Western democracy, for example—to condemn slavery. Thus, he not only encouraged revolt, but also laid the foundation for the cooler arguments of men such as Frederick Douglass. Though the *Appeal* caused great commotion upon publication, including a raft of new pro-slavery arguments designed to counter it, its long-term impact was greater than the immediate controversy it stirred. A leading historian calls it "the most radical, brilliant and uncompromising assessment" of the blacks' situation before the Civil War and "one of the classic documents in the history of American civilization" (Davis, p. 287).

For More Information

Aptheker, Herbert. *"One Continual Cry": David Walker's Appeal to the Colored Citizens of the World.* New York: Humanities Press, 1965.

Davis, David Brion. *Antebellum American Culture.* Lexington, Massachusetts: D.C. Heath & Company, 1979.

Stewart, James Brewer. *Holy Warriors: The Abolitionists and American Slavery.* New York: Hill and Wang, 1976.

William Lloyd Garrison

1805-1879

Personal Background

William Lloyd Garrison was born on December 10 or 12, 1805, in Newburyport, Massachusetts. His parents, Abijah and Fanny Lloyd Garrison, had moved there from Saint John, a port city in the Canadian maritime province of New Brunswick. They had come with two children, James and Caroline; Lloyd, as William Lloyd Garrison was called, was born soon after. Fanny Lloyd had been a deeply religious woman when she married, and she was forced to rely on her faith as she worried about her husband, who stayed at sea for long periods of time. She also had to face his growing alcoholism, which was made worse by months of joblessness. Shipping was more active in Massachusetts than in New Brunswick. Fanny hoped that the move to Newburyport would provide Abijah with enough work to make him give up drinking.

Desertion. In 1807, President Thomas Jefferson, trying to avoid war with Britain and France, declared an embargo, or ban, on foreign trade. Stillness fell over the once-busy harborfront as shipping came to a stop. The following year, Lloyd's five-year-old sister Caroline died after eating some poisonous flowers. Abijah began drinking steadily, spending time in waterfront bars or bringing a drinking crowd home. One day Fanny threw his drinking friends out of the house and smashed his bottles. Abijah walked out and was never heard from again.

▲ **William Lloyd Garrison**

Event: Speeches and protests against slavery; publication of *The Liberator* (1831-1865); founding of New England Anti-Slavery Society (1832).

Role: For his refusal to compromise in his opposition to slavery, writer William Lloyd Garrison became known as the conscience of the abolition movement. He rejected political discussion of the issue and in his newspaper *The Liberator* called for immediate emancipation on moral grounds alone.

Proud boy with a tin bucket. Fanny was left alone to raise two boys as well as a new baby girl, Maria. She found it hard to get by. They roomed with a family called the Farnhams, and Mrs. Farnham often looked after the children while Fanny worked as a nurse, looking after elderly or sick people in the big houses of the wealthy. When he was old enough, Lloyd often went out to sell molasses candy on the street. Often, too, his mother sent him out with a tin bucket to collect scraps of leftover food from some of the big houses where she worked. On his way home he was usually stopped by bigger boys of the neighborhood, who crowded around him, making fun and demanding to see what was in the bucket. For Lloyd, these times were especially difficult. Not only was his family poor, but he was at the older boys' mercy because he had no father to protect him. A stubborn pride began growing inside him, a desire to show that he was as good—and as strong—as anyone else.

Painful penmanship. When he was not needed for work or collecting food, Lloyd attended the school across the street from the Farnham house. Because he was left-handed, he had trouble learning to write. Every time he started to write naturally, using his left hand, the teacher slapped his knuckles with a ruler and forced him to use his right hand. His writing skills lagged behind those of the other children, and his reading suffered also. Finally, he forced himself to practice writing with his right hand, and his penmanship gradually became the best in the school. Examples of Lloyd's writing were put on public display in Newburyport; for the rest of his life he would be known for his neat, finely shaped letters.

Odd jobs. When Lloyd was about seven, Fanny took James, her oldest and favorite child, to live in nearby Lynn, where she hoped to find more steady work for herself. She also hoped to apprentice James to a shoemaker. Lloyd stayed in Newburyport living with the Bartletts, the family of the local Baptist minister (whose church the religious Fanny had attended). He continued in school for awhile, but the Bartletts, far from wealthy themselves, needed him to help pay his way. He took whatever temporary jobs he could find—selling apples, sawing wood, or making "lasts," the wooden models used by shoemakers. At age nine, Lloyd, like James, became apprenticed to a Lynn shoemaker.

Baltimore and Newburyport. The following year Fanny

took the children to Baltimore, Maryland, where a friend planned to start a shoe factory. Lloyd missed Newburyport and the Bartletts, so after a few months, his mother sent him back to live with them once more. He enrolled in school again. Fanny, not convinced that schooling was as worthwhile as good old-fashioned work, soon arranged to have Lloyd apprenticed to another tradesman, this time in Haverhill, a town about fifteen miles from Newburyport. The homesick boy tied his belongings together in a bundle and headed back once again to the Bartletts. Finding a stagecoach bound for Newburyport, he waited until it was moving, then climbed upon the rear luggage rack. He amazed passengers during the journey. As the horse-drawn coach slowed for a stop, he would jump off. While it was stopped, he would walk happily by the waiting passengers, then repeat his trick of climbing on when the coach started moving again. At each stop, the passengers were surprised to see that the small boy on foot was keeping up with them with ease. Meanwhile, in Baltimore, James, following in his father's footsteps, had begun drinking and losing the jobs his mother kept finding for him. Like his father, too, he started taking sailor's jobs, alternating between months at sea and periods of idleness in waterfront bars.

Newburyport *Herald.* At age thirteen, Garrison began work as apprentice to a newspaperman, E. A. Allen, owner-editor of the Newburyport *Herald.* Garrison soon realized he had found a trade that he loved. He enjoyed setting up the type (the movable letters) in long racks to make a page of news and running the presses. He moved in with the Allens and was soon put in charge of the paper's presses and office work. Also, even more than with the Bartletts, Garrison enjoyed the security of living with a solid family. He became friends with some of the older printers working at the *Herald,* one of whom continued Garrison's education, teaching him some Latin and encouraging him to read works of English and American literature. Mr. Allen, who owned a large collection of books, also encouraged the boy to read in his spare time.

"An old bachelor." After three-and-a-half years of working hard and reading both books and other newspapers, Garrison wrote an article himself, a letter complaining about girls who sued when their boyfriends refused to marry them. He signed it "an old bachelor" and turned in the piece without letting Allen know who had written it. Allen read it out loud to the staff, handing it to the boy to put into type. Soon "an old bachelor" was making regular contributions to the *Herald,* though it was months before his identity was discovered.

On his own. In 1826, when Garrison was twenty, Allen loaned him enough money to buy his own small newspaper, which he called the *Free Press.* Although the paper lasted only a few months, it was as owner-editor of the *Free Press* that Garrison discovered a young man who would become one of America's most famous poets, John Greenleaf Whittier. Whittier's sister had secretly sent one of his poems to the paper, and Garrison, recognizing the talent of its author, searched him out. Two years younger than Garrison, Whittier would later become not only a famous poet but a major abolitionist in his own right, protesting against slavery in many of his poems.

After the failure of the *Free Press,* Garrison worked as editor at other newspapers, including Boston's *National Philanthropist,* a "reform" paper dedicated to fighting drinking. This subject matter—morality rather than politics or current events—appealed to Garrison, who had adopted the strongly religious views of his mother (who had died a few years earlier). Christian morality, along with the pride created by his difficult childhood, would drive his personality in the struggles to come.

Participation: Antislavery Movement

Benjamin Lundy and the *Genius.* When he was twenty-two years old, Garrison met Benjamin Lundy, a mild-mannered Quaker sixteen years his senior and an early voice in the movement to abolish slavery. Lundy had started his own newspaper in 1821, the *Genius of Universal Emancipation,* which was dedicated to the gradual freeing of the slaves. Lundy also supported the idea of sending groups of free blacks to areas outside of America. Called "colonization," this plan had achieved popularity among liberal whites who disliked slavery but hesitated over blacks and whites living together as equals in society. Impressed by Lundy, Garrison wrote several enthusiastic pieces for the *Philanthropist,* praising his work. Lundy responded by asking Garrison to join him in Baltimore as co-editor of the *Genius.* Garrison would eventually accept the offer.

Immediate freedom vs. gradual freedom. While he was in Boston thinking over Lundy's offer, Garrison was also preparing to devote himself and his life to the cause of freeing the slaves. He decided that his own views differed from Lundy's in two important ways. First, he rejected the widely held idea of gradual emancipation. Instead, he thought that anything other than *immediate* freedom was unacceptable. Second, he saw colonization as an unfair and unworkable option. All Americans had the right to stay in America, he reasoned, and in attempting to get rid of freed blacks, the colonizers were merely avoiding any real solution to the problem. Garrison would develop his thinking on these positions in future years, but these two demands would always be central to his crusade. In 1829, after careful consideration, he decided to accept Lundy's offer.

Before going south to Baltimore, Garrison was asked to give a speech at Boston's Park Street Church. Among those in the congregation was eighteen-year-old Harriet Beecher, daughter of the church's abolitionist pastor, Edward Beecher. More than a decade later, Harriet Beecher would write the famous antislavery novel *Uncle Tom's Cabin* (see **Harriet Beecher Stowe**).

Jailed for libel. A few months after joining the *Genius,* Garrison wrote two articles attacking a merchant from his hometown of Newburyport for carrying slaves in his ships. In the second article, he called the man and other slave traders "highway robbers and murderers." The man sued the newspaper, and a jury found Garrison guilty of criminal libel (knowingly writing false and hurtful statements about somebody). Because he could not pay the fine of $50 plus legal costs, the judge sent Garrison to jail.

Garrison enjoyed his time in jail, writing poems and articles describing his experience, as well as sending letters to friends and opponents (such as the judge who had sentenced him to jail). He was treated respectfully by the warden and by his fellow prisoners. All in all, this and other such experiences appealed to his highly developed sense of drama. As his enemies often pointed out, he was not a modest man, and being sent to jail allowed him to paint himself as the persecuted leader of a noble cause. The publicity he won drew the attention of a wealthy New York merchant and future abolitionist, Arthur Tappan, who paid his fine. Garrison left jail after seven weeks, more famous and more dedicated to opposing slavery than before.

The Liberator. His differences with Lundy eventually prompted Garrison to start his own newspaper, *The Liberator.* The first issue appeared on January 1, 1831. Garrison's co-publisher was his old friend Isaac Knapp from Newburyport, who had also worked on the *Herald.* Reliable and easygoing, Knapp was happy to follow Garrison in taking up the cause of American slaves. He would do much of the day-to-day printing work for *The Liberator.* Money for the paper came mostly from free black subscribers, many of whom Garrison had written to asking for help. The cost was $2 per year, but some bought more than one subscription and passed the extra copies out to friends. A black sailmaker in Philadelphia, Pennsylvania named James Forten, for example, sent $54 for twenty-seven subscriptions. The first issue was only four pages, with **THE LIBERATOR** in bold at the top of page 1, and the slogan "Our Country is the World—Our Countrymen Mankind" underneath. Near the top of the page, in the fashion of the day, was a poem greeting the public and describing *The Liberator*'s aims. Below the poem came Garrison's own statement in plain language. Its effect was more stirring than the poem itself.

"I will be heard." Garrison's statement includes the most famous passage that he ever wrote. It reflects his absolute refusal not only to compromise, but even to soften the very language he used in his attacks on slavery:

> I am aware, that many object to the severity of my language; but is there not cause for severity? I *will* be as harsh as truth, and as uncompromising as justice. On this subject I do not wish to think, or speak, or write, with moderation. No! no! Tell a man whose house is on fire, to give a moderate alarm; tell him to moderately rescue his wife from the hands of the ravisher; tell the mother to gradually extricate her babe from the fire into which it has fallen;—but urge me not to use moderation in a cause like the present. I am in earnest—I will not equivocate—I will not excuse—I will not retreat a single inch—AND I WILL BE HEARD. (Merrill, p. 45)

Objecting to slavery was not new. What Garrison did, however, was to reject the idea of allowing it to continue for another minute.

"Reasonable," "moderate" abolitionists who wanted to discuss the issue and different methods of emancipation were as guilty as the slave holders and slave traders themselves, Garrison claimed. It was not a position calculated to win him popularity. But then Garrison had no desire to be popular. He only wanted to be heard.

Questions of peace and violence. The 1820s had been a time of growing unrest among slaves in the South—and among free blacks in the North. In 1829, a free black Bostonian named David Walker wrote *Appeal to the Colored Citizens of the World,* a pamphlet that not only condemned slavery but also called for violent rebellion against it (see **David Walker**). Garrison, who as a Christian believed in peace as much as he hated slavery, at first disapproved of Walker's call for violent revolt. After Walker's mysterious death, however, Garrison reprinted the *Appeal* in an early issue of *The Liberator.* In August of the same year (1831), a Virginia black named Nat Turner led a slave revolt in which more than fifty white men, women, and children were killed and mutilated.

Outrage. Nat Turner's rebellion outraged whites in both the North and South. In the South especially, alarmed whites blamed Walker and Garrison for encouraging the violence. Walker's death left Garrison as the main target of their anger. Throughout the South, fines were set for people found circulating or even reading *The Liberator.* In Georgia, the legislature offered a $5,000 reward for capturing Garrison and bringing him to that state for trial. A number of southern mayors protested to the mayor of Boston, calling for action against Garrison. Predictably, Garrison did nothing to lessen the southerners' rage. Instead, he welcomed it and the growing fame that it brought. And while he continued to reject violence, he laid the blame for it squarely at the door of the whites who allowed slavery to exist, rather than blaming the rebels themselves. Turner and his followers had done nothing worse than "our fathers in slaughtering the British" (Merrill, p. 52). If Americans celebrated the Founding Fathers for fighting for freedom, he argued, how could they condemn the slaves for doing the same thing?

Radical thoughts, gentle manners. For all of the strength of his words, Garrison himself was a gentle and friendly man. From his early thirties he was almost completely bald, except for a fringe of dark hair around the side of his head. Tall and slender, with delicate features and small oval glasses perched on a narrow nose, he looked more like a meek schoolteacher than a fire-breathing fanatic. Once, when he and some friends were traveling by ship on their way to Philadelphia, one of his friends, the Reverend Samuel May, began chatting with another passenger. Learning that May was an abolitionist, the man began arguing with him. Garrison came up and joined the conversation as a crowd gathered, eventually persuading the man to accept his views. "If all the Abolitionists were like you, there would be much less opposition," the man said. "But, sir," he continued, "that hair-brained, reckless, violent fanatic, Garrison, will damage, if he does not shipwreck, any cause." At that point, May stepped up, saying, "Allow me, sir, to introduce Mr. Garrison, of whom you entertain so bad an opinion. The gentleman you have been talking with is he" (Merrill, p. 77).

New England Anti-Slavery Society. For some time Garrison had wanted to form an organized group dedicated to the goal of immediate abolition. In 1832, he did so; the New England Anti-Slavery Society was the first American antislavery group founded on "immediatist" ideas. His leadership of the society confirmed his place at the forefront of the abolition movement in America. Garrison dominated the society, which included many free black members. Aside from its antislavery work, it ran educational and other programs in support of the free black community. In doing so, it differed sharply from such abolitionist groups as the American Colonization Society, which wanted to remove the free blacks from America. The Colonization Society, as Garrison rightly pointed out, believed that blacks could not be educated. Garrison's 1832 pamphlet *Thoughts on African Colonization* sharply attacked the colonizers' ideas and virtually ended that movement's influence. As always, he used harsh language. The pamphlet's chapters, for example, had titles like "The American Colonization Society Is Nourished by Fear and Selfishness" and "The American Colonization Society Deceives and Misleads the Nation."

Riots. Garrison's refusal to soften his positions made him enemies in the North as well as the South. Several times in the 1830s, he was endangered by violent mobs in Boston. In his usual style, he welcomed such confrontations with little concern for his own safety, sticking to the peaceful principles he called "nonresistance." The worst riot happened on October 21, 1835, when Garrison and George Thompson, an English abolitionist and Garrison's good friend, were scheduled to give speeches to the newly formed Boston Female Anti-Slavery Society. Garrison had received several threats, one of which offered a reward of $100 to the man who would be the first to lay violent hands on Thompson. The reward was offered by a number of "patriotic citizens" who declined to sign their names. Thompson stayed away from the meeting, but Garrison—despite the protests of local merchants who feared violence—insisted on making his planned appearance. A mob gathered outside the building, and from inside he could hear cries of "*Garrison* is there! Garrison! Garrison! We must have Garrison! Out with him! Lynch him!" (Merrill, p. 106). Garrison realized that he would not be able to reason with them. As he tried to make an escape, however, they seized him and wound a rope around his body. His clothes were shredded as the angry crowd manhandled him along the street. He narrowly missed being lynched and had to spend the night in jail—this time for his own protection.

Gaining ground. Such occurrences grew rarer, however, as more and more people joined the antislavery movement. From the late 1830s to the 1850s, abolition became less of a "radical" cause and won supporters among the common people. (Some, in fact, joined because of the violence against men like Garrison, wishing to uphold the abolitionists' right to freedom of speech.) Garrison's finances, often shaky in the early years, also became more stable as *The Liberator* enjoyed a broader readership. He married a pretty, dark-haired young woman named Helen Benson in 1834, and their first son, George Thompson Garrison, was born in 1836. He was named after his father's friend, the English abolitionist. Helen, who came from a family of abolitionist Quakers, had seen Garrison speak when still in her teens. Later he had become friends with her father and brothers, and the two had fallen in love on his visits to the Benson home in Brooklyn, New York. Helen thought he was the most courageous man she had ever met, and her warm support gave him an emotional base that he had lacked since childhood. They had six children in all, five sons and a daughter.

Frederick Douglass. In 1841, at an abolitionists' meeting on the Massachusetts island of Nantucket, Garrison heard about an escaped slave who was doing odd jobs nearby. Garrison persuaded the man, who had taken the name Frederick Douglass, to come to the meeting. He then asked him to tell the audience about his experiences as a slave. A large, powerful man, Douglass proved to be a captivating speaker, holding the audience spellbound with his life's story. Over the coming years, Douglass would continue to tell his story, eventually becoming a famous abolitionist and black spokesman (see **Frederick Douglass**).

Conscience of a nation. During the 1840s, Garrison's uncompromising "moral" approach drove a wedge between his followers and more moderate abolitionists, who wished to find a political solution to the problem. Leaders such as Theodore Weld lessened Garrison's influence within the movement by creating separate societies that favored political change, such as passing new laws in Congress. Garrison, by contrast, stuck to his demands, refusing to accept any negotiation at all with slavery's supporters. By the 1850s, it had become clear that political efforts were getting nowhere, as the slave states blocked attempts to free the slaves by law. As the issue created a growing gulf between North and South, Garrison's stubborn refusal to compromise won him new and lasting respect as a national symbol of integrity and courage.

Aftermath

A purpose fulfilled. Abraham Lincoln's election as president in 1860 was followed by the Civil War (1861-1865), a bloody sign of the failure to resolve the question of slavery by political means. With northern victory came the Thirteenth Amendment, which ended slavery in the United States forever. Garrison, now almost sixty years old, saw his mission as accomplished and ended publication of *The Liberator*. He continued to call for reform in other areas, as he had done well through the newspaper's three decades of publication. In numerous articles and speeches, he supported women's rights (especially the right to vote), the prohibition of alcohol, and the rights of native Americans and Chinese immigrants.

Both his and Helen's health declined during the 1870s. Helen died in 1875. William Lloyd Garrison died four years later, on May

24, 1879, as he lay peacefully in bed, surrounded by children and grandchildren singing his favorite hymns.

For More Information

Archer, Jules. *Angry Abolitionist: William Lloyd Garrison.* New York: Simon and Schuster, 1969.

Faber, Doris. *I Will Be Heard: The Life of William Lloyd Garrison.* New York: Lothrop, Lee and Shepard Company, 1970.

Merrill, Walter M. *Against Wind and Tide: A Biography of William Lloyd Garrison.* Cambridge, Massachusetts: Harvard University Press, 1963.

Frederick Douglass

1817-1895

Personal Background

Experience as a plantation slave. Frederick Augustus Washington Bailey (he took the name of Douglass only after his escape to freedom) was a slave for the first twenty years of his life. He was born on a plantation at Tuckahoe, Maryland, in 1817, the son of a slave named Harriet Bailey and an unknown white father. The infant was separated from his mother and lived with his grandmother until he was about eight years old.

In his autobiographies (he wrote three), Frederick Douglass recounts the horrors of being a slave. He recalls being so poorly fed at times that he competed with plantation dogs for scraps of food. He saw, and experienced firsthand, the beatings slaves received for the slightest offenses. He witnessed the cruel breakup of slave families and was outraged when his own grandmother, considered too old to work any longer, was turned out of her cabin and sent into the woods to die.

Experience as a city slave. In 1826, at the age of eight, Douglass was sold to the family of Hugh and Sophia Auld in Baltimore, Maryland. Life with the Aulds, at least in the beginning, was much easier than on the plantation. Douglass's only jobs were to run errands and to care for the Auld's infant son, Tommy. Sophia, who frequently read aloud to Tommy, began to teach Douglass how to read.

▲ **Frederick Douglass**

Event: Antislavery struggle; publication of the *North Star.*

Role: Frederick Douglass was an escaped slave who became one of the abolition movement's most effective spokesmen. His publication of his own antislavery newspaper and his views on how best to abolish slavery led to his break with William Lloyd Garrison, the foremost white abolitionist of his time.

He quickly learned the alphabet and how to spell words of three or four letters. Sophia was proud of his progress. But her husband demanded that the teaching stop. He believed that Douglass would be unfit to be a slave if he learned to read. Auld's attempt to prevent Douglass from reading had the opposite effect: "The argument which he so warmly urged, against my learning to read, only served to inspire me with a desire and determination to learn" (Douglass, p. 37).

Self-schooling. Douglass proceeded to learn to read on his own, befriending poor white children who gave him reading lessons in exchange for bread. To earn a little money for himself, he became a bootblack (he shined boots). He spent his wages on *The Columbian Orator,* a book of speeches and essays.One of the chapters in *The Columbian Orator* featured a master and his slave debating the justice of slavery. They finally agree that slavery is wrong and that no man has the right to hold another in bondage. (Douglass was fond of quoting passages from this book to the end of his life.)

Through his reading Douglass also learned about the abolition movement, much discussed in Baltimore's newspapers. Added to his own experience as a slave, his reading helped shape his views:

> The more I read, the more I was led to abhor and detest my enslavers. I could regard them in no other light than a band of successful robbers, who had left their homes, and gone to Africa, and stolen us from our homes, and in a strange land reduced us to slavery. (Douglass, p. 42)

He dreamed endlessly of escaping to freedom, a fantasy that saw him through many dark days.

Douglass vs. the slave breaker. In Baltimore Douglass lived under conditions far less harsh than those on the plantation. He was allowed to leave the Auld household to work in the city's shipyards. He was hired out, working for the same wages that were paid to his master. Douglass hoped he might be allowed to earn enough extra money to buy his freedom. But in 1833 his hope was crushed. His master died, and a quarrel over Douglass's ownership resulted in his being sent back to a plantation. The move was a difficult adjustment for a slave who had experienced the freer atmosphere of the city.

On the plantation, Douglass tried to share his learning. He

established a "sabbath school" for the slaves, but it was destroyed by an angry mob of white church leaders. Suspicious of slaves who showed any talent for leadership, slave owners regarded him as troublesome property. Consequently, Douglass's master sent him to the farm of Edward Covey, a "slave breaker." Covey worked slaves very hard—spying on their every move and whipping them for the slightest reason. Douglass was beaten several times during his first six months at Covey's farm. When Covey beat him for collapsing from the heat, Douglass walked to his master's farm and begged to be allowed to stay. His master ignored his plea, ordering him to return to Covey.

Covey intended to make an example of Douglass for complaining to his master. For his part, Douglass resolved to resist any further beatings. When Covey surprised the sixteen-year-old slave in the stables and attempted to tie him up for another whipping, Douglass decided to fight back: He seized Covey hard by the throat, and the two men grappled for nearly two hours. Covey finally let him go, Douglass later wrote, "saying that if I had not resisted, he would not have whipped me half so much" (Douglass, p. 74). The truth was that Douglass had not been whipped at all, and Covey never again laid a finger on him in anger. This act of resistance was a turning point for Douglass. It gave him a sense of power that remained with him in the days to come."My long-crushed spirit rose, cowardice departed, bold defiance took its place; and I now resolved that, however long I might remain a slave in form, the day had passed forever when I could be a slave in fact " (Douglass, p. 74).

After leaving Covey's place, Douglass's mind was filled with the possibility of escape from the farm. In 1836, nineteen-year-old Douglass and four other slaves planned to run away by taking a boat up the Chesapeake Bay and then sailing north. Their plan was betrayed by another slave, however, and they were arrested the morning they were scheduled to leave. All expected to be sold "down the river" or even sentenced to death. Miraculously, after a brief prison stay, they were returned to their masters. Rescued by Thomas Auld, Douglass was promised that he would be set free at the age of twenty-five and sent back to Thomas's brother, Hugh Auld, in Baltimore. He would be hired-out to work in Baltimore's shipyards.

Escape to freedom. Douglass was not welcomed by the

white workers in Baltimore's shipyards. They nearly knocked out one of his eyes. His master attempted to have them punished, but no white witness was willing to testify, and the testimony of blacks was unacceptable in southern courts. After he recovered from his injuries, Douglass returned to work.

Socially, Douglass's life was much improved. He met a free black woman named Anna Murray, to whom he became engaged. Unhappy at being forced to turn over all his earnings to his master and determined to marry only as a free man, Douglass decided to escape. On September 3, 1838, with money borrowed from Anna, a set of clothes, and "protection papers" borrowed from a free black sailor, he boarded a train bound for Philadelphia and New York. The trip north was a tense one. Douglass saw several white men who knew him, but for some reason they did not identify him as a runaway. His closest brush with capture came just as the train was crossing into the free state of Pennsylvania. At this point a conductor asked to see his "papers." Douglass's looks did not at all match the physical description in the papers given to him by the black sailor. Fortunately, the conductor merely glanced at them and moved on. The train had crossed the border. Douglass was free.

Settling in the North. Douglass was excited and relieved to reach free soil. His first feelings of joy were quickly replaced by insecurity and loneliness, however. Fearing capture and a return to slavery, he wandered aimlessly around New York for several days, afraid to speak to anyone. When his money finally ran out, he asked for help. David Ruggles, a local black leader, gave him a place to stay. Ruggles also arranged for Douglass to marry Anna (she had followed him to New York) and helped the newlyweds move to New Bedford, Massachusetts, a much safer place for runaways than New York. It was in New Bedford that Frederick Bailey at last changed his name to Douglass, taking it from the hero of Sir Walter Scott's poem, the "Lady of the Lake."

Participation: Antislavery Movement

Prejudice in the North. Although Douglass had escaped slavery in the South, he did not escape prejudice in the North. He could not practice his trade as ship's caulker in Massachusetts because the white shipyard workers threatened to quit if a black worker was hired. He had to make do with lower-paying unskilled jobs. Anna could only find work as a house servant. Furthermore, northern churches refused to accept black worshippers, and public transportation was segregated. The one hopeful sign Douglass saw was the spirit of reform in northern society.

The most active reform movement of the time was the abolition movement. Its strongest followers believed slavery was a sin and slave owners were criminals. Slavery, they preached, violated every principle on which the American nation was based. Douglass, who was given a gift subscription to *The Liberator,* was quickly drawn to the teachings of the publisher, William Lloyd Garrison (see **William Lloyd Garrison**). Garrison advocated complete, immediate emancipation of the country's slaves and rejected all proposals to relocate them to Africa (or any other area of the world). Most of the northerners did not yet agree with Garrison's views. Douglass, however, read *The Liberator* with keen interest, attracted by Garrison's zealous opposition to slavery.

Public speaking. In 1839, Douglass joined an antislavery society in New Bedford. Before long he was speaking at meetings, arguing against plans to colonize American blacks outside the United States. On August 9, 1841, he met Garrison, who had come to speak in New Bedford. No man, Douglass stated, ever made a greater impression on him. Two days later both men attended an antislavery convention on Nantucket Island. It was at this meeting that the former slave gave his first great public speech. An imposing figure at six-feet tall, Douglass had a handsome face and a magnificent speaking voice. He felt nervous and spoke haltingly at first, but his words began to flow more easily as he told of his experiences as a slave. He held his audience spellbound. His commanding presence and flowing speech gave the lie to southern claims about the natural inferiority of blacks. When he finished, Garrison rose to speak:

> "Have we been listening to a thing … or a man?" he asked.
>
> "A man! a man!" the audience shouted with one accord.
>
> "Shall such a man be held a slave in a Christian land?" called out Garrison.…
>
> "No! No!" shouted the audience. (McFeely, p. 88)

Douglass spoke again at the evening session of the Nantucket convention. Garrison and the other antislavery leaders were so impressed by his story that they offered him a job as a regular speaker on the antislavery circuit.

Autobiography. Douglass paid a heavy price to lead the life of an antislavery speaker. He was separated from his wife and children for long periods. Hostile audiences often threw rotten eggs and vegetables at him and he and his fellow speakers were sometimes viciously beaten. As an escaped slave, Douglass ran an extra risk of being captured and sent back to his master. He even endured insults from friends who suggested that he speak more like a plantation slave and less like an educated free man. This Douglass refused to do; he would not compromise his dignity. When some critics questioned whether a man with his gift of speech and intelligence could ever have been a slave, he made a courageous move. He wrote and published his first autobiography, *Narrative of the Life of Douglass.* In this book he revealed his real name and mentioned the place and people he had known as a slave, including his various masters. The book sold well, and in 1845 Douglass embarked on a speaking tour of England, beyond the reach of southern slave catchers.

Time in England. Douglass remained in England from 1845 to 1847, enjoying a huge success as a public speaker there. Slavery had been abolished throughout the British empire in 1833, but Douglass urged antislavery forces there to keep up the pressure for emancipation in the United States. He was treated so well that he considered staying in England permanently. Though he ultimately decided not to stay, he made some important friends in England. One of them, Ellen Richardson, started a successful fund-raising drive to buy his freedom. A sum of $1,250 was raised and paid to Thomas Auld, who signed and legally registered a document certifying that Frederick Bailey, or Douglass as he called himself, was a free man.

The *North Star.* Perhaps bolstered by his experiences in England, Douglass decided to start his own antislavery newspaper, which he named the *North Star.* Although the paper was widely praised, it was not a financial success. Donations from friends, his own savings, and even a mortgage on his home (now in Rochester, New York) were necessary to keep the paper going. It did not begin to prosper until the arrival of a friend from England, Julia Griffiths.

An excellent businesswoman, Griffiths helped put the paper on a sound financial basis. The *North Star* (after 1851 called *Douglass's Paper*) allowed Douglass and several other black writers to express their views. It also became a symbol to all blacks of what they might achieve.

Douglass vs. Garrison. Douglass's relations with Garrison's wing of the abolition movement were severely strained by his newspaper. Some of his old friends resented his independence and thought Douglass was ungrateful. Critics accused him of acting more haughty after his trip to England. They spread rumors about his relationship with Julia Griffiths, who as his business manager lived for years with Douglass and his wife and children. He refused to buckle under to the scandal mongers, but Griffiths moved out and later returned to England.

The final causes of Douglass's break with Garrison were their different viewpoints. Douglass came to disagree with Garrison on a number of issues. Though Douglass supported political action to encourage laws to abolish slavery, Garrison felt only moral argument, or persuasion, could succeed. Douglass supported various political parties that opposed the spread of slavery, including the Liberty Party, the Free Soil Party, and, finally, the Republican Party.

The first break came in 1851, at a meeting of the American Anti-Slavery Society. In a speech delivered there, Douglass stunned many of the delegates by announcing that he would urge the readers of his paper to use political power in the fight against slavery. Although Garrison's paper bitterly attacked Douglass's position, Douglass persisted in calling for political action to bring about emancipation.

Underground Railroad. Douglass was furious at the passage of the Fugitive Slave Laws, which required northerners to aid in the capture and return of runaway slaves. Consequently, he became active in the Underground Railroad (the system created to help runaways escape capture and reach a free sanctuary). His home, located in northern New York near the Canadian border, became an important hiding place for slaves trying to reach Canada, where slavery was outlawed. In the 1850s, hundreds of runaway slaves found shelter in the Douglass home, where at one point eleven were hidden at the same time.

Friendship with John Brown. Throughout most of his career as an abolitionist, Douglass opposed the use of violence. In the 1850s, however, his views began to change. He argued that slaves had the right to resist violence with violence, and openly urged his readers to oppose the activities of the slave catchers with force. He developed a friendship with John Brown, who felt any means was justified in the battle to do away with the slave system.

Brown stayed with Douglass for several weeks and outlined to him a plan for using armed men to protect runaway slaves. He also spoke of establishing a state in the mountains for slaves seeking refuge. Douglass supported these schemes but never approved Brown's plan to attack the government arsenal at Harpers Ferry, New York. Brown tried for two days to persuade Douglass to join his small band, but Douglass refused. The plan, he believed, was suicidal. In fact, Brown and his entire band of twenty-two men were either killed or captured at Harpers Ferry.

Among the papers on Brown when he was captured was a brief note from Douglass (dated two years earlier). The note almost led to Douglass's arrest as a participant in the plot. Fortunately for him, the telegraph operator who took down the message for his arrest was an abolitionist who delayed delivering it for three hours in order to forewarn Douglass. Though he was innocent, Douglass fled to Canada and from there sailed to England.

Douglass stayed in England only a short while. He returned home when he learned that one of his children had died. By then, the furor over John Brown had quieted down and Douglass was no longer being sought for arrest. In fact, his ties to Brown, who had since died, became an advantage in the North, where the antislavery warrior was regarded almost as a saint. Brown's memory would be recalled often by Douglass, who said he had not had enough courage to go with the old man on his daring raid.

Pre-Civil War politics. Douglass played a part in the presidential campaign of 1860. Although he was at first hesitant to support the Republican Party because its stand against slavery was not

▶ **Douglass was one of several prominent free black men who fought for the emancipation of slaves**

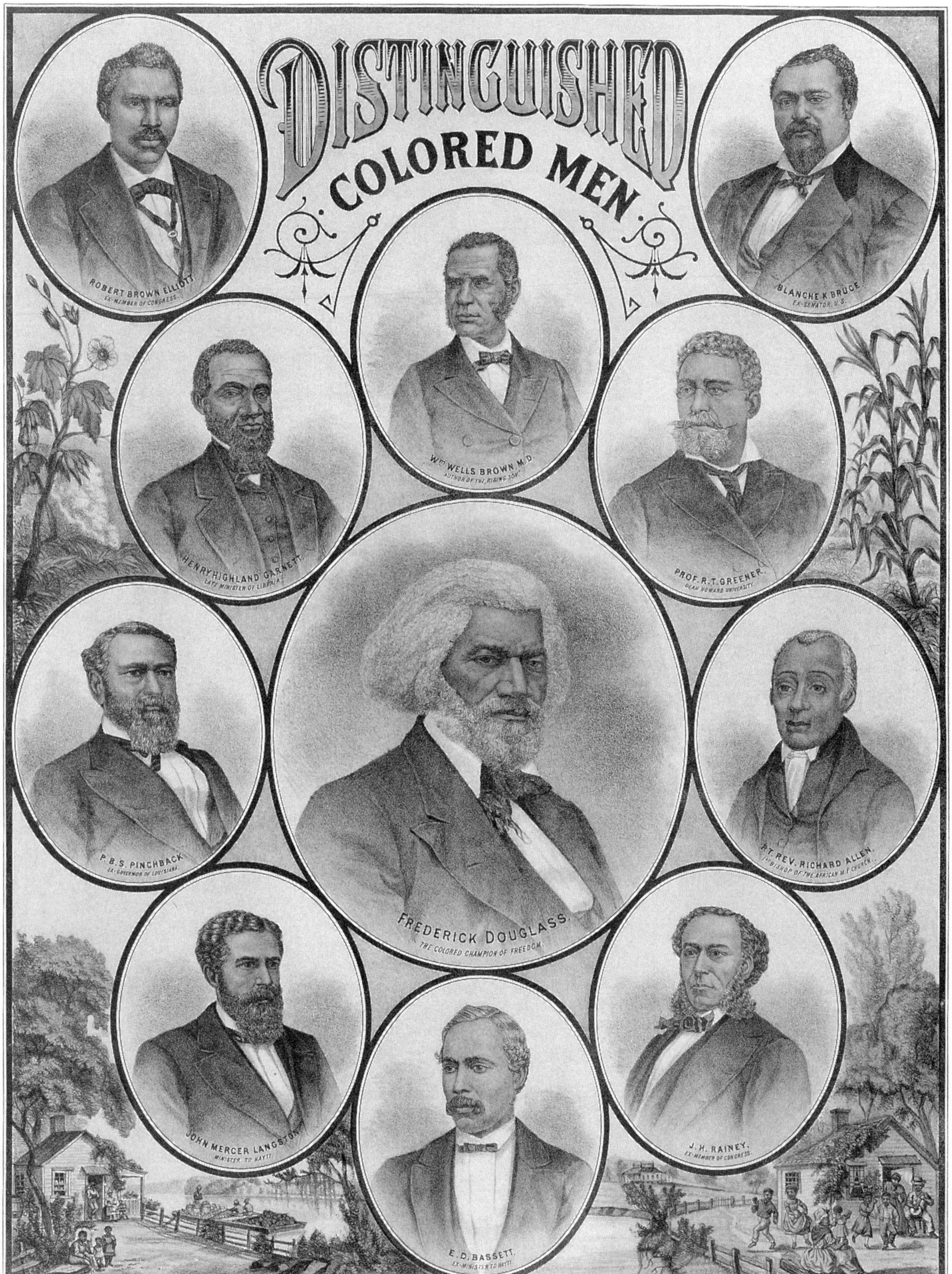
DISTINGUISHED
COLORED MEN
ROBERT BROWN ELLIOTT
EX-MEMBER OF CONGRESS.
BLANCHE K. BRUCE.
EX-SENATOR, U.S.
Wm WELLS BROWN, M.D.
AUTHOR OF THE RISING SON.
HENRY HIGHLAND GARNETT.
LATE MINISTER OF LIBERIA.
PROF. R.T. GREENER.
DEAN HOWARD UNIVERSITY.
P.B.S. PINCHBACK.
EX-GOVERNOR OF LOUISIANA.
FREDERICK DOUGLASS.
THE COLORED CHAMPION OF FREEDOM.
RT. REV. RICHARD ALLEN.
1st BISHOP OF THE AFRICAN M.E. CHURCH.
JOHN MERCER LANGSTON.
MINISTER TO HAYTI.
J.H. RAINEY.
EX-MEMBER OF CONGRESS.
E.D. BASSETT.
EX-MINISTER TO HAYTI.

strong enough to suit him, he finally did endorse Abraham Lincoln's candidacy. Lincoln's election (as Douglass had known it would) caused the South to secede and finally to fire on Fort Sumter, South Carolina, starting the Civil War.

Aftermath

Civil War role. Once the war had begun, Douglass did his best to transform it into a conflict to abolish slavery. Slavery alone, he argued, had caused the war and it would be the height of foolishness to end the conflict without destroying the evil which had brought it on. Although he felt that Lincoln should have moved more quickly, Douglass applauded the Emancipation Proclamation. He called January 1, 1863, the date it went into effect, "the turning point in the conflict between freedom and slavery" (Nash, p. 260). At a huge rally in Boston, he led a joyful crowd in singing hymns of freedom.

Douglass's greatest contribution to Union victory was his constant support for the enlistment of black troops. When the War Department finally allowed blacks to enlist, he became the foremost recruiter, traveling thousands of miles in his efforts. The creation of the heroic 54th Massachusetts Regiment, in which two of his sons enlisted, was largely the work of Douglass.

Next, Douglass fought for the black troops to receive equal treatment in pay and opportunities for advancement. He also argued that they be allowed to fight rather than be restricted to support services. He believed the nation would never support full equality for the former slaves unless they proved they deserved it by fighting and sacrifice. He also believed that his people would gain self-respect by fighting for their own freedom. Altogether around 200,000 blacks served in Union armies. Their participation was an important factor in the defeat of the Confederacy.

Douglass and Lincoln. Perhaps one of the most remarkable stories of the Civil War is that of Douglass, the former slave, who became an adviser to the president of the United States. Douglass journeyed to the White House twice to meet with Lincoln. He was charmed by the president and convinced that Lincoln was moving as fast as circumstances allowed in ending discrimination against black troops. Their second meeting, which occurred when Lincoln was afraid he might be defeated in his 1864 bid for reelection, was a somber affair. Lincoln asked Douglass to prepare a plan (to be used if he lost the election) for bringing north as many slaves as possible before his successor took office. Much to Douglass's delight, Lincoln triumphed at the polls. A short time later Douglass was shocked and grief stricken at the news of Lincoln's assassination.

During Reconstruction (1865-1877), Douglass continued to fight for equal rights. He campaigned vigorously for the fourteenth Amendment, which made former slaves full citizens, and for his favorite cause during these years, the vote for black Americans. He considered the fifteenth Amendment, which guaranteed the right to vote regardless of race, a great milestone in the history of freedom.

Douglass was at times bitterly criticized for his activities during these years. The women's movement felt betrayed by his support for the fifteenth Amendment, which did not extend the vote to women. And his own children found fault with his decision to marry a white woman, Helen Pitts, after the death of his first wife. Douglass shrugged off his family's criticism, commenting that his first wife was the color of his mother, and his second, the color of his father.

Douglass campaigned for equal rights to the end of his life. He fought the Jim Crow laws, which permitted segregation. (Once, when being forced to move to the black seating section of a train, he held on to his seat so tightly that it was carried off with him.) He joined Ida B. Wells Barnett in condemning the lynching of black men. And, after a time, leaders of the women's movement welcomed him back into service on their behalf. After speaking at a women's suffrage meeting on the evening of February 20, 1895, Douglass collapsed and died at home while excitedly describing to his wife the activities of the day.

For More Information

Douglass, Frederick. *Narrative of the Life of Douglass.* Garden City, New York: Doubleday, 1973.

McFeely, William S. *Douglass.* New York: W. W. Norton and Company, 1991.

Nash, Roderick. "Douglass." *From These Beginnings: A Biographical Approach to American History.* Vol. 1. New York: HarperCollins College.

Russell, Sharman. *Douglass.* New York: Chelsea House, 1988.

Sojourner Truth

c. 1797-1883

Personal Background

Sometime around 1797, in an area of upstate New York settled by Dutch immigrants, a baby girl was born to a slave couple named James and Elizabeth. The couple were the property of the wealthy Hardenberghs, one of the area's oldest "patroon," or landowning families. Called Isabella, or Belle for short, the girl grew up speaking Dutch. Her mother, known as "Ma-Ma Bett," was a strong woman who tried to help her daughter cope with a slave's harsh life. She told Belle to obey her masters so that she would not be punished. Belle's eight older brothers and sisters had all been "sold away" to other masters. Her mother would tell her remaining children—Belle and her younger brother, Peter—stories about their brothers and sisters. Michael and Nancy, for example, at five and three had been taken by a white slave dealer who put them into his horse-drawn sleigh one cold winter morning. Comforting herself and her children, Ma-Ma Bett would say that their brothers and sisters were still under the same moon and stars, even if they were far away. Belle's mother also taught her to say her prayers to a God who lived up among those stars.

New masters. Belle was sold for $100 to the Neelys, an English-speaking family who lived nearby. She was very unhappy with them. Mr. Neely beat her with rods tied together, and Mrs. Neely, not

▲ Sojourner Truth

Event: Lectures and protests against slavery and discrimination.

Role: Born a slave named Isabella, Sojourner Truth took her new name in her forties, after claiming her freedom. For the rest of her life, Truth preached her message of equality and justice for both blacks and women in America.

realizing that Dutch-speaking Belle could not understand orders given in English, punished her as well. Meanwhile, her father, once so straight and strong that he was called "Baumfree," or "tree," had grown weak and bent by a life of hard labor. When Belle's mother died without warning, there was no one left to care for her husband. (Too old to work very hard, the two had been freed at about the same time that Belle was sold.) Stooped with arthritis and nearly blind, he was allowed to continue to live in the damp cellar at the Hardenberghs, which had been the family home. From there, when he was strong enough, he sometimes visited Belle at the Neelys.

After two unhappy years with the Neelys, Belle again was sold, this time to a kinder couple named Schryver, who ran a tavern in the port of Kingston, New York. She enjoyed work in the tavern and for the first time heard talk (by now she understood English) of exciting cities like New York and Boston, and of foreign lands like Africa and the West Indies. After about a year and a half, a customer at the tavern offered Schryver the large sum of $300 for her. A poor man, Schryver accepted. Belle had been sold again—for the last time, as it turned out.

"Better to me than a man." Her new owners, the Dumonts of New Paltz Landing, would own Belle for seventeen years. Mr. Dumont was generally kind and understanding, but Mrs. Dumont was strict and scolded Belle often. Belle's work began early in the morning when she went from the kitchen to the barns to milk the cows, then to the fields to care for the corn, and finally back to the house to clean it up at night. While working for the Dumonts, Belle grew into a slim but strong young woman, tall and graceful, with dark skin and striking looks. She worked very hard. As Mr. Dumont was fond of saying to his friends, Belle was "better to me than a man—for she will do a good family's washing in the night and be ready in the morning to go into the field, where she will do as much raking and binding as my best hands" (Ortiz, p. 26).

A local girl, hired as kitchen help, saw how hard Belle worked and jealously tried to get her into trouble with Mrs. Dumont. Every morning, Belle had to scrub and boil the day's potatoes. Much as she would scrub them, however, there were always little bits of dirt floating around in the potato pot. It was the Dumont's ten-year-old daughter, Gertrude, who discovered that the local girl was putting ashes in the pot after Belle left for the fields. After that early incident, life with the Dumonts became easier. Even Mrs. Dumont (though always hard to please) recognized how hard Belle worked.

Freedom on the horizon. In 1817, when Belle was about twenty, the New York Legislature passed a law stating that the last of its slaves were to become free on July 4, 1827. By this time, Baumfree had died, alone and ill and without enough food to eat. Also, Belle had begun having children, by a slave named Thomas whom Mr. Dumont had chosen for her. Belle herself had fallen in love with a different man, Bob, who belonged to a neighbor. Bob would visit her, but on one occasion his owner followed him to the Dumonts and began beating him. Dumont kicked the man off his property but made sure Bob was not beaten further. But Belle never saw him again, and soon heard that he had been forced to marry a woman who belonged to the same owner. With Thomas, Belle eventually had five children, four of whom survived: Diana, Peter, Elizabeth, and Sofia. Her two older daughters were sold away as children, and for the time being, Peter and Sofia remained with her at the Dumonts. In 1824, Dumont promised Belle that if she continued her good work, he would free her a year early.

Claiming her freedom. As the date approached, Belle grew more and more excited at the prospect of being free. There was a setback, however. Shortly after Dumont made his promise, Belle had cut her hand badly on the sharp scythe she used to mow the grass. Because she did not want to take time off, the cut did not heal properly. When July 4, 1826, finally arrived, Mr. Dumont changed his mind. He said he would keep her the extra year after all because she had missed valuable work due to her injured hand. Shocked at first, Belle soon realized that the experience had opened her eyes. For the first time, despite his past kindness, she saw Dumont for what he was: a man who could think of other human beings as property. Without a doubt in her mind about the rightness of her action, she took her baby daughter, Sofia, and simply walked away.

Participation: Antislavery Movement

Birth of an abolitionist. Although she did not take the name until later, Sojourner Truth was born the moment Belle left the

Dumont farm. She had always been an obedient and humble slave, thinking of her master as almost godlike. Now, in a single moment, she had changed. For the first time, she had not only disobeyed but defied her master. She had done it because she believed that right was on her side. She did not know where she would spend the night, or how she would feed herself and her baby. Truth just refused to wait any longer for what she was owed. God, she was convinced, would look out for her. This was a new path of independence that she would stay on for the rest of her life, a path that would lead her to fight for herself, for her people, and for other women.

Quaker refuge. As she walked along, Truth remembered a man named Levi Rowe, whose home was nearby. Rowe had once before offered to help her. After a night by the side of the road, she made it to his house, exhausted. Sick in bed himself and unable to help, Rowe sent her to the nearby home of a Quaker couple, Isaac and Maria Van Wagener. There Mrs. Van Wagener welcomed her without hesitation. After her husband returned, the two offered her work, meals, and a bed. When Dumont arrived to claim his property, Isaac Van Wagener explained firmly that he did not recognize anyone's ownership of another human being. However, he did offer to pay Dumont to leave Truth alone. "I will pay you twenty dollars now if you leave her in peace. And I will pay five dollars for the child. I am not buying your slaves. I want no slaves. I only want their freedom" (Claflin, p. 37). Dumont accepted. Truth was finally free.

Victory in court. Before she left the Dumonts, Truth's son, Peter, had been sold to a neighbor, Dr. Gedney. While she was working for the Van Wageners, Truth learned that Peter had been sold again to Gedney's brother, who had in turn sold him to an Alabaman named Fowler. Fowler, Truth found out, had taken the boy from New York back to Alabama. When she returned to the Dumonts to question them about it, Mrs. Dumont made fun of her: "Ugh! A fine fuss to make about a little nigger!" (Ortiz, p. 31). Outraged, Truth was suddenly determined to get her son back. "I was sure God would help me get him," she later said. "Why, I felt so tall within—I felt as if the power of a nation was within me" (Ortiz, p. 31). It was illegal to sell a slave to someone in another state, so she had the law on her side. She found lawyers willing to help, and though it took several months, she won her case. Peter had been badly beaten by his new master, but at least she had him back. And she had accomplished what at that time was unheard of. She, a black woman, had challenged a white man in court, and she had won.

New York cults. In about 1829, Truth moved to New York City, where Peter had been offered a chance to go to school. She took the name Truth Van Wagener. Looking for a church to attend, she joined first the John Street Methodist Church and then, when told she could not worship at white services there, the African Zion Church. Truth, now in her early thirties, had by this time become extremely religious. She experienced visions and heard voices that she believed came from God. Soon she joined the cult founded by religious leader Elijah Pierson, who also claimed to have such mystic experiences. Over the next two years, she became closely involved with Pierson's movement. It was collecting money, supposedly to help New York prostitutes, and Truth gave all of her own savings to Pierson. Soon another fanatic appeared on the scene, Robert Matthews, who called himself "Mathias" and claimed to be the Messiah. The two joined forces, with Matthews posing as the Messiah and Pierson as John the Baptist. Truth believed in them and in 1833 moved to their commune "The Kingdom of God" outside of New York City.

Scandal. For another two years, Truth continued to have faith in them, despite their increasingly strange behavior. After Pierson died under mysterious circumstances, Matthews was charged with murder, and Truth herself—described in newspaper stories as "the colored woman"—was linked with the scandal. A couple, the Folgers, who had also been followers of Matthews and Pierson, accused her not only of guilt in Pierson's death but of trying to poison them as well. Once again, Truth went to court, this time to clear her name. With the same stubborn determination as before, she collected testimony from the Dumonts, the Van Wageners, and others about her good character. She was also helped by a book about the affair that praised her behavior and proclaimed her innocence. The court awarded her $125 in damages against the Folgers.

Life in New York. For the next eight or nine years, Truth lived peacefully in New York City, working as a household servant for several families. Her main concern, at least at the beginning of this period, was her troubled son, Peter. The boy, now fourteen, had problems in school and with the police, and more than once Truth had to get him out of jail. She finally refused to come get him at all. A man named Peter Williams, whose last name Peter had been using in his scams, was curious about the boy and went instead. He ended up arranging a job for Peter on a whaling ship, which genuinely interested the boy. Soon he shipped off to sea. Truth received a few letters from Peter over the next two years. After that, she never heard from her son again.

While in New York, Truth began to question the kind of life that she felt people were forced to live in the city. It seemed like a constant struggle for money and possessions. Still deeply religious, she wondered how good material things were for the soul. Restless with city life, Truth felt as if she were being summoned to some greater purpose. With only an old pillowcase half-filled with belongings and two shillings (about four or five dollars today), she left New York in the early summer of 1843.

"The Lord gave me Sojourner." She had explained to her employer that she was going farther east "because the Spirit calls me there and I must go" (Ortiz, p. 44). Often, she had spoken at religious meetings and noticed that people always seemed to respond to the deep beliefs behind her words. The pilgrimage east would allow her to share her deeply held spiritual beliefs with more people. She decided to take a new name that would reflect her aims. "I went to the Lord and asked him to give me a new name," she later recalled. A sojourner is a traveler who stays in one place briefly, then moves on. The determined woman explained, "And the Lord gave me Sojourner, because I was to travel up and down the land, showing the people their sins, and being a sign unto them" (Ortiz, p. 44). As a slave, her last name had always been that of her master. Her new master, she decided, was truth, so that was the last name she now took.

Summer on the road. Sojourner Truth spent the summer walking east across Long Island, Connecticut, and Massachusetts, taking odd jobs as they came along and, at first, often sleeping in the open. She attended prayer meetings wherever she found them (in the 1800s they were common events), speaking and singing when the impulse moved her. As the summer wore on, her popularity grew and people began to request her as a speaker at the meetings. Now a woman in her mid-forties, she looked younger than her years. She had a dignified but friendly manner and she often used humor to make a point or tell a story. One religious group she encountered, for example, believed that Christ was planning to return in 1843. They spent time in fearful and noisy prayer getting ready for his arrival. She gently made fun of their meetings and their preparations, saying, "Why are you making such a to-do? You are in such a state, the Lord might come, move all through the camp, and go away again—and you would never know it!" (Claflin, pp. 64-65).

Northampton Association. By winter, Truth had joined a Massachusetts community, the Northampton Association, which had been founded a few years earlier by George Benson. Benson was the brother-in-law of William Lloyd Garrison, America's most famous abolitionist (see **William Lloyd Garrison**). Founded on ideas of equality and freedom, the community supported itself by breeding silkworms, an activity in which all members shared the labor. Everyone lived together in an old factory building, and membership included abolitionists and other social reformers. Aside from Garrison and others, Truth also met the famous abolitionist leader Frederick Douglass, who, like herself, had been an escaped slave (see **Frederick Douglass**).

Truth stayed at Northampton for three years altogether. It was her first exposure to the antislavery movement and it changed her deeply. The restlessness that had driven her to leave New York and the stubbornness and independence that had earlier led her to walk away from the Dumonts now found a direction. Truth became firmly committed to the abolitionist cause.

Westward. The Northampton Association broke up in 1846, but for several years Truth remained in the Benson household as an employee and guest. She continued giving antislavery speeches in Massachusetts, with abolition leaders like Garrison and Douglass publicizing her appearances in antislavery newspapers. Her reputation grew steadily, so that she was attracting large audiences by the time she began heading west in the 1850s. Throughout Ohio, Missouri, Kansas, and Indiana, she spoke at antislavery meetings that also featured Frederick Douglass and others. At the same time, she began calling for equal rights for women, which she saw as being part of the struggle for equality for all people.

Narrative. Truth had told her life story to Olive Brown, a writer who put it into book form as *The Narrative of Sojourner Truth.* When the book was published in 1850, she began to support herself by selling it at meetings. She continued to draw large crowds with her colorful style. At one point, when proslavery forces started a rumor that she was actually a man, she showed one of her breasts to a crowd. She often faced angry proslavery listeners, but had a way of calming them with her good humor and no-nonsense way of addressing them.

Sojourner Truth on the Constitution

"Children, I talks to God and God talks to me ... This morning I was walking out, and I ... saw the wheat a-holding up its head, looking very big. I went up and I took hold of it. You believe it—there was no wheat there! I said, 'God, what *is* the matter with this wheat?' And He said to me, 'Sojourner, there is a little weevil [insect] in it.'

"Now I hear talking about the Constitution and the rights of man. I come up and I take hold of this Constitution. It looks *mighty big,* but when I feel for *my* rights, there ain't any there. Then I say, 'God, what *ails* this Constitution?'

"He says to me, 'Sojourner, there is a little weevil in it!'" (Claflin, p. 88)

Home in Michigan. In the mid-1850s, Truth settled in Battle Creek, Michigan, which would be her headquarters for the rest of her life. Her daughters, now grown women, came to live with her there. When the Civil War began in 1860, she immediately started walking through Michigan, collecting donations of food and clothing for the black volunteer regiments that fought for the Union. In 1863, Harriet Beecher Stowe, whose 1852 novel *Uncle Tom's Cabin* had done so much to sway public opinion against slavery, wrote an article about Truth for the *Atlantic Monthly.* Stowe praised her accomplishments, calling her "the Libyan Sibyl," a phrase meaning "African prophet" (see **Harriet Beecher Stowe**). The following year, shortly before his assassination, Sojourner Truth went to Washington and met President Abraham Lincoln.

Aftermath

Continuing the fight for equality. After the end of the Civil War, in 1865, blacks were legally free. As they found out, however, free did not mean equal with white Americans. Now an old woman of nearly seventy, walking with a cane, Truth took up the struggle to win an equal place for black citizens in American society. She was appointed "counselor to the freed people" at Freedmen's Village in Virginia, where black children were being kidnaped by whites from Maryland. She organized a group of soldiers to fight off the kidnapers and win the release of the children. Many of her campaigns foreshadowed the civil rights protests of nearly a century later. In Washington, D.C. for example, she protested segregation on streetcars and suffered a dislocated shoulder after being shoved by a conductor. She sued the conductor, who was fired; shortly after that, segregation ended in Washington streetcars. For several years, she fought to establish a "Negro State" in the West. The campaign failed, but nevertheless she is believed to have been responsible for the westward migration of many blacks.

"Oldest truth." Her health declining, Truth went home to Battle Creek in 1875. Nearly 80, she in fact believed herself to be nearer 100. In 1879, four years before she died, a Kentucky newspaper proclaimed, "The oldest truth nowadays is Sojourner" (Ortiz, p. 140). Visitors streamed into her home at the rate of hundreds a year, right up to her death. She died on November 26, 1883.

For More Information

Claflin, Edward Beecher. *Sojourner Truth and the Struggle for Freedom.* Hauppauge, New York: Barron's Educational Series, 1987.

Ortiz, Victoria. *Sojourner Truth: A Self-Made Woman.* Philadelphia and New York: J. B. Lippincott Co., 1974.

Harriet Beecher Stowe

1811-1896

Personal Background

Harriet Elizabeth Beecher was born on June 14, 1811, in Litchfield, Connecticut. She was the sixth of eight children in a family that was already well on its way to becoming almost legendary. Her father, the Reverend Lyman Beecher, was the most famous American church leader of his time. A New England Puritan preacher who moved constantly from one parish to another, Lyman Beecher mixed a strong element of social reform into his popular religious sermons. He opposed drinking, for example, and called for equal treatment of men and women in society. Though widely known himself, Lyman Beecher would be outstripped by his talented children, who were religious and social reformers in their own right. In time Beecher would be called "the father of more brains than any other man in America" (Gerson, p. 2).

Mother's death. Roxanna Foote Beecher, Lyman Beecher's first wife and Harriet's mother, died when Harriet was four. Her father remarried, and although the children accepted their stepmother, much of their mothering came from the oldest child, Catherine. Eleven years older than Harriet, Catherine had a strong personality, and her brothers and sisters relied on her. Yet Harriet missed her mother. The four-year-old went to live with her Episcopalian grandmother and aunt, the Footes, at their farm on the Con-

▲ **Harriet Beecher Stowe**

Event: Publication of *Uncle Tom's Cabin* (1852).

Role: Harriet Beecher Stowe is the author of *Uncle Tom's Cabin*, a moving story about slaves in the South. An immensely popular novel when it was published, it had a huge impact on public opinion. The novel caused outrage against slavery in the North and outrage against its author in the South. Historians count *Uncle Tom's Cabin* as an important factor in bringing on the Civil War.

necticut shore for one winter. No longer allowed to climb trees or play with her male cousins the way she had with her brothers, Harriet instead had to memorize answers to religious questions in order to please her strict aunt. Using the Bible and other religious works, her aunt and grandmother also taught her to read, and to recite a wide variety of hymns, poems, and other Biblical passages.

Library refuge. Harriet felt a bit overwhelmed by all the religious studies, but reading excited her, as it would for the rest of her life. On returning home early the next summer, she began attending "Ma'am Kilbourne's" school on nearby West Street, walking there every morning with her younger brother Henry Ward. Soon Harriet was reading fluently, and growing impatient at the limited selection of books available (in those days, far fewer books were written for children).

In the attic, the Beecher children's favorite place to play, Harriet found barrels of her father's old sermons mixed with pamphlets of all sorts. Her search through the barrels produced an old copy of *The Arabian Nights,* which she read over and over. The romantic tales of far-off desert lands thrilled her, providing comfort when her older brothers refused to take her along on their adventures. By the time she was eight, her father had rewarded her progress by giving her free use of his library, where he wrote his sermons at a big desk surrounded by high, book-lined walls. There she found Cotton Mather's *Magnalia,* two volumes of short stories set in her own New England instead of in a faraway land. It became her new favorite, and she often found a snug corner where she read happily while her father worked.

Proudest moment. As a student at the Litchfield Academy, Harriet was writing essays at age ten that impressed her teachers with their discipline and clarity. When she was twelve, the Academy's students each wrote a term paper, several of which were chosen to be read at graduation by the headmaster, Mr. Brace. Harriet's was one of those chosen. She later recalled her father's reaction:

> When mine was read, I noticed that father, who was sitting on high by Mr. Brace, brightened and looked interested, and at the close I heard him ask, "Who wrote that composition?" "Your daughter, sir," was the answer. It was the proudest moment of my

> life. There was no mistaking father's face when he was pleased, and to have interested him was past all juvenile triumphs. (Stowe, p. 14)

Studies with Catherine. That same year, Harriet went away to study at Hartford, Connecticut, where her oldest sister, Catherine, had just founded a school for girls. Having a few years earlier suffered her fiancé's death at sea, Catherine had decided to devote herself to improving women's education in America. At this time, women were not expected to stay in school past their early years. Instead they were supposed only to prepare themselves for a life of child-rearing and housework. Strong-willed and intelligent, Catherine believed that a woman's desire to have a family did not mean she had to close herself off from a career or from developing her mind. With typical Beecher zeal, she devoted over half a century to her cause, never again considering marriage. Up to this time, Harriet's best friend had been her brother Henry Ward. Over the next decade, she remained close to him, but spent her time first studying under her sister, and then working for her as a teacher. Both relationships would remain among the most important in her life.

Move to Cincinnati. In 1832, when Harriet was twenty-one, the family moved to Cincinnati, Ohio, where Reverend Beecher had been offered a job as head of the Lane Theological Seminary. Here, Catherine established another school, the Western Female Institute. Harriet continued to work for her, helping her open the school, teaching classes, and even writing a geography textbook when one was needed. In Cincinnati, Harriet and the other Beechers saw much of their mother's brother, Samuel Foote. A sailor and world traveler, Foote provided a balance to Beecher's narrow Puritan view of the world. Whereas Lyman Beecher looked down on Catholics and Jews, for example, Foote defended his friendships with them. He also was said to have had an affair with a Turkish Muslim woman during his travels. Despite Beecher's accomplishments as a public speaker, he had trouble countering Foote's arguments in favor of tolerance.

Foote was a romantic and sophisticated figure to Harriet. He, in turn, had a special fondness for his niece and broadened her cultural horizons. He took her to the theater, where she was especially captivated by *Hamlet* and *Romeo and Juliet.* Thereafter, Harriet would always count Shakespeare among her very favorite writers. Foote also brought her to meetings of the Semi-Colon Club, where Cincinnati writers and others held weekly discussions on literature.

Getting published. For some time, Harriet had been dissatisfied with limiting her life to teaching and working for her sister. Always an enthusiastic letter writer, she now began thinking of trying to write articles and stories as well. Encouraged by Judge James Hall, a Semi-Colon Club member and editor of the magazine *Western Monthly,* in 1833 she submitted first a short article and then a story called "A New England Tale" to the magazine. Both were accepted and published, and she was paid $50 for each. Twenty-two-year-old Harriet Beecher was now a professional writer.

Participation: Antislavery Movement

Tensions in Cincinnati. Growing up in New England, Harriet had not really thought much about slavery other than as a vaguely unpleasant institution that existed in the distant South. Her father opposed it in general, but had also frequently spoken against the abolitionists, whom he saw as stubborn, single-minded fanatics. He especially disliked the idea of immediate emancipation, which was supported by abolitionists like William Lloyd Garrison (see **William Lloyd Garrison**). Lyman Beecher, who had spoken out against Garrison in Boston a few years earlier, thought that the slaves should be freed gradually so they could be prepared through education to take a place in society. Unlike New Englanders, people in Cincinnati lived with slavery close by, just across the Ohio River in the slave state of Kentucky. Feelings on both sides of the issue were stronger, as abolitionists clashed with those who had business dealings with the South, such as cotton or tobacco merchants. Cincinnati, up until the end of the Civil War, remained the largest stop on the Underground Railroad, the system of routes which brought escaped slaves to Canada. By 1833, as Harriet began her writing career, few in Cincinnati remained neutral on the issue of slavery.

Across the Ohio. That same year, Foote took Harriet to visit some friends who owned a large plantation in Kentucky. Harriet did not seem comfortable in the South. She objected to the abundant meals, where seemingly huge portions of fine foods were laid out in fancy bowls and platters. According to her Puritan upbringing, excess and waste were considered sinful. As for the slaves, she simply appeared not to notice them at all. Harriet's friend Mary Dutton, who accompanied Harriet and her uncle on the trip, later recalled how Harriet had actually been observing her surroundings carefully:

> Hattie did not seem to notice anything in particular that happened, but sat much of the time as though abstracted [lost] in thought. When the negroes did funny things and cut up capers [joked around], she did not seem to pay the slightest attention to them. Afterwards, however, in reading "Uncle Tom" I recognized scene after scene of that visit portrayed with the most minute fidelity [accuracy], and knew at once where the material for that portion of the story had been gathered. (Gerson, p. 39)

Marriage. Harriet's life in Cincinnati was brightened by the arrival, also in 1833, of her brother Henry Ward. The following year, she received news of the death of a close Cincinnati friend, Eliza Stowe. She had met Eliza and her husband, Professor Calvin Stowe, through the Semi-Colon Club. Calvin Stowe was a large, powerful man with a deep voice and full beard. He taught Biblical literature at Lane Theological Seminary, now headed by Harriet's father. Eliza and Harriet had become close friends, though Harriet's relations with Calvin had remained formal. In the year or so after Eliza's death, however, the professor visited the Beechers more and more frequently. Finally in the fall of 1835, he and Harriet announced their engagement. They married in January 1836, and within a few months the new Mrs. Stowe was pregnant.

Family and writing. In those days most pregnant women withdrew into the privacy of their homes or bedrooms until giving birth. Stowe, however, did just the opposite, enthusiastically taking up her briefly interrupted writing career. She would do the same in future pregnancies, never allowing them to stop the writing that grew increasingly important to her. The writing was in fact necessary to support her growing family, because her husband made very little money at teaching.

During the spring and summer of 1836, she sent off essays, articles, and short stories to be published in the *Western Monthly.*

She also wrote almost daily pieces for a local newspaper, the *Journal,* where Henry Ward had taken a job as editor. Tensions in Cincinnati over slavery were especially high that year, as pro-slavery mobs attacked and burned the offices of an abolitionist publication, the *Philanthropist,* and threatened other newspapers. Henry Ward began carrying pistols to work, though his sister was confident on her visits to the *Journal* that no one would attack a pregnant woman. Like their father, both opposed slavery in general, yet both also still thought that the abolitionists were violent fanatics whose methods would only make the slaveholders more stubborn. Stowe wrote several articles that summer making fun of the abolitionists, and Henry Ward also opposed them in his editorials for the *Journal.*

Changing views. In the fall, Stowe gave birth to twin girls. They were named Eliza and Harriet, after their father's two wives, who had been such close friends. Pregnant again by the following summer, Stowe began to suffer from exhaustion due to her busy schedule of writing and serving as a housewife and mother. Concerned for her health, Calvin insisted that she take a vacation, so she went to stay with her brother William and his wife in Putnam, Ohio. Staunch abolitionists, her brother and sister-in-law were active in the movement and received in their home a steady stream of abolitionist friends and colleagues. Rarely did they discuss any other topic. Unaccustomed to spare time, Stowe spent her vacation reading pamphlet after pamphlet attacking slavery's cruelty and injustice. Although opposed to violence, she came to agree that slavery must be stopped and that the abolitionists might not be fanatical after all.

In 1839, after the arrival of a third child, Henry Ellis, the Stowes hired a black woman from Kentucky to work for them. The woman had been a slave whose mistress had left her in the free state of Ohio. Legally, therefore, she was free. Soon, however, Calvin heard that her master had come to Cincinnati to claim her. Arming themselves, he and Henry Ward brought the woman to a friend's farm outside the city until the man gave up looking for her and went home. Stowe later used the episode in *Uncle Tom's Cabin.*

Antislavery writings. During the 1840s, Stowe wrote steadily for various magazines, focusing more and more on the problem of slavery in her stories and articles. It was a decade of great productivity for her professionally, while her stories gained a wider audience. At times she supported the family with her writing alone, as in 1848 when her husband's health problems forced him to take a year off from teaching. She also continued to have children: Frederick in 1840, Georgianna May in 1843, and Samuel in 1848, who died in a cholera outbreak the next year. Soon after, Professor Stowe was offered an attractive job at Bowdoin College in Brunswick, Maine. Eager to return to the East, in April 1850 Stowe took three of the children with her on the three-week journey to Maine. She would look for a house and wait for her husband to join her. He soon followed with the other children when someone had been found to replace him at Lane.

Fugitive Slave Law. Soon after arriving in Maine, Stowe gave birth to another son, Charles. Her growing family as well as the expenses of moving meant that she would have to write almost full-time to avoid the family's falling into bankruptcy. Like many in the North at the time, the entire Beecher family was deeply concerned about an 1850 law that forced citizens in the North to turn in escaped slaves. Highly unpopular, the law sharply increased northern support for abolition. Stowe's brother Henry Ward had moved to Brooklyn, New York several years earlier, where he was beginning to become well-known as a preacher (several of the Beecher boys had followed in their father's footsteps). Henry Ward brought a runaway slave to one of his sermons, raising the money right then and there to buy the man's freedom. The wife of another brother, Edward, wrote to Stowe in late 1850: "Now Hattie, if I could use a pen as you can, I would write something that would make this whole nation feel what an accursed thing slavery is" (Gerson, p. 64).

Uncle Tom's Cabin. In the summer of 1850, Stowe had written a story called "The Freeman's Dream," which had been published in the antislavery magazine *National Era.* Prompted by letters calling for more stories like it, Gamaliel Bailey, the magazine's editor, asked Stowe to write another. She could not think of an idea, however. Undiscouraged and believing in her talent, the editor sent her the large sum of $100 as an advance payment for another antislavery story. Stowe's mind still remained blank—until at church one cold February morning in 1851 she had a vivid image of an old slave, beaten to the point of death, gently forgiving his master before dying. She began writing that day. Bailey published a chapter each week in his magazine, and the story soon grew into a full-length novel. She researched the details for it by reading widely. The autobiography of the freed slave and abolitionist Frederick Douglass especially moved Stowe (see **Frederick Douglass**). After she finished in 1852, *Uncle Tom's Cabin* was published as a book. No one expected many sales. Yet it sold 3,000 copies the first day, and soon went on to become a publishing legend as one of the best-selling books of all time.

The story. *Uncle Tom's Cabin* tells the story of two slaves, Tom and Eliza, who must be sold to pay off their kindly master's debts. To escape being separated forever from her young child, Eliza escapes north across the Ohio River and is later joined by her husband, George. The very religious Tom, however, after several adventures, is sold to evil Simon Legree, a plantation owner who eventually beats him to death even as Tom forgives him.

Stowe's Most Successful Venture

Uncle Tom's Cabin was reprinted in 120 editions in its first year alone (which means the publisher ran out 119 times), with total American sales of about 350,000 copies. In 60 years, it had sold nearly 4 million copies in the United States and an equal amount in foreign translations. Within two years, it was translated into French, Spanish, Danish, Finnish, Dutch, Flemish, Polish, Russian, Bohemian, Hungarian, Serbian, Armenian, Illyrian, Romaic, Wallachian, Welsh, and Siamese.

The impact. Stowe's simple, melodramatic story touched the hearts and minds not only of Americans but also of readers in foreign countries. For Americans, though, it seemed to crystallize the moral issues that were increasingly dividing the nation. Stowe rose to overnight fame in the North, where she was compared to illustrious authors like Charles Dickens. In the South, however, she was accused of lying and distorting the facts to achieve an emotional response from readers. A cousin who lived in Georgia told her that she was afraid to receive mail with Stowe's return address on the envelope. Stowe herself received sacks of mail from outraged southern readers. While critics argued about whether the book was well-written or overly sentimental, the public continued to buy it, talk about it, and be swayed by the feelings it aroused. Later, when Stowe was introduced to President Abraham Lincoln during the Civil War, it was reported that Lincoln said: "So this is the little lady who made this big war" (Gerson, p. 163).

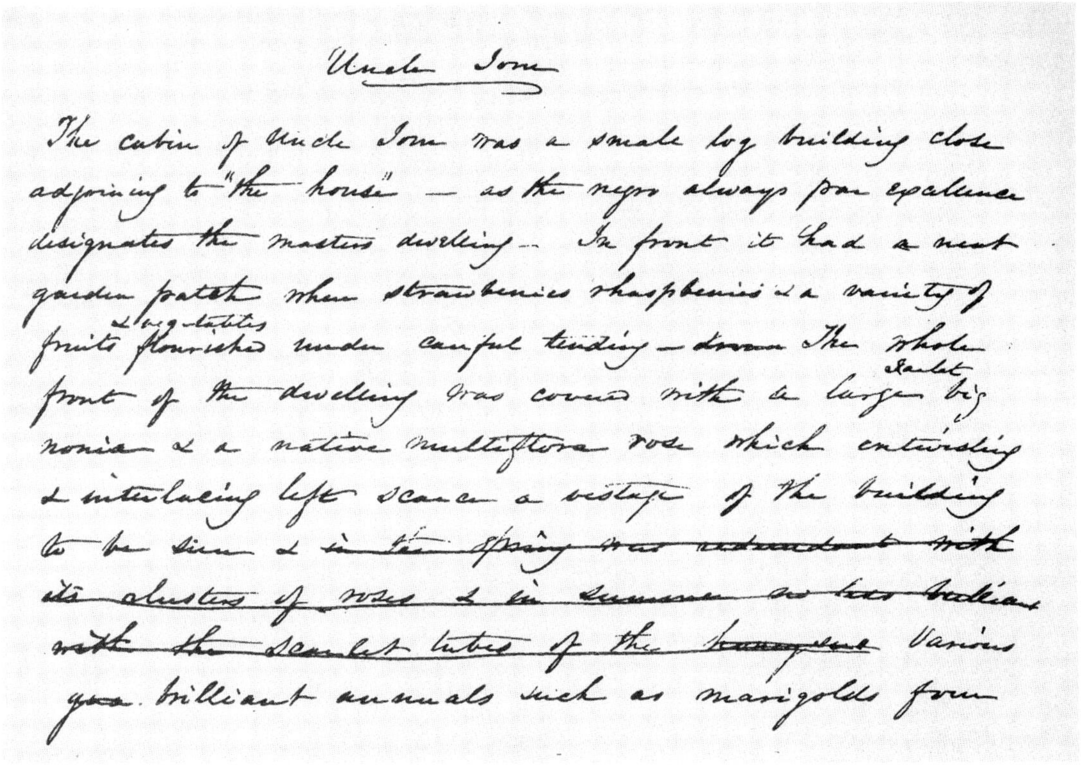

Uncle Tom

The cabin of Uncle Tom was a small log building close adjoining to "the house" — as the negro always par excellence designates the masters dwelling — In front it had a neat garden patch where strawberries raspberries & a variety of fruits & vegetables flourished under careful tending — ~~down~~ The whole front of the dwelling was covered with a large scarlet bignonia & a native multiflora rose which entwisting & interlacing left scarce a vestige of the building to be seen & ~~in the spring was redundant with its clusters of roses & in summer no less brilliant with the scarlet tubes of the honeysuckle~~ Various ~~gay~~ brilliant annuals such as marigolds four

▲ **Manuscript from *Uncle Tom's Cabin***

Celebrity and abolitionist. In the decade between the publication of *Uncle Tom's Cabin* and the outbreak of war, Stowe enjoyed celebrity status. No longer did she have to struggle to support her family. She traveled widely in Europe, where she met the English monarch Queen Victoria among other famous people of the day. On her first visit to England, huge crowds waited at the docks just to catch a glimpse of her, and English abolitionists showered her with gifts to help support the cause in America. (One gift, for example, was a gold bracelet in the form of a slave's shackle; another was a solid gold pen for writing additional antislavery works.) With the money Stowe made from her book, the family moved to Hartford, Connecticut (where their next-door neighbor was a young writer named Samuel Clemens, later famous as Mark Twain).

Aftermath

Other works. *Uncle Tom's Cabin* had been an immediate success, and Stowe's subsequent books were highly popular as well. Some, such as *Dred: A Tale of the Great Dismal Swamp,* also featured an antislavery message and central characters who were black. Others, like *The Pearl of Orr's Island,* told of Stowe's native New England. She continued to write at a furious pace until the late 1870s, when she was nearly seventy.

National figure. Stowe's seventieth birthday in 1881 turned into a national celebration, with newspaper articles and speeches honoring her achievements. Her favorite brother, Henry Ward, now himself the most famous preacher in America, devoted one of his Sunday sermons to her.

In 1886, Calvin Stowe died, after which Stowe grew increasingly senile. She spent most of her final years in bed in the winter home that she and her husband had bought in Florida after the Civil War. It was there that Harriet Beecher Stowe died, in her sleep, on July 1, 1896.

For More Information

Gerson, Noel. *Harriet Beecher Stowe.* New York: Praeger, 1976.

Jakoubek, Robert E. *Harriet Beecher Stowe: Author and Abolitionist.* New York: Chelsea House, 1989.

Stowe, Charles Edward. *Harriet Beecher Stowe.* New York and Boston: Houghton Mifflin & Company, 1889; reprint, Detroit, Michigan: Gale Research, 1967.

Bibliography

Aptheker, Herbert. *"One Continual Cry": David Walker's Appeal to the Colored Citizens of the World.* New York: Humanities Press, 1965.

Bailyn, Bernard, et al. *The Great Republic: A History of the American People.* Vol. 1. Lexington, Massachusetts: D. C. Heath, 1992.

Bemis, Samuel Flagg. *John Quincy Adams and the Union.* Westport, Connecticut: Greenwood Press, 1956.

Besson, Terry. *Nat Turner.* New York: Chelsea House, 1988.

Birney, Catherine H. *Grimké Sisters: Sarah and Angelina Grimké: The First American Women Advocates of Abolition and Women's Rights.* Westport, Connecticut: Greenwood Press, 1970.

Brent, Linda. *Incidents in the Life of a Slave Girl Child.* Edited by L. Manu. Orlando, Florida: Harcourt Brace Jovanovich, 1973.

Brown, Richard D., and Rabe, Steven G., editors. *Slavery in American Society.* Lexington, Massachusetts: D. C. Heath, 1976.

Chapman, John L. *William Lloyd Garrison.* New York: Birkman Publications, 1933.

Cosby, Ernest. *Garrison the Non-Resistant.* Englewood, New Jersey: James S. Ozar Publisher, 1905.

Crozier, Alice. *Novels of Harriet Beecher Stowe.* New York: Oxford University Press, 1969.

Douglass, Frederick. *Narrative of the Life of Douglass.* Garden City, New York: Doubleday, 1973.

DuBois, W. E. B. "Douglass." In *Dictionary of American Biography,* Vol. 3. New York: Scribner's Sons, 1977.

Dudley, William, editor. *Slavery: Opposing Viewpoints.* American History Series. San Diego: Greenhaven Press, 1992.

Frederickson, George, editor. *William Lloyd Garrison.* Englewood, New Jersey: Prentice Hall, 1968.

Garrison, William Lloyd. *William Lloyd Garrison On Non-Resistance.* Brooklyn, New York: Haskell House Publishers, 1973.

Grimké, Archibald H. *William Lloyd Garrison, the Abolitionist.* New York: AMS Press, 1891.

Grimké, Sarah. *Letters on the Equality of the Sexes and Other Notes.* Edited by Elizabeth Bartlett. New Haven, Connecticut: Yale University Press, 1988.

Hagan, William T. *The Sac and Fox Indians.* Norman: University of Oklahoma Press, 1958.

Iskoubek, Robert. *Harriet Beecher Stowe.* American Women of Achievement Series. New York: Chelsea House, 1989.

Killens, John Oliver. *Great Gittin' Up Morning.* New York: Shamal Books, 1980.

Kraditor, Aileen S. *The Ideas of the Women Suffrage Movement.* New York: Columbia University Press, 1965.

Limpus, Lowell. *Disarm!* New York: Freedom Press, 1960.

Lofton, John. *Denmark Vesey's Revolt: The Slave Plot that Lit a Fuse to Fort Sumter.* Kent, Ohio: Kent State University Press, 1983.

Martin, Christopher. *The Amistad Affair.* New York: Abelard-Schuman, 1970.

McKissack, Patricia, and McKissack, Frederick. *Douglass, Leader Against Slavery.* Hillside, New Jersey: Enslow, 1991.

Merritt, Elizabeth. *James Henry Hammond, 1897-1864.* Baltimore: The Johns Hopkins Press, 1923.

Nash, Gary, et al., editors. *The American People: Creating a Nation and a Society.* Vol. 1. New York: Harper and Row, 1986.

Oates, Stephen B. *The Fires of Jubilee: Nat Turner's Fierce Rebellion.* New York: NAL-Dutton, 1982.

Reynolds, Moira H. *Uncle Tom's Cabin and Mid-Nineteenth Century America.* New York: Stowe-Day, 1978.

Ross, John. *The Papers of Chief John Ross.* Edited by Gary Moulton. Norman: University of Oklahoma Press, 1985.

Ruchames, Louis. *The Abolitionists.* New York: G. P. Putnam's Sons, 1963.

Scott, John Anthony. *Hard Trials on My Way: Slavery and the Struggle Against It, 1800-1860.* New York: Alfred A. Knopf, 1974.

Scott, Winfield. *Memoirs of Lieutenant General Scott.* New York: Sheldon and Company, 1864.

Simonds, Christopher. *Slater's Mill and the Industrial Revolution.* Englewood Cliffs, New Jersey: Silver Burdett Press, 1990.

Smith Arthur D. *Old Fuss and Feathers: The Life and Exploits of Lieutenant General Winfield Scott.* Salem, New Hampshire: Ayer Company Publishers, 1975.

Stampp, Kenneth M. *The Peculiar Institution: Slavery in the Ante-Bellum South.* New York: Vintage Books, 1964.

Stanton, Elizabeth Cady. *ECS, Diary and Letters.* Edited by Theodore Stanton and Harriot Stanton Blatch. New York: Harper & Sons, 1922.

Tragle, Henry I. *The Southampton Slave Revolt of 1831: A Compilation of Source Materials.* Amherst: University of Massachusetts Press, 1971.

Tucker, Barbara M. *Sam Slater and the Origins of the American Textile Industry.* Ithaca, New York: Cornell University Press, 1984.

Villard, Fanny G. *William Lloyd Garrison on Nonresistance Together with a Personal Sketch by His Daughter and a Tribute by Leo Tolstoi.* Englewood, New Jersey: James S. Ozer Publisher, 1972.

Walvin, James. *Slavery and the Slave Trade: A Short Illustrated History.* Jackson: University Press of Mississippi, 1984.

White, George S. *Memoir of Samuel Slater.* Fairfield, New Jersey: Augustus M. Kelley Publishers, 1967.

Wilkins, Thurman. *Cherokee Tragedy: The Story of the Ridge Family and the Decimation of a People.* New York: Macmillan, 1970.

Index

Boldface indicates profiles.

G

H

I

J

K

L

M

N

O

P

PROFILES IN AMERICAN HISTORY

Significant Events and the People Who Shaped Them

Volume 5: *Reconstruction to the Spanish American War*

Reconstruction
Andrew Johnson, Thaddeus Stevens

Indians and Government Policy
George A. Custer, Carl Schurz, Chief Joseph

Labor Movement
George Pullman, Samuel Gompers, Mother Jones

Struggle for Civil Rights
Ida B. Wells Barnett, Booker T. Washington, W.E.B. DuBois

Realism in American Literature
Mark Twain, Helen Hunt Jackson, Stephen Crane

Social Reform
Elizabeth Cady Stanton, Josephine Shaw Lowell, Frances Willard

Spanish American War
William McKinley, William Randolph Hearst, Theodore Roosevelt

Volume 6: *Chinese Exclusion to the Women's Rights Movement*

Immigration
Yung Wing, Bartolomeo Vanzetti, Abraham Cahan

Social Welfare
Jane Addams, Herbert Croly, Louis Brandeis, Upton Sinclair, Ida Tarbell

World War I
Woodrow Wilson, John Pershing, Oliver Wendell Holmes

Industrial Growth
Henry Ford, John L. Lewis

Scopes Trial
Clarence Darrow, William Jennings Bryan

Harlem Renaissance
Marcus Garvey, James Weldon Johnson, Zora Neale Hurston

Women's Rights and Roles
Charlotte Perkins Gilman, Margaret Sanger